ROBBIE
RUGBY WARRIOR

THE AUTOBIOGRAPHY OF

ROBBIE HUNTER-PAUL

WRITTEN WITH

CHRIS IRVINE

GREAT NORTHERN

Great Northern Books
PO Box 213, Ilkley, LS29 9WS
www.greatnorthernbooks.co.uk

ISBN: 978-1905080-10-6

Design and layout: David Burrill

Printed and bound by CPI Group (UK) Ltd, Croydon, CR0 4YY

CIP Data
A catalogue for this book is available from the British Library

I dedicate this book to mum and dad for all of the values and love they instilled in me over my first 18 years and also to my wife for her patience and support

Acknowledgements

Too many people to thank here – you know who you are – but there are two people to whom I owe absolutely everything. Besides, without them, I wouldn't be here. Mum and dad blessed me with the tools to become a rugby player and so much more. From them came the drive, the pursuit of excellence and the values I hold dear, which I like to think have held me in good stead. They also produced Henry, who set the benchmark, raised the bar and is so much more to me than simply a brother. He is a best friend who I can depend on and turn to. We are similarly blessed with the great mates we grew up with and are still our best mates now, and our extensive *whanau* of family and friends. All have played their part on my life's journey. To every coach who offered me new tools and skills, every club and team I played for and every player who I appeared alongside, it was my privilege.

This book wouldn't have been possible either without the unstinting efforts of my co-writer Chris Irvine. His patience with me and dedication to the cause during countless early morning and late night sessions, sustained only by cappuccinos and egg and bacon muffins, left his wife Patricia bereft, who I must also thank. Working on this book has been a joy in putting me in touch with my past and who I am. A big thank you to Jason Robinson, Brian Noble and Dave Swanton in helping produce so many kind words in the forewords; to all the team at Great Northern Books for their faith, guidance and expertise; Matt Johnson Photography for the cover shot; and Greg Brown, Nathan Mill, Matthew Green and Dr Graeme Close for their expert help with the High Performance sections.

Without the love and support of my wife Natalie, I wouldn't be me. I owe her everything along with my daughters, Iesha and Mia. The fact that I've grown up and matured the last few years is entirely down to the influence of the three of them.

CONTENTS

Chris Irvine lives in Leeds and is rugby league correspondent for *The Times* and *Sunday Times*. He has covered the sport since 1992. He is a regular Sky Sports pundit and also works as a senior lecturer in sports journalism at the University of Huddersfield. His journalistic career began in 1981 at the *Warrington Guardian* where he developed his love of rugby league. He worked there as a news reporter and also at the *Coventry Evening Telegraph*, *Yorkshire Post* and *Scotland on Sunday* before launching his own sports writing business in 1991 and reporting on rugby league, rugby union, football, cricket, tennis and various other sports for *The Times*. He is married to Patricia and they have a son, Hamish.

Foreword

by Jason Robinson OBE

I had been playing in the Wigan first team for about three years before the evolution of summer rugby. The winter season closed down and we all prepared for the great unknown of playing rugby league in the summer, beginning in 1996. Some clubs worked overtime in promoting Super League and one of those was Bradford Bulls with "Bullmania".

Robbie Paul was promoted well by the Bulls and given the No 1 jersey. He was only very young at the time and I asked his brother Henry about him. Henry said that Robbie was a special talent and that he would do well; he wasn't wrong. Playing against Robbie was always a challenge in that he had great vision and mobility and was a gamebreaker in every sense of the word. He could spot an opportunity and his ball-handling skills were exceptional. I played under several coaches in rugby league and when it was time for a team meeting ahead of playing against Bradford, one name would always be mentioned to keep an eye on. That was Robbie Paul.

After Wigan's eight-year stranglehold on the Challenge Cup was broken, St Helens and Bradford Bulls played each other in the 1996 and 1997 finals. Robbie scored a hat-trick on the losing side in 1996 as a rare beaten finalist to win the Lance Todd Trophy as man of the match for his remarkable feat. In the winter of 1996, several rugby league players tried their hand at rugby union. Henry Paul and I went to Bath, Va'aiga Tuigamala returned to his native code at Newcastle and Robbie and Gary Connolly went to Harlequins. It was an interesting experience at the time, especially playing against my Wigan team-mate Gary Connolly along with Robbie, who took to the 15 man code game very quickly.

I played against Robbie for Great Britain against New Zealand and he showed that he could take his club skills on to the international stage without any problems. Robbie also played in several games where the Kiwis beat Australia. The combination of Robbie and Henry at Bradford Bulls was amazing and they were responsible for so many people taking an interest in the sport in the Bradford area and beyond. This was at a time when Bradford City were also riding high as a football team in the city.

Robbie picked up many medals along the way before he suffered a badly broken arm, but he recovered well and continued to excite rugby fans with his skills. Robbie eventually moved from Bradford to Huddersfield Giants and helped kick start them from a sleeping giant to become a force in Super League and finally called it a day from playing after a spell with Leigh Centurions. Robbie remains a stand out character in the game of rugby league both on and off the field. He will be remembered fondly down the years as one of the greats in the game and rightly so. His contribution deserves that.

Jason Robinson played rugby league for Wigan and Great Britain from 1992-2000 before he crossed codes to rugby union with Sale Sharks and won the Rugby World Cup with England in 2003.

A Hooker's Foreword

by Brian Noble

Whenever I think of Robbie Paul, Robbie Hunter-Paul now, I can't help but smile. He does that to you. I'm privileged to call him my friend. I was his coach and these days we're television colleagues. The bloke can light up any room, just as he lit up the rugby pitch with lightning feet and breathtaking skills that can be summed up in two words – world class. More than that, he is an icon. An icon of Bradford Bulls and of rugby league itself. I've never spoken about a player like this before, let alone commit the words to the written page, but the first name on any team sheet of mine would be Robbie's. I love the guy, the way he played and everything he stands for. The sport is lucky to have him now blazing a marketing trail.

If I could have 13 Robbie Pauls, I would have the ultimate dream team. For a glorious decade he was Mr Bradford Bulls. He was the marquee player, the face of the club and the guy without whom the Bulls would not have been the phenomenon they became in the first 10 years of the Super League era. He was the team and yet when Chris Caisley, Bradford's chairman, took a brave punt on signing him in 1994, on the basis of Henry Paul saying he'd a kid brother back home in New Zealand better than him, no-one had heard of Robbie. Less than two years later, he was the name on everyone's lips after a phenomenal performance at Wembley in the classic 1996 Challenge Cup final.

By that stage, I'd returned to the club from Wakefield to be an assistant coach and I took to Robbie from the first minute I met him. He was no ordinary teenager. I won everything with Bradford in my playing days but never reached Wembley, so to be invited to lead the team out by Brian Smith, the head coach, was an honour. The guy behind me as we emerged from the tunnel that blisteringly hot day was Robbie, a bag of nerves spinning the ball around his fingers. What followed is etched into my memory and all those who witnessed it. Three tries – the first hat-trick in a Wembley final – the Lance Todd Trophy as man of the match, youngest cup final captain, who still ended up on the losing side that day. He grew from that experience.

Win or lose, Robbie kept me smiling. There was a joy that he transmitted when he played. It was like dealing with a force of nature. He had the most unbelievable footwork and speed, which was why I was always in his ear: "Run Robbie, just keeping running." Those who watched him and those who meet him now can't help but come away with a smile on their faces. He is a lover of the sport and a lover of life, for whom I have the utmost respect. Time in his company is always time well spent. If I have a regret with Robbie, it is not having spent more time with him when I effectively had to let him go from Bradford at the end of the 2005 season. In the hurly burly of working life, sometimes you lost sight of what is important.

I like what he does away from rugby, that he is an artist, that he reads books and is an intelligent fella who you can have a proper conversation with. The fact that he did a marketing degree at the University of Huddersfield, because he is interested in that field and wanted to further educate himself, is a sign of the man. He can be a force in the game for many years to come because rugby league needs guys like Robbie, who effectively ran the Bradford Bulls brand for 10 years in fulfilling the vision of people there like Chris Caisley and the late Peter Deakin, the Bulls' marketing guru.

The side people don't really see of Robbie is his meticulous preparation and selflessness. There was no better team man. I told him before a semi-final once that I was going to bring him off the bench. For a player of his calibre to be told that could be seen as a blow to his ego, yet Robbie stuffed it in his back pocket, came on after 20 minutes and killed the opposition, as I predicted he would. Nor did people see the hard work with Robbie. They saw the fun and the flamboyance, but behind all that was a guy who worked his socks off in the gym, for the team cause, just whatever was required. He never once whinged.

I'm not sure whether anyone knew his best position, because he could play so well in so many. Brian Smith's philosophy with Robbie was that it didn't really matter what his number was, just get him to dummy half and run, and cause mayhem for the opposition. That's precisely what he did. Stand off, scrum half, full back and, latterly, hooker, where he encountered a few blokes with baseball bats ready to ruin his good looks, he was exceptional. He played more than 30 times for New Zealand and nearly half of those he jumped on a plane, helped beat Australia often as not, and would be back in less than a week at

Bradford raring to go again.

The good thing about Robbie was that he never made the same mistake twice, otherwise his father, Walter, would have battered him. Walter and Gail, Mr and Mrs Paul, were very much part of the Bulls' family and it's not hard to see where Robbie and Henry get their values from. They're a close-knit family and the club was blessed the day we got the two brothers at Bradford. We had a particular move called "snapper" featuring the pair of them. More often than not we'd score from it. It was Henry coming across Robbie, or vice versa, with Jimmy Lowes organising in and around the sticks. Depending on which side of the field, if Robbie got it, he'd step off his right. If Henry got it, he'd come off his left. Their footwork just bamboozled opponents.

They were both headstrong. A few times it erupted between them, with Tevita Vaikona, a big Tongan, stepping in to referee two scrapping Maori boys, and Scott Naylor winding them up again. Video sessions could be like the clash of the titans. The thing with Henry was to plant the seed in him three weeks before and let him think it was his idea, while Robbie would run with everything you asked of him like a man possessed. As the older brother, Henry would try and knock Robbie down. "Shut up, pup," while Robbie would be going "yap, yap, yap". But they were breathtakingly good together. When both of them were on, it was a case of sit back and admire the fireworks. They were fabulous runners of the ball, like spinning tops at times. Who wouldn't want Robbie and Henry Paul in their team? The two of them were box office.

The 2001 Super League Grand Final, Henry's last for Bradford, was just the most sublime performance for them to sign off as a pair for the Bulls. Without Henry, we had to be more structured as a team and Bradford's 2003 clean sweep reflected the importance of Robbie, Jimmy and Paul Deacon together. With Deacs' kicking game, Jimmy's crafty kicks and Robbie's running, there was no stopping us but, if I'm being honest, 2005 was my favourite Grand Final success with Bradford. Robbie's role in that triumph from the turmoil of the first half of the season was enormous, for which I'll always be grateful to him.

Robbie confronted me in my office. When you have your head up your backside, sometimes you forget the intimacy of the team. I pulled myself away from contract negotiations when Robbie bluntly told me that I was losing the plot and in danger of losing the team. It was tough for him putting me on the spot like that, but it had the desired effect. His approach was the catalyst for me to front up to the problem, and when the air was cleared, it was as if the club returned to a familiar "one for all and all for one" mentality. We rose from mid-table to win the Grand Final for a third time in five years. At the time I could never imagine a Bradford side running around without Robbie Paul, the club's emotional leader. When the parting of the ways came, we parted best of mates; he still is and always will be.

Brian Noble is the only coach to win three Super League Grand Finals, with Bradford Bulls in 2001, 2003 and 2005. He also coached Wigan Warriors, Crusaders and Great Britain to the 2004 Tri-Nations final. He captained Great Britain on the 1984 Australia tour and made more than 400 appearances for Bradford Northern.

Introduction

I grew up reading sporting autobiographies – Wally Lewis, Jonah Lomu, Michael Jordan, to name just a few – tapping into their experiences and feelings, getting a sense of what drove them to such great heights. I wanted to be inspired because these were people I aspired to be. I have always scraped as much information as I can from wherever I can get it. Being a voracious reader and sponge for knowledge, I am always anxious to figure things out in order to improve myself. I love people who are creative, innovative and arresting characters. If I was going to do a book, it had to amount to more than purely my life story so far. I wanted to get across some practical messages to athletes, future athletes and people in all walks of life.

As a big fan of text books, especially since doing a degree in sports marketing and public relations, the theory is all well and good. What I really like are the practical case studies in text books that bolt all the theory together. That explains the "Play like a Professional" aspect to the book through my HP, or High Performance sections. These frameworks fit in between each chapter of the journey through the rugby-playing first half of my life. The real inspiration for this somewhat different approach to an autobiography was coming from the first generation of players in both rugby codes, who were all fully professional and perhaps didn't all have the necessary tools to deal with life as best they could beyond the full-time sport environment.

I've not exactly lived a rock and roll lifestyle, though I've had my moments. There are warnings, advice, tips and information hopefully of value to people contained in my story that I wanted to flesh out in a practical way. The outcome is a two books in one principle – the second being a guide to how to be a better person mentally and physically, and is aimed at both adults and children. The tools and skills I have learned playing rugby are what have set me up for the rest of my life. Mental strength, physical wellbeing and having the right attitude transcend sport in all areas of life. Psychological strength is the same with Lance Armstrong on a bike as it is with Sir Richard Branson in the boardroom. That is a message I have been anxious to get across in more than purely the narrative of my playing career, which ended after 18 years as a professional in September 2011.

After hanging up my boots, I thought long and hard about doing a book, simply because I didn't see my story as complete. The journey of being a professional athlete was about introducing me to the rest of my life. I'm a stickler for doing things the right way and I saw the approach taken here as the best way of offering not just an insight into me and the way I tick but giving readers proper working knowledge. The first half of my first non-rugby year since the age of three was spent working with Chris Irvine, *The Times* and *Sunday Times* rugby league correspondent and senior lecturer in sports journalism at the University of Huddersfield, on hopefully achieving those two goals in *Robbie: Rugby Warrior*.

For athletes walking the same professional pathway as I did, there is a need to have an eye on more than just the prize on the playing field. Spread your wings, embrace educational and trade and workplace opportunities, because careers are finite. No rugby player in either code earns enough money from playing to last a lifetime so, of course, you've got to be prepared for life after sport. In my case that was taking the academic route as a mature university student that ultimately led to my first post-rugby career role as business development manager for the Huddersfield Giants club in Super League.

I remain completely passionate about rugby, though I am by no means defined by it. What inspired me as a kid growing up in New Zealand, as part of a warrior race, and what motivated me as an athlete were an intoxicating mix of competitiveness, stretching my boundaries, learning and discovery of an inner strength. Rugby was my life but my artistic side also flourished. A ball or a paintbrush, sometimes it didn't matter which, as long as it was food for my soul. In the glass half full/glass half empty debate, I'm definitely a glass half full guy and passionate about everything I do. As a rugby player, I've always been seen as someone a little bit different. I define myself as a bloke with a foot in two rich cultures. I'm proud of my British and Maori heritages. I'm not British and I'm not Maori. I'm both, that's the way I see it.

My sport and the people around me have allowed me to live my dreams. As I went through the process of putting together the book, I found it a really humbling experience. I would not have been in the privileged position I am were it not for the natural gifts bestowed by my parents, without whose support over the years I'm not sure where I would have been. In walking my rugby pathway again, I have experienced for a second time the joy, the laughs, the love, the heartache, the embarrassment, the anger, the despair and the euphoria. The memories are from my perspective. Others may see them differently and the truth will lie somewhere in between, but this is my story and where better place to start it than that great sporting mecca, Wembley Stadium.

Chapter 1

Wembley, Rock God

Get it down, just get the thing down. Brain's whirring. I'm at full tilt. It's for the hat-trick, I know that. Ball safely tucked under one arm. No one-handed trickery. I'd learned that to my cost at London Broncos a few months earlier. Far too fancy and I'd got my backside slapped. The ball slipped out as I went to plant it over the line. Bloody daft. We lost that game. Now, it's two hands or dive over the line. I'm nearly there. Rather than slide and get grass burns, I roll. It's as I come up, fist pumping, that it hits me with a blinding force. A wall of 30,000 Bradford Bulls fans losing their minds, pouring all their love at me. Positive energy raining down from the terraces, and I drink it in. Joy unconfined and, for that one fleeting, glorious moment, I knew just how it felt. To be a rock star.

Once savoured, never forgotten. People say it's about the money. If so, I would have gone and played rugby union for the rest of my career. This was me doing what I loved, playing rugby league on the greatest of stages, doing what makes me happy, playing a sport I truly love, providing me with food for my soul. That is what makes you really wealthy – in spirit. Mind you, there was the small matter of £10,000 as the first player to score a hat-trick of tries in a Wembley Challenge Cup final, and the Bradford boys were in for their slice of that cheque, as Graeme Bradley, a bruising and brooding presence in our team, never stopped reminding me.

The moment passed with the realisation that we were back in a classic final, two points adrift of St Helens at 34-32, with nine minutes left on the clock. Unbelievably, we had been leading 26-12 just 14 minutes earlier. Our tormentor, Bobbie Goulding, had one last trick though. A reverse pass and Apollo Perelini dived over for the clinching try. Euphoria turned to desolation. Winner of the Lance Todd Trophy as man of the match, scorer of the first hat-trick at Wembley, youngest captain of Challenge Cup finalists at 20 years and 84 days, and I would still swap those records and accolades for a winner's medal. To this day, I carry a bag of bricks on my back from a final that made my name as a player; the best of days and worst of days. The real magic of the Challenge Cup is winning it. I didn't discover that until much later.

My brother Henry and I had been big fans of the Challenge Cup from little kids growing up in New Zealand. Mum and dad would wake us at 3am to watch the live TVNZ feed from Wembley. We just knew that it was a fabulous occasion at a great stadium and that a glamour team called Wigan always seemed to win the match. We would be on the look-out for the Kiwi boys and were massive fans of the Iro brothers, Kevin and Tony. Those two were always in the thick of it in the cherry-and-white of Wigan. Kevin "The Beast" scoring tries for fun and Tony pretty much unstoppable on the wing. Then the great Dean Bell would lift the trophy. You could not help but be inspired.

Wigan were still an unstoppable force in 1995, the year Henry played in his first Challenge Cup final. I was not there that day, but was sat at home in Bradford watching big brother have a wonderful game as Wigan dismantled Leeds. If someone had told me then that I would be at Wembley 12 months hence, I would have laughed in their face. Bradford were a long way from such heady heights, their last Challenge Cup success having been in 1949. So when it came to Saturday April 27, 1996, I was green, utterly naive and, as it turned out, completely fearless when it came to game time. That day I was saved by my ignorance.

Some of my team-mates could not sleep the night before, they were so nervous. I slept like a baby and wolfed down breakfast. Others were throwing theirs back up. I knew that it was a big game but had no inkling of the occasion's significance. Even on the traditional eve-of-final walkabout at Wembley, I had just thought that I had never been to a stadium quite so old, or seen a pitch quite so perfect. A glorious green sward. The place was vast but empty. I did not foresee the thunderbolt coming, even on the team bus to the stadium. The likes of Graeme Bradley, Paul Loughlin, Sonny Nickle and Bernard Dwyer knew all right. Like a silly kid, I was more interested in our police escort. Rather than via the M25, the driver went directly through the middle of London, going on the wrong side of the road sometimes and mounting kerbs after some roads were closed. Police motorcycles weaved in and out and I was leaping out of my seat in boyish excitement. How one of the guys didn't strap me down and shut me up was a miracle. The match was the furthest thing from my mind, until we came past Wembley Way.

I had never seen so many people in one space, a bobbing ocean of humanity all headed to a stadium that had come alive like some great beast. That was the first uppercut. The second came lining up before the match in the tunnel. We emerged from our respective dressing rooms, I gave the obligatory nod to Bobbie Goulding, the St Helens captain, and I was suddenly fixated by the view of the mouth of the tunnel, myriad people in the distance shimmering in the heat, with an energy pouring towards us. I began quivering, shaking my legs, spinning the ball on one finger. On the BBC commentary, Martin Offiah reckoned that maybe I was a bit cocky. Actually, it was a nervous reaction. I don't know why I was spinning the ball, only that I was trying to take the focus away. We then began the longest walk of my life, 100 yards that felt like 100 miles.

When we emerged into the cauldron, the energy slamming into us from 76,000 people screaming their heads off was enough to knock me off my feet. My heart was going a million miles an hour, the rush of blood felt like my head was going to explode and electricity flew across my skin, to the point where I could feel every hair on my legs and arms prick up. The emotional power left a steely bitterness in my mouth. If I had known it was going to be like this, I would probably have run a mile. Ignorance was my saviour.

I have no recall of lining up or shaking hands with dignitaries, as if a defence mechanism kicked in. My next memory is of being beckoned close by a senior player, who was knelt down. I thought that as he had experience of the Wembley cauldron, he wanted to pass on a pearl of wisdom. What he wanted was a wee. As I cocked my head to try and catch what he was saying in the din, all I felt were sprinkles on my leg. He just did not want his pre-match leak caught on camera.

The heat was intense – 95 Fahrenheit in the middle of the pitch, according to the BBC – and the whole feel to the day was one of renewal and opportunity, with the first Challenge Cup final of the new Super League era and Wigan's eight-year Wembley monopoly finally at an end. Bradford and St Helens were the coming teams. Into this mix the Challenge Cup sponsors, Silk Cut, announced a £10,000 prize to the first player to score a hat-trick in the final, perhaps safe in the knowledge that no-one did that sort of thing in the Wembley pressure cooker. That did not stop the media hyping up the chances of Danny Arnold doing so, as he had scored 15 tries on the right wing for Saints in the first nine games of the 1996 season.

I had addressed a Bradford team meeting as captain, at which I said that wingers were nothing more than muscly linesmen. In other words, finishers who got all the plaudits off the backs of others. I pointed out that hat-tricks were not the product of one player's work and emphasised that should anyone be lucky enough to manage the feat at Wembley, they should keep £5,000 and give the rest to the team. Our wings Jon Scales and Paul Cook scratched their heads and muttered that they didn't know about that, while front rowers like Jon Hamer and Karl Fairbank began leaping off their seats in excitement at the thought. Vote passed; talk about Sod's Law.

The cheque, however, looked to be in the pocket of the St Helens full back Steve Prescott. He scored after three minutes, then again 14 minutes later. A third try beckoned for him when Bobbie Goulding put a chip kick in near our posts that reared up and came back off the bar. Steve was underneath and dived, only for the ball to bounce into my arms, fortuitously. Unfortunately for Steve, a lick of paint denied him that prized first Wembley hat-trick and the ten grand. From that point, the game changed on its head and swung our way for 40 minutes.

Jon Scales scored out on the edge, Paul Cook converted and added a penalty, before Nathan Graham, our full back, who was having a sensational game, made a break that again had Saints on the back foot. I forged another 20 metres from dummy half, Bernard Dwyer created room and I flew on to the ball. Party time five metres out. I sidestepped Paul Newlove, bounced off him and scored under the posts. It was an easy place-kick for Cookie in putting us 14-12 ahead at the interval. There was no emotion from Brian Smith, our coach, just the technical know-how to ensure we got our hands on that precious trophy which, after all, was made in Bradford by the silversmiths Fattorini and Sons.

Bernard, one of the trio of former Saints in our side with Loughlin and Nickle, got a try seven minutes into the second half. We were seemingly on an irresistible roll. After 53 minutes, we tapped a penalty and the forwards hit the ball up with quick play-the-balls. My job specification in those situations was to get into acting half back and, like Forrest Gump, just run. Someone flew out of the St Helens line at me, I spun round and straight into the brick outhouse, Vila Matautia. As I sidestepped, though, his power helped propel me between two defenders. As I fell, the line was within reach. He still had a grip on my shorts as I dotted the ball on the whitewash. In the action of pulling away from Vila, my little fella popped out. My team-mates tried to pick me up. The reason I clung to the ground was because I was trying to sort myself out. I didn't really fancy being exposed in front of six million television viewers.

Cookie was on fire with the boot and converted my second try. Fourteen points is a massive lead in a final, even with 23 minutes to hang on or continue going for broke. We had momentum, complete control of the game and had been dominating across the park when the first St Helens bomb went up. It was a pure speculator from 30 metres out. We were not having our line put under any pressure. It was just perfect technique on Bobbie Goulding's part. St Helens had done their homework on Nathan Graham, who kept his hands low under the high ball and not high, a commonplace technique nowadays. To our eternal shame, we all stood open-mouthed and watched the ball arc crossfield. It dipped down, Nathan let it bounce in-goal and Keiron Cunningham came up with the try in his first final. Nathan, though, was left exposed by all of us. The sport itself learned a lesson that day. Every time a high kick is put up now, people run from all over the place to offer protection. The trouble was that Bobbie had got the taste and his fusillade intensified.

The next two high balls were put right on Nathan's head. Again no-one came to his assistance. Simon Booth claimed one try and Ian Pickavance a third in the space of seven agonising minutes. Brian Smith defended Nathan at the after-match press conference in the face of opponents coming at him with knives and baseball bats, as Brian described it. The truth was that he had been let down by all of us. Nathan was wrongly vilified when, in fact, Bradford would not have been in a fantastic position to win the game had it not been for his attacking influence in returning the ball and putting us on the front foot. The problem for Nathan was that the club had signed Stuart Spruce from Widnes, a young full back champing at the bit. Nathan never properly got the chance to make amends, although he did not need to answer the critics. The Bulls did not have the muscle memory in the bank at that stage to protect him that day. That came with time and the emergence of the likes of Jimmy Lowes, Glen Tomlinson and Steve McNamara, who were cup-tied for Wembley.

A four-point deficit had become eight with Arnold's second try for

Saints. However, when their defence subsequently parted 40 metres out, I came off my left foot into the hole, leaving me one on one with Steve Prescott. He began backing off, a smart thing to do against a side-stepper, because it gave him space on his side to try and run me down. Usually a full back will come straight at you. Not Steve, he was too clever, although a fraction too clever on this occasion. I tried to move him to my right, then swerved to the left. He head faked but did it too soon. His centre of gravity was going the wrong way, because he had thought one step too early. That was the tenth of a second I needed to go clear. Touchdown number three, a bit of history to boot, and that glorious, mind-bending adulation.

Ultimately, it meant nothing. Not in terms of winning, which was all that really mattered when I looked up and saw the 40-32 score after 80 minutes. I would happily be the guy who did nothing in a final as long as the team won. I joined a select band of individuals in collecting the Lance Todd Trophy in a beaten cause, having been privileged to play in a classic final of the modern era that boasted the highest score, most points by a losing team, the biggest points and tries aggregate and, yes, the first Wembley hat-trick of tries, which probably nicked me the man of the match vote by the Rugby League Writers' Association over Goulding and his inspirational hat-trick of bombs.

The disappointment of losing my first final still lingers. The Lance Todd Trophy means so much to me but, as a whippersnapper less than two years in England, I didn't know what to think in the aftermath. The whole team felt destroyed. I was an emotional wreck. To be so close to tasting success and watching Saints lift that wonderful old trophy, the hat-trick achievement felt soured. I got presented with the Lance Todd and a giant cardboard cheque on the field in a Maxfli cap, for which my mate Jaz Athwal, the first Asian golf captain in the country at Waterton Park in Wakefield, had promised me a set of clubs if I wore it. I had said I would only do it if we won, but one of the boys tossed me the cap anyway. I still use those clubs; I'm too tight to buy new ones.

Matt Calland was a wild man, but as I was sat on the bus leaving Wembley so solemn and desolate, he grabbed me around the neck and said: "Snap out of it, you had one of the greatest games you'll ever play in your life and you did it at the right moment. Get your head around that." To have one of your peers tell you that certainly helped. I was so driven that I wanted our labours to bear fruit that day, not appreciating then that this was the beginning of the journey for the Bulls. It was also the start of something special for me.

Coming in as such heavy underdogs, the nature of the game was celebrated by our growing army of fans on an open top bus tour through Bradford. The club had momentum and Peter Deakin, the Bulls' marketing guru, positioned everything perfectly. It was not so much that we lost that day but that we were growing. Peter rolled with the positives. He was spot on, too. The dominance that Bradford went on to exert in the new Super League era sprang from us losing the 1996 Challenge Cup final, although for Graeme "Penguin" Bradley there was the small matter of his slice of the hat-trick money. The real cheque took ages to arrive. Every day for three months Peng pestered me about whether it had come. You do not get a bigger wind-up merchant than Bradley and he was relentless. When the money finally came, it was the hardest cheque I have ever had to write, because I knew it'd get pissed up the wall at the end-of-season bash in Tenerife, which it did.

But those three tries were also a springboard for me. Opportunities came thick and fast, varied and exotic. There were times during my career when the tag of first Wembley hat-trick scorer would frustrate the life out of me. Was that all I was good for? But, as you get older, you appreciate that you do not have too many games like that, not on the big stage. It took another four years to get that Challenge Cup monkey off our backs, but the Bulls were up and running, and the reason for me playing rugby league 12,000 miles from my homeland was about to be realised. A seed that had been planted in me in New Zealand as part of a proud warrior culture.

High Performance – An introduction

The concept of the High Performance, or HP sections, in between the chapters of my life story in rugby, is to offer an insight into many of the factors that go into the life of a professional rugby player both on and off the field.

It was never enough for me to do just a straightforward autobiography. I wanted to offer the added value of a "how to be a professional" guide – a guide to being a better player mentally, physically and professionally, with practical tips that people can take on to the pitch, or, equally, into the board room, based on my own experiences and information gleaned over many years at the rugby coalface.

What does it take to be a professional sportsman or woman? Yes, it takes skill and dedication, but also feeding, nurturing and looking after the human machine. Possibly I got the idea from the car manuals my dad would avidly read from cover to cover.

My rugby dreams, aspirations, highs and lows are interlaced with real rugby world information and practical advice aimed not just at aspiring sports professionals but kids, parents, adults, indeed anyone interested in what it takes to perform at your peak.

My approach to professional rugby has also been the same approach I took to studying at the University of Huddersfield and in to my first "real world" job at the Huddersfield Giants as Business Development Manager. Some may even say that the unrelenting nature I have was born out of the desire to compete at the highest level as a professional sportsman.

The discipline needed to stay singled-minded has allowed me to focus on the smallest detail that I needed to give me the edge on competition. I don't really see the difference between a pitch and a board room. To me they are both places I can compete in and places I need to be on my "game" in.

I have compiled the HP sections with the idea that there will be something for everyone in them. The themes are wide ranging and cover a vast area that involves the life of a professional rugby player. I look at areas as simple as nutrition and exercise for children all the way through to training programmes for weights, speed and fitness. I give insight into my own personal psychological approach to success, as well as dealing with helping potential professionals understand what their responsibilities as a professional sportsman and woman will be, if they are fortunate enough to make it that far.

I have tried to keep much of the information simple and practical and attempted to steer well clear of the massive amounts of scientific and descriptive text that can become tedious to a reader. I have also tried to keep the HP frameworks brief and to the point. I have a favourite saying, "Tell me and I'll forget, show me and I may remember, involve me and I'll understand." That lies behind the HP sections.

In many of the sections, starting with children's nutrition after the next chapter, I have also added small insights and stories that are not in the autobiography but should help to add to the fuller picture of who I am as a person.

Chapter 2

Born Free

When I think of myself and Henry leaving New Zealand to live and play rugby on the other side of the world in England, I am reminded of another young wanderlust, our grandfather. William Allen was born in Liverpool. He lied to the merchant navy that he was 18 and set sail for New Zealand as a 15-year-old. He was also a navy boxing champion, which is something I did a little of as a youngster before the rugby took over. Grandad was also an artist and his father was a naval painter. When I was born, Robert Rawiri Paul on February 3 1976, I dipped a long way into the Allen gene pool.

Grandad still has a brush in his hand as a painter and decorator. He and my grandmother, Mary, had five children. At one time they owned a highly popular restaurant in Auckland City that was big on the jazz scene. When my grandmother was pregnant with my mum, they went to see the great Nat King Cole while he was touring New Zealand. When he came off stage, he spotted that my grandmother was pregnant and sang 'Unforgettable' to her and her bump, so to speak. I've always loved that story. When I married Natalie in 2010 that was the song we danced to, after having some professional lessons.

My mum, Gail, is of English descent and my dad, Te Whata, who everyone knows as Walter, is a Maori. They met at a time in the 1960s when mixing of the different cultures was generally frowned upon, unbelievable as that attitude seems now. Mum was born and brought up in Auckland City, my father in Whangarei, the northernmost city in the country. They certainly hailed from two entirely different worlds. Dad is one of 21 siblings. Mary Paul, my grandmother on my father's side, was the matriarch of this vast family, who we all knew as Big Nan. She had 16 children and my grandfather, Monty, had another five. There are so many of us that my love of family is hardly surprising. Mum was brought up in white upper middle class New Zealand, at a time when a more liberal and tolerant society was just starting to emerge. My parents were at the forefront of this peaceful revolution.

Mum was sent away to boarding school at Whangarei Girls. My dad was at Whangerei Boys. At school they tried to beat his culture out of him. If you spoke the Maori language in his day, you would get the cane. New Zealand now celebrates its rich Maori culture and heritage but not in those less enlightened times. Mum and dad were the trailblazers, who created a first generation of the likes of Henry and myself, mongrels, half breeds, mixed race kids, and bloody proud of it. They helped break the back of the old cultural stranglehold. Until then there was no intermingling, let alone intermarriage, and my parents encountered prejudice in those early days because it was seen as so different. Dad didn't really talk about it, but I know that mum copped a lot from both sides in coming into the Maori fold. She also happens to be a lot tougher than me, Henry and my dad put together. She had to be to put up with the three of us.

My parents' early relationship wasn't easy for a variety of reasons. Dad met mum in Whangarei in their early teens through Henry, dad's brother, who my brother is named after. Times were tough in Whangarei, as one of a huge family in a deprived area. Dad was 14 when he ran away from home to Auckland. He was caught in a stolen car there and sent to borstal for a year. Mum would write to him. Once he got out, they were inseparable. They moved back north to Whangarei and were living in a house there with a few of my uncles when someone fell asleep while smoking. The house burnt down. Thank goodness no-one got killed or injured, but that prompted my parents' move to the forestry town of Tokoroa in the Waikato region, 250 miles away, encouraged by the opportunity of work.

My Uncle Rob was working as a lumberjack there. Tokoroa was a two-horse forestry town, somewhat of a backswood place close to State Highway 1, built on the back of the lumber industry. Forest Products was the main employer and dad worked for them. They lived a little way out of town at Atiamuri in a house that was easy to spot from the road. The company painted homes in an agreement with the local authority. They had run out of white paint by the time they got to mum and dad's place. You could see it like a shining beacon from State Highway 1, the only house in bright purple.

When Henry came along, he was a freak. He weighed 11lbs at birth. Our Mum is 5ft nothing. I weighed in at 8lbs 9oz and mum reckoned she spat me out after Henry. Not long after I was born, Henry was taken sick at the age of two. He was in hospital with pneumonia. You wonder at any age what makes you be what you are, but Henry proved very early in life that he was a fighter. He nearly died. When mum speaks of it now, you can still hear the fear in her voice. Maori people use the word *whanau*. It is not about just looking after your own kids but the extended family. When Henry was taken ill, mum was at the hospital all day and dad was still working in the forest. Family rallied round, with the consequence that for pretty much the first year of my life I lived with family up north. I think there was a bit of an issue afterwards in getting me back, but dad wields a pretty big stick in the family and I rejoined my brother in Tokoroa, after his protracted battle with pneumonia. There was no stopping Henry after that. Dad would go fishing on the dam – there's no shortage of water around Tokoroa with 45 lakes – and he would tie Henry to a tree to stop him jumping in. He was just a ball of energy.

Mum and dad were happy in Tokoroa, but our lives changed when dad had an accident in the bush. A tree came down on him, crushing both legs. It meant a move to Auckland City, where dad underwent rehabilitation and we moved in with my grandparents in Ponsonby in Herne Bay. Mum began work at a betting shop, while dad spent a year in hospital. The tree had crushed the femur and tibia in both legs; the old man still gets pain but you never hear him complain. While Henry was at playschool, I could not have been more than two when I got out of the house. I had made my way across two busy roads when an old lady scooped me up and took me to the local police station, where an officer fed me tomatoes and chocolate. The next time I got out, I actually made it to mum's work. I did not quite get the delighted reaction from her that I had been hoping for.

They eventually set up house in Te Atatu, a peninsula that juts out into Waitemata Harbour, some seven miles from Auckland City. There was one way on and one way off the peninsula, a wonderfully safe place, where everyone knew each other. For two little tearaway kids, it was the best place that our parents could have picked for us to live. There was space to breathe and games to play. Henry had already picked up his first rugby ball in joining the Ponsonby club at the age of four. It was not long before I followed him, because that is what kid brothers do when it comes to living up to their elder siblings.

If Henry had not been so driven, I doubt whether I would have been as successful in my rugby career. He had fought his way through illness, he was hard on himself and he made sacrifices to better himself in order to reach his goals. They were life lessons for him and were traits I recognised as a kid looking up to my big brother. As his younger sibling I was dragged along with the things he did. I followed him everywhere. Bless his cotton socks, he was not one of those older brothers who get fed up of his little bro. He accepted me. Henry was the first person to take me nightclubbing, the first person to buy me a beer and he remains my best friend. He is someone I trust implicitly. That does not mean things always run smoothly, as anyone who has seen us going hammer and tongs at one another can testify, but even as kids we were a tight-knit twosome.

Dad was well again by the time we moved to Te Atatu and began a welding career, while mum worked for Databank and would bring us home stacks of paper. We both loved drawing. With his hand-eye co-ordination, Henry was a good artist but did not quite share the passion for art that I had developed at an early age. Henry could look at a picture and just recreate it. He was more content, though, pulling things apart and putting them together, especially electronic equipment. In school Henry was in the top set. I was in the middle set, until I reached the giddy heights of the top set at Rutherford High School, now Rutherford College, where mum teaches mathematics and information technology.

My creative side was fostered by my maternal grandmother Mary Allen, who had a massive influence on me, due in no small part to her liberal outlook on life. When I returned home for my wedding in 2010, I found Jehovah's Witnesses round at her house. Most people hide when they see them coming. Not my grandmother. She ended up educating them. They were the ones desperate to get out of the house. She was the person who helped broaden my horizons and had a knack of communicating with me like no-one else. She read the Bible and various religious texts, simply to gain a better understanding and knowledge. She hailed from a white, privileged background, but she is a worldly wise woman, proud of the fact that one son married a Maori woman, another a Samoan and a third a Malaysian, while a daughter married a Samoan man and my mum a Maori.

Ponsonby, where my grandparents lived, was a liberal area inhabited by a lot of artists. My grandmother had a drapery business. At Christmas and in the summer, mum would send me round there to act as a sort of security guard to ward off thieves. I stayed in the top floor room of the house, which was also my grandfather's art room. I loved waking up and looking at the paints and canvases, surrounded by his extensive collection of jazz records. It was like Jackson Pollock's dream studio, with a beautiful light streaming through. It was an inspiring place to visit let alone work in. He would travel a lot to the United States and back to England – the Pauls have family in Salford, Cumbria, as well as his native Liverpool – and his relationship with my grandmother had reached that stage when they did not need to be in each other's pockets. I never saw a finished piece in that studio by him, but by the time I had reached my GCSE-equivalent year in New Zealand, we had found some common ground.

For the first time we properly connected. He was fascinated by my use of really vibrant colours in my artwork. I converted a back room in my parents' house into a working studio. My grandfather isn't that tall but is very much an alpha male. He would come in shouting, "Robbie, Robbie, what are you doing?" We'd chat about perspective and vanishing points. I learned some great lessons from him, including one day at the beach him sitting me down with pen and paper and teaching me the necessary technical details. My grandmother looked after the creative side in opening my mind up. She would take me into town to look at paintings, tapa or bark cloths, or simply share her amazing knowledge. We would sit for hours and just natter.

Mum describes herself as a socialist. She certainly gets frustrated with the capitalist system and only a few having a lot, but I would say that she is a fusion of education and open-mindedness in her approach to life. I am like her in that I do not think that there is one recipe or that you can place yourself on one political flank. People want to rush and call you something, but sometimes you are not easily defined. It is why I do not like being pigeonholed and get frustrated with people who talk badly about other people. It is interesting to hear their thoughts, but what I always want is to experience things for myself, not for people to try and make decisions for me. If people want to treat me badly, that is their loss. I am a happy person, who finds it difficult to say no and, in that respect, I am very much like my parents.

We grew up with what I referred to as street kids. They were kids who needed foster care. Lots of my older cousins moved to Auckland and came to live with us. They left a legacy of connections with young people. Often they were kids who would need a bed for a couple of nights. Mum and dad would help them out and liaise with social services or their families. One of those who came to stay was Mark Elia, who went on to play 10 games for the Kiwis. Mark was with us for a year. Henry and I shared bunk beds and were woken one morning by Mark screaming. We all went running into his bedroom to discover him covered in goo. The cat had given birth on him. I did not quite connect that figure with the player who went on to represent his country. I remember being so jealous of Henry that Mark brought him back a St Helens jumper after he had joined Saints in 1985. But he was just one of many teenagers who needed somewhere to live at that time. That informal fostering at my parents' continues today. I will go back there and kids will shout, "Hey, Robbie" and I have no idea who they are. Often as not, though, I do know their parents.

It was just part and parcel of our lives growing up. The house was always full of people, although my dad had made a conscious decision, having come from such a huge family, just to have Henry and me. The thinking was that they wanted us as kids to have every opportunity in life. People crack me up when they ask whether there are any more Paul brothers running around a rugby pitch. I simply explain that my dad had his knackers tied after they had me. What we had was a full-on childhood. It was an awesome upbringing. I never wanted for company and we never went without. As brothers, we competed in different sports every day. Henry's friends would run after me to try and beat me up. Henry would stand there, laughing and telling them that they would never catch me. I would sidestep them and tease them even more. It was constant competition. Countless windows in the house would be smashed, and when it was too wet to play outside, we would clear everything out of the dining room and create our version of hockey. This would consist of strapping baseball pads to our knees and wielding tennis rackets at a makeshift ball made from Sellotape.

Dad put in a swimming pool. The whole peninsula would flock to our house. We would spend the entire summer in that pool, for which the old man did not bring in contractors but built the thing himself, including the veranda around it. I cannot remember a tradesman visiting our house. For a man who dropped out of school at 13, it was remarkable how he would pick up an engineering book, go through it from back to front, be able to fix cars, you name it, and ended up studying for a degree in horticulture. We never had carpet in the house.

It would only rot from kids running in and out with wet feet. It was a house made for folk to come and go. My parents did not spend money on it, knowing it would just get wrecked. A chandelier got ripped off in a pillow fight once. There was a hole in the front room for 12 years. All the money mum and dad had was spent taking us to tournaments and buying sports kit. They would take us on every school trip, come on school camps and basically live their lives through us. It has been the bane of my own children's lives that I am the only dad to turn up for their sports day. That is because my parents were conspicuously the only ones there at our sports days. They would have a ring of children around them, because everyone knew Mr and Mrs Paul, either through living with us at some point or just coming round to swim and play.

Then there was the food bill. It did not hit mum until Henry and I had left home that she no longer had to fill up three baskets when she popped to the supermarket. We wouldn't have three square meals a day – we'd have six. We consumed ridiculous amounts of carbohydrates. We were just eating-machines, because we were training every night and playing sport every weekend. Our house was also next to a play park, a quarter of an acre of land for sporting matches of every description. It is a potential goldmine for a housing development, but mum and dad aren't interested, and I can fully understand why. They bought the house for NZ$20,000 in 1979. It has not changed much but the waterfront itself is no longer the scruffy place it once was. Some posh houses have sprung up, although Te Atatu itself remains divided in two. One of the reasons I played rugby league and not rugby union was a matter of basic geography. The league club was in Te Atatu North, where we lived, while the union club was based in Te Atatu South. There was also the small matter of my dad having played both codes but infinitely preferring both playing and watching league. The game was his passion and it quickly became mine.

Naturally, I followed Henry into rugby league. Like him, I took up the game at four years of age. Mind you, I cannot remember a single boy I grew up with who did not play rugby. My debut came alongside my brother. Henry was six and the star of the Te Atatu North minis. The instruction was to pass to Henry, because he was the one who could score the tries. He was bigger, stronger and faster than everyone else. It turned out to be the last game we played together until the senior team. Mum described it as Henry playing rugby and me digging holes in the pitch, but one glorious moment stood out. I got the ball and just ran and ran. I eventually got tackled and got up to play the ball. However, the referee said I had scored a try. Henry came over to congratulate me. In that moment, I knew that this was the sport for me.

Our life from that point on was really built around the rugby club, although we were conscious of another side of life in Auckland. Gang culture was around. One of my uncles had a 21st birthday party at which people had to take their "patches" off – identifying their gang affiliation – because the code was to fight those wearing other badges. There can be a Maori intolerance to alcohol and a by-product of that could be violence. We saw people being beaten, but you just got away from that sort of thing. My dad might have taken that path but he got sorted out by Big Nan pretty early on that score. He had also moved to a world in which his sons' weapon of choice came oval-shaped.

Children's nutrition

Making sure your child gets the correct nutrition is really important for building a strong foundation for them reaching their HP potential. Some argue that it is at this time habits are formed in creating your future self. If so, the important thing here is to make sure the habits that we are instilling are the correct ones to help our kids realise their dreams.

Rather than science-related education, my parents stumbled upon making sure my brother and I received a balanced diet. Healthy portions of carbohydrates, low fat meats, dairy and, most importantly, vegetables and fruit were always the order of the day.

I remember both mum and dad piling greens on to our plates. I can't remember a single time when we never demolished our plates without massive smiles on our faces. To this day I absolutely love my veggies, especially salad. All of the nutrients and vitamins that are the building blocks to growth, strength and intelligence are produced by nature and are a gift to us, and as such we should embrace them.

One of the first marketing activities I engaged in at the Huddersfield Giants was helping to develop a platform where the Giants players could go into schools and deliver healthy living messages to kids. The focus was on nutrition and exercise. The feedback was and continues to be absolutely brilliant, because the kids receive healthy living life messages from their heroes.

Through our community department we decided to team up with the local Change4Life campaign and use their key messages as our focal points.

Key nutrition messages for children are:

- **5 a day:** We all know the 5 fruit and vegetables portions a day rule is based on making sure we have a healthy balanced diet (a balance of anti-oxidants, fibre, minerals, vitamins and other micronutrients). But did you also know that of the 5 a day, at least 3-4 should be vegetables? Another thing to consider is that many products claiming to be 1 of your 5 a day on the tin or pack can come with a host of other additives and bad elements with them. My rule of thumb here is always get and eat fresh vegetables when it's convenient. They taste better too.

My top 5 vegetables and fruit

Spinach (Packed with iron, calcium and lutein. Popeye's a big fan also!)
Blueberries (Packed with anti-oxidants, vitamin C, polyphenols, and taste great too)
Broccoli (Vitamin C, calcium, iron and fibre. Eat raw and get extra punch)
Beans (Fibre, protein, healthy fats and carbohydrates. I like mine baked)
Tomatoes (Vegetable or fruit? You decide. What we do know is that they defend against many types of cancer)

- **Me Sized Meals:** We have a tendency to over eat. If you are like me, I used to worry Henry would eat everything, so I would stack my plate and leave myself at bursting point every now and again. But making sure your portion sizes are correct for you will set you right. I've always found listening to my body is the best way to know when you are full. Did you know it takes the stomach about 20 minutes to send the signals to the brain to say 'hey you've had enough, stop eating'? As a sports professional, the approach I've always had is to take my time with meals and not to take too much. Slow down and enjoy your food. Once the message has arrived that my stomach is full, I've never worried about stepping away from my plate. When eating I also always start with the greens first, so I never leave any of that behind. Get those "super foods" in you.

- **Sugar swaps and snack checks:** Simply put, think about swapping sweets, fizzy drinks, etc. that have a high sugar count with lower options like dried fruit and nuts and sugar free cordial. Spend more time understanding what goes into the products you snack on, as it will be beneficial for you to understand the sugar, salt, calorie and fat content of your snacks, and try to swap them for products that are better for you.

- **Water, why do we need it?** Our bodies consist of 70 per cent water. As we make our way through the day we use the water in our bodies to help fuel our activities. To keep your body topped up you should drink at least 6-8 glasses of water each day. If the weather is warm or you are being active, you should drink more. Staying hydrated is an athlete's golden rule as dehydration can lead to a drop in performance of over 20 per cent – and when your team depends on you to make another tackle, you don't want to let them down. Something to remember: if you're thirsty, you're already dehydrated.

Chapter 3

The Seed is Planted

Henry was two when I was born, despite him still telling everyone that I am older than him. Mum and Dad instilled strong family values. Our culture was always one of coming back to our extended *whanau*, or family, and even though Henry and I can be apart for months at a time, when we come back together we're still the thick-as-thieves brothers we were growing up in New Zealand and later playing alongside one another for Bradford Bulls.

Like most younger brothers, I was anxious to follow in Henry's footsteps. We both played a sport we were passionate about and we had a go at every sport imaginable. Softball was a particular favourite. Henry was a pitcher and I acted as his catcher. When you are competing with and against someone two years older, you get dragged along at his pace. Henry also had only one gear. That was ramming speed. I have still got my old baseball glove. When Henry comes round it occasionally comes out. Just throwing the ball to each other in the backyard left the left side of my body in bits and pieces on one occasion.

When we meet up, the pair of us just fall into our natural pattern. He is big brother and somehow I have got to stop him. When it came to rugby as a kid, it involved me halting someone more physically advanced than I was. Sometimes I managed it, sometimes I didn't. Henry always set the benchmark though. Like brothers do, we would fight and scrap, although there was nearly a case of fratricide when Henry kneed me once while I was watching television. I was enraged, raced after him and grabbed a machete that I threw at him. It resembled a scene from the film *The Matrix*, the world going into slow motion as the thing spun through the air. At the last moment, Henry ducked. The machete missed him by a whisker.

When he took up martial arts, naturally I had to follow him. We would go cycling together. Henry got hit by a car once and it frightened the life out of me. I didn't cycle, I ran all the way home screaming that Henry was hurt. You consist of rubber and springs when you are young and he was okay after an overnight stay in hospital, although as a kid he did break his arm playing rugby and it kept him out for much of one season. I was always a passive, happy kid and loved hanging out with my mates, whereas Henry was always competing. I have never known him as anything other than a fighter, whether it was battling pneumonia when he was two, or on the pitch. Once he has set a goal, Henry will do everything in his power to achieve it. It has meant that at times he has not always played well alongside others. He could be the most infuriating player to have in your team. The dude is never wrong. It was the same playing a board game. Henry would even change the rules if they did not seem right to him. He would have thrived in an individual sport like tennis.

I am a different animal, more of an individual working to a team goal. The trouble with Henry was that as a great player he expected everyone to see the game the way he did. With team sport, though, you are only as strong as your weakest link. We got into a massive argument once at Bradford because Henry effectively broke our attack system, purely because he was such a phenomenal player. The bloke outside him was just playing to our system and did not possess the same skills set. Nor was he able to see what Henry could in terms of changing the line of attack. Henry was fuming at a video session. He has mellowed in older age and adapted, but as a great player he could see what a merely good player could not, and it would frustrate the life out of him.

It is always a matter of perspective. As kids, no-one bothered about the difference between rugby league and rugby union. I played a bit of union, as the world's smallest flanker. I was fast and got to the breakdown before anyone else. I should have gone on to play schools' representative level in union, but the union code's rules in New Zealand then were that you could not play both representative union and league. Rugby league didn't care, it just got on with it, partly because union was, and still is, a New Zealand institution. One of my softball mates was the All Black prop Kees Meeuws, who played union for Te Atatu South. The union club was too far away for dad to take us. Besides, he preferred league. In order to practice with us, dad began coaching-clinics at Te Atatu North. He was very much an innovator and wanted us to do things that others couldn't. He would have us tipping the ball on our fingertips while running, which perhaps explained the odd fancy trick we liked to indulge in. Playing basketball, I would spin the ball on every finger and my wrist to while away my time on the bench. It was not often that I was seen without a ball of some shape, spinning it around my fingers and hands.

Dad got immersed in coaching with the league governing body in Auckland and had his nose stuck in coaching course books by the likes of Wayne Bennett and John Lang. He introduced us to weights training exercise when I was 13 and Henry was 15. Dad was a big admirer of the great Balmain and Australia forward Wayne Pearce. Once he discovered that Pearce was exercising with weights, dad introduced them to us. He turned the garage into a gymnasium, with a bench press and multigym. All the kids in the neighbourhood would be round toning up to look good on the beach. Some of the weights were begged, stolen and borrowed and others did not even fit on the barbell, but dad knew what he was doing and Henry and I learned early on that building up the right muscles formed an essential part of training. The gym is still there at the house and kids go round to do their stuff, although by the time I was playing junior representative rugby league a proper gym membership was part of the package. It was not, however, until Matthew Elliott arrived at Bradford that I appreciated what real explosive power could be generated from proper weights training.

We mainly played rugby union at school and league for Te Atatu North. I had several heroes as a kid, all league players, such as Ellery Hanley and Andy Gregory in their Wigan pomp and the great New Zealander Mark Graham, who looked like a god and was built like a brick outhouse with a big booming voice to match. He was a good Kiwi boy from the sticks and solid all the way through. But no-one could quite match my true rugby league hero. Wally Lewis, captain of Australia and a player simply known as "The King", was actually the bane of my existence as a kid supporting the New Zealand team. He just had this knack of always beating us. We seemed to have the game in the bag and Wally would come up with something sensational. Always Wally, what a player.

When you think of the skill sets of players like Benji Marshall, Darren Lockyer, Johnathan Thurston and Sean Long, you wonder whether Wally would have hacked it in the modern game. The skilled guys nowadays are athletes, whereas Wally was more of a barrel. But he possessed such vision and game sense that he transcended appearance, especially to this particular six-year-old. That was the age when dad chucked me on to the pitch at Carlaw Park after a Test match against Australia. I just headed for my hero, little legs going like the clappers, programme clutched tight in one hand and pen in the other. I have still got Wally Lewis's autograph from that day, proudly at mum and dad's. It was the day, too, that the seed was planted.

From Wally giving me his autograph, I knew precisely what I wanted from life: to play international rugby league for New Zealand. That Wally scribble straight after that match also imprinted an understanding and appreciation of how important it is to engage with young kids. Twelve years later, dad only gave me one piece of advice when I left Auckland for Bradford. He was quite confident that I could take care of all the athletic aspects, but he reminded me to make sure that I signed every single kid's autograph book. It does not matter if you are in Workington and have to take a taxi home because the team bus has left without you. You stand there and sign every autograph, then hail a cab. You can make that difference to a kid. From Wally's signature came a huge internal drive to go on and one day play for the Kiwis.

That was my epiphany moment and nothing was going to stop me. Agility and speed were my obvious strengths growing up. The Polynesian and Maori kids exploded in size really early. They matured so quickly but, luckily for me, mum and dad had blessed me with good skills, plus I was smart. I would take the big blokes on. Dad would tell me to run at the strapping guys and put some footwork on them. I ended up doing that virtually my whole career, until I eventually slowed down. I also had good timing in terms of my defence. If people made an ill-informed decision to target me, they found that out to their cost. It does not matter how big an opponent is, if your technique is good in putting all your energies into hitting people the right way, you can hurt them. Fortunately, mother nature also blessed me with a big backside. Your power comes from your trunk and I was able to use it the right way.

At 16 I began to really physically mature. That coincided with my discovery along with Henry that pasta was the thing to eat before you play. We would boil up loads, flavourless and without any sauce, and devour the lot on the understanding that it was good for us. Maybe it did me some good because I got my first real breakthrough in the Auckland under-17s team. The original choice as scrum half got injured, I got drafted in and had a stormer. Up until that time, I had concentrated on developing my skills in touch rugby. The upshot was that I then got selected for New Zealand under-17s ahead of Stacey Jones who, truth be known, was always the better player. We both punched a year above our weight, but while everything was going swimmingly in one sense, I seemed destined for disappointment in those formative teenage years.

Scouts from the Australian competition always made a beeline for the national tournament in New Zealand. When I was 15 and 16 Auckland Warriors were the new kids on the block. I watched as the new franchise signed up Stacey Jones, Awen Guttenbeil, Logan Swann, Joe Vagana and Nigel Vagana, contemporaries of mine and slightly older. Henry had signed for them too, but no-one from the Warriors came knocking on our door for me. I felt left out because it was such an exciting time for rugby league in New Zealand. The Warriors were following a simple remit to develop the best squad from big existing names and exploiting the amazing league talent emerging in the country at that juncture.

Money appeared to be no object and the club was brilliantly promoted. "The Warriors are Coming" was the basis of the publicity campaign. Not for this kid, though. They signed up Dean Bell, John Kirwan from rugby union, various Kiwi legends and the best up and coming players in the land. With all my peers being signed along with Henry, it was hard to handle. Those who did sign got a NZ$3,000 contract for two years, which was hardly the best business deal in the world. What it was, however, was your place in the whirl of the Warriors' arrival. It was sold as, this is your team and this is your duty, and it proved very persuasive. The money was paid up front along with a gym membership, effectively payment in kind. Henry also got free boots but, more especially, the precious Warriors gear. Of course I was jealous. Everyone seemed to be signing these contracts, apart from me.

The Australian competition was massive and here it was finally arriving in New Zealand. Growing up, I supported Manly Sea Eagles during the Des Hasler years and admired little Geoff Toovey strutting his stuff. I later swapped allegiance to Canberra Raiders, probably on the basis that they were the red hot team at that time. They had the likes of Quentin Pongia, Brent Todd, Laurie Daley and John "Chicka" Ferguson. I did have some contact with Canberra when I was 16 but that fell through, while the Warriors seemed a distant prospect. They were about ten players deep in the halves, so the last thing they needed was another little bloke.

It wasn't until the 1994 Junior Kiwis tour to Australia that my fortunes turned around, although I was gripped at that stage by my passion for art. I left school at 17 to study at the art and design college at Auckland Institute of Technology. I actually got on the course before completing all my exams at school. It makes me angry still that I fobbed off those exams. I studied art and design, graphics and design art history, painting and English for my bursary, or A levels. I prided myself on working hard, even though I was not exactly the brightest kid in the world. By my final year, painting was what stirred me and it was my great good fortune to have two outstanding art teachers in Mr Moody and Mr Shaw.

I have always had good hand-eye co-ordination. I could always see something and translate it to paper or canvas, like replicating a photograph. I could even grab a Rembrandt and do a reasonable copy. But one day Mr Moody lost his rag with me. I had done another picture perfect copy – who knows, I could have gone on to a be a fairly decent counterfeit painter – when Mr Moody grabbed an ice cream container, scooped up some white paint and began chucking it on my black and white sketch. I don't know quite what happened but something in me just clicked, thanks to my teacher's inspired act of vandalism. My whole way of looking at art was transformed. They had been trying to talk to me about interpretation. In that moment, I got it.

By the end of that final school year I was producing giant canvases but never actually having wielded a paint brush. I used bits of plastic, anything I could lay my hands on, to create different landscapes. Contrasting colours fascinated me and still do. My understanding of expressionism then was still very basic and needed to be developed but I got a school prize for one of my pieces. It was a stepping stone to getting a real job, whatever that would be, and living a real life, I guess. A massive part of my life was still rugby, but the reality was that you cannot always do what you want. I had just turned 18 when I began college. That light bulb moment having come some months earlier, art was no longer schoolwork but a passion. In my down time from the rugby, I would be thinking creatively, just as I do now. Artwork is in my mind's eye. I paint in my head. I will see a painting or work that I admire and it will send me off into my own little creative world.

The course was a foundation year, learning the basics and how to use the tools during the first two semesters. I never actually got to the third semester because life changed for me on many fronts in 1994. Although I had not been offered a contract by the Warriors my aspirations still burned brightly. I was performing at the highest level on the wing for the Te Atatu premier team and making Auckland and New Zealand representative squads. My disappointment about the Warriors ran deep but it was not like my dreams were disappearing. It just made me more determined. I am a person who digs his heels in and works harder. I trained every day. I honed my skills in touch rugby and got bigger in the gym.

I never had any trouble with the crazy teenager bit. Growing up alongside so many talented athletes, I appreciated the importance of self discipline. If there was a party on, I tended not to go. If I did, I did not drink and would be home at a respectable time. I had some goals and wanted to achieve them, backed up by my parents' strong moral code. They trusted us as kids, knowing full well that we were hardly going to be perfect. Dad would utter his favourite saying: "If you make a mistake, it is not your fault. Make the same mistake, it is your fault, because you have not learned the lesson." I would love to say that I have not repeated mistakes in my life but I would be lying, but dad's words remain in my conscience and motivate me to always improve.

Early in 1994 I was pursuing three dreams at the same time: education, being a rugby league professional and my first long-term relationship. I had met Antonia in a bar the previous August. I was 17 and not short of a girlfriend. Playing a popular sport and having the gift of the gab, you did all right on that score, but there was never anyone serious. New Zealand culture then was slightly slower than now. I would drive Henry's car. It was a rickety old thing and in New Zealand you did not need insurance to drive. We had full driving licences at 16. A couple of my mates were petrol heads and went around in souped-up cars. But never being lost for a word or three, I never had to impress any girl with talk of a shiny car. Besides, cars have never really interested me. I have always been a confident person and that is again down to mum and dad. I know who I am and I have never tried to be someone I am not. I have always hung on to those values. If I do not like somewhere, I will take myself out of that place and avoid it next time. "Everyone isn't the same, so do not try and treat them the same," as my grandmother would tell me.

It was the 18th birthday of Wendell Sisnett, one of my best friends, when I first met Antonia. We went to South Auckland to celebrate. I was 17 with a face of a 15-year-old. Little wonder I got turned away from one bar where you had to be 21 to enter. All my mates got in, so my other great buddy Ueta Siteine came with me to another bar around the corner. The place was empty. We walked up to the bouncer, who suddenly grabbed us and whipped us upstairs. Ueta looked at me and I looked at him and the guy said: "Henry, whatever you want to drink, it's on the house." It was one of the very few times that being mistaken for my brother came in handy. Henry was on a residents team tour of Australia at the time and was already making a name for himself, but I could not live with myself after that first beer and owned up, much to Ueta's disgust that he had been denied a free night on the pop.

We came back to the city to a nightclub where I saw Antonia, began chatting and swapped phone numbers. Within four months we were in a full-blown relationship. She was from the city, I was from the suburbs. I was discovering a new world of art that was stretching my imagination and she was living a life completely at odds with what I had experienced. It was very seductive. She had her own place and a month-old baby daughter. I fell in love with Iesha as much as Antonia, whose upbringing in an upper middle class New Zealand European family was far removed from my growing up in a basically Maori culture, even though mum is of European extraction. We came from opposite sides of the track. She was interesting, fascinating, but at the same time vulnerable as a young single mother.

Antonia and I were two passionate people with completely different internal drive systems. I came from a hard-working background, she from what I saw as a laid back world in which people were more interested in entertaining themselves than being productive with their lives. That is part of the reason Antonia and Iesha came to live with us after my first semester at art college. I wanted our relationship to be more productive in an environment where you roll your sleeves up, not just hope to be lucky in life. She was not working and I thought she could get back on her feet if she came to live with me. And, of course, mum and dad fell in love with Iesha instantly.

Over 13 years, mine and Antonia's relationship was akin to train tracks that come together and drift apart. We never married. We talked about it once. It was a wedding or a kitchen. We bought the kitchen.

Over the years we broke up a few times but always tried to do the best thing by Iesha and Mia, who was born in 1995. Even when we were together we basically led separate lives. When we eventually called it quits it was probably the best thing to happen for both of us. We get on so much better now because we no longer take energy off each other. That is what used to happen with sometimes spiteful consequences. The reality was that we were two different people who wanted different things out of life.

The one aspect of my life that began to suffer when Antonia moved in was my art education. I was producing okay work but nowhere near the standard of which I was capable. I was in love, we had got a beautiful baby with us and other things were distracting me. I had received some television exposure with Te Atatu Roosters in the national competition and also at under-19 representative level. Then I got the player of the tournament award at the 1994 nationals with Auckland in a competition featuring the likes of Willie Talau, David Kidwell, Joe Vagana and Nigel Vagana. In partnering Stacey Jones at stand off, I had a storming series of matches in which we destroyed all-comers. That earned me selection for the Junior Kiwis and caused Auckland Warriors finally to come on the scene. They waved the same NZ$3,000 contract they had at Henry, but that Junior Kiwis tour to Australia changed everything. Mick Withers was in the Australian Schoolboys side we beat in that series. "The first Australian Schoolboys side to lose on Australian soil," as Joe Vagana and I would endlessly taunt Mick in our days together at Bradford.

Henry had chosen a similar path after school in getting into teacher training college before events took off for him after the 1993 Junior Kiwis tour to Great Britain. The Warriors structure had been in place for over a year. However, the team was still another two years from their first season in the Winfield Cup, so Henry was given a release to play in the English championship at Wakefield Trinity. He had been there over Christmas and the January of 1994 when I received a call from him, the day before I started art college. David Topliss, the Wakefield coach, wanted to know whether I would fancy playing the rest of the season with them.

The only way I could resolve this dilemma was to admit to myself that, although this offer was a dream come true, I did not fully believe I was ready. I had played a season of first team rugby on the wing for

Te Atatu but was only just making my way in terms of the new New Zealand Super League competition, otherwise known as the Lion Red Cup, for Waitakere City Raiders, which was a step up. Not quite enough at that stage, I believed, in turning Toppo, Wakefield and Henry down with the heaviest of hearts. Nevertheless, interest in me had been building. Before the 1994 Junior Kiwis tour, Peter Brown, a player agent for many of the Kiwi boys, who was acting on my behalf, had a couple of deals on the table from Hull FC and Oldham. They were not that great. But when I went to speak to Auckland Warriors, the sales pitch of Ian Robson, the club's charismatic chief executive officer, was masterly. I was all prepared to sign that piece of paper there and then when Peter pulled me aside. "If you sign this pathetic contract," he said, "I'm going to give you a bloody good hiding."

The best deal on offer was one by a new Australian club, South Queensland Crushers, under the former Castleford Tigers coach Darryl Van de Velde, although it was only a semi-professional contract. Henry, in the meantime, had been making waves in England, notably in a league fixture against Wigan. Once Henry emerged on Wigan's radar, they wanted him. All the time he was at Wakefield, though, Henry was selling the English game to me and how I would love it over there. He even gave a press interview talking about his kid brother back in New Zealand better than himself; perhaps he meant better looking. At long distance I could see Henry's career taking off. Wigan did a swap deal plus cash with Auckland Warriors for Denis Betts and Andy Platt to move there for the 1995 launch. All I could see on my horizon in New Zealand at that stage were part-time contracts or scholarships, a long way from the seed planted by Wally Lewis some dozen years earlier.

Henry, however, was persistent. He told David McKnight, who was representing him in England, just how much he would love to have me over. David told him he would see what he could do. It was at that point he told the Bradford Northern chairman Chris Caisley that he had Henry Paul's little brother if he fancied signing him. That was one weekend and I had my answer on the Monday via a fax machine that mum and dad had invested in to keep in touch with Henry, as it was cheaper than phoning. When it came through, the fax had distorted lines all over it, but when I picked up that piece of paper, I just thought wow. A fully professional contract to become a rugby league player in Bradford, England. I signed there and then. What they got back at the other end was probably little more than a black smudge. For a kid finally on his way to the big time, I was just so excited about the prospect, without really knowing anything about this team called Bradford Northern.

I had watched Challenge Cup finals and Test matches from England but Bradford was a mystery. Wigan were the team who won everything, the team Henry had signed for, for whom the Iro brothers, Dean Bell, Sam Panapa and Frano Botica paraded the cup at Wembley as proud Kiwis in the famous cherry-and-white colours. Ellery Hanley, Martin Offiah, Shaun Edwards, Andy Gregory, English legends of the game, none of them played for Bradford, but the 1993-94 championship table didn't lie, surely? Wigan finished top, again, but with Bradford up there with them in second place on the same number of points, both having won 23 games and lost seven. This was the Bradford I was joining, a team as good as Wigan. I could not wait to whisk Antonia and Iesha on to that plane.

Exercises for kids (and adults)

Over my years as a professional sportsman I have been asked many times to suggest a weight training programme for children. I must admit it has always made me uncomfortable to do this. The reason I feel it is inappropriate is that weightlifting can be dangerous if you do not use the correct technique. Also, for children in their teens, forcing growth through an unnatural process like weightlifting can have a bad effect on the body's natural growth pattern as children go through puberty. As a rule of thumb, I suggest that kids don't start weight training until they are at least 15. Saying that, I do feel it is appropriate to teach them technique before they turn 15, then they will be ready to hit the ground running. Can I also suggest using a qualified professional to teach them these techniques.

I have always believed that extra training will benefit anyone, so I have decided to list a few of my favourite plyometric exercises that anyone can do, including children of all ages, that will help develop some core rugby-using muscles.

All exercises will help improve strength, muscle density and explosive power.

Squat jumps *(Major muscles of the leg)*
With feet planted just wider than your shoulders, bend down into a sitting position so your thighs are at right angles to your shins, then explode upwards into a jump, raising your knees up to your chest. Upon touching the ground repeat the full process. Ten squat jumps represent one set. Complete 3 sets having a 1 minute rest between sets.

Explosive hops *(Major muscles of the legs and increased agility)*
Set up 4 hurdles half a metre apart (whatever height is comfortable). The aim is to hop sideways over the four hurdles with only a single bound in between hurdles. Upon clearing the fourth hurdle, still facing the same way, hop straight back over the four hurdles in the other direction. Upon reaching the start position change legs and repeat the process. This is one set. Complete

3 sets having a 1 minute rest between sets.

Explosive press up *(Chest, shoulders and triceps)*
Start in a normal press up position with your arms straight and your hands placed on the floor, shoulder width apart. Make sure your body is flat like a board. Bend your arms and allow your body to slowly go towards the floor. When your chest touches the floor explode upwards, so that your body and hands leave the floor. Ten explosive press ups represents one set. Complete 3 sets having a 1 minute rest between sets. As you build your strength, you will eventually be able to clap your hands before your hands make the start position.

Side throws *(Lower back muscles and waist)*
Using both hands, hold a football 30cm away from your belly button and standing side-on place yourself 3-5 metres away from a flat wall. Powerfully twist towards the wall releasing the ball straight at it in a side rugby passing motion. Allow your hips to rotate with your torso but keep your feet firmly planted. Pick up the ball and repeat the process. 20 throws both left and right represent one set. Again I suggest doing 3 sets with 1 minute rest between sets.

This workout completed in full will help develop all of the muscles needed for rugby and will also give you a good blow out and work your muscles.

Chapter 4

Barefoot in Bradford

There was a three week turnaround from signing the contract with Bradford to boarding the flight. The weekend before we set off I settled down at home to watch a film on the one movie channel they had those days on Sky NZ. Up popped *Rita, Sue and Bob Too*, a raw, working class portrayal of, yes, Bradford. I could not quite believe it. This wasn't what Bradford was like, was it? I swear I still had a part of mum's skirt held tight in my hands as I got on the plane.

I looked at Iesha – she was named after a song by a group called Another Bad Creation – and wondered whether I was really doing the right thing. Antonia had been in a relationship that had ended early and had been bringing up Iesha alone. My family had got to benefit from their arrival and here I was moving them 12,000 miles to a place I had some vague notion of from a film that, to say the least, hardly portrayed it in the best light. I was 18, a little scared but imbued with an overriding sense of responsibility. The way I reconciled it, I had to be strong and lead because I had a partner and child depending on me. No room for weakness; you bury the fear. Get on with business, that is the way I was brought up. If you are old enough to do this, you are old enough to accept the responsibility. Old enough in one way, not in others, however. I still had one work to complete before quitting art college, a steel sculpture. I borrowed dad's welding gear, but in my haste ripped off the protective mask to try and finish it a little quicker. I had been staring at the bare light. When I got up the next morning it was as if someone had stuck razor blades under my eyelids.

Truth be told, I probably would not have gone to England at that time had Henry not been there. As much as I was driven, it was comforting to know that big bro was not far away. In late August we all set off together, me on my way to Bradford and Henry to join Wigan. My contract was for three years and I was to get £25,000 over the first ten months. Not that I really knew how much that was. I was so green it is frightening looking back. I had only travelled as far as Australia before and en route to England we broke up the journey with a couple of days in Los Angeles, where Iesha amazed us all by taking her first steps and Americans stunned me also by putting sugar in their milk.

This was going to be a different life in every sense. When we eventually touched down in Manchester, after what seemed an eternity, we were greeted by a typical British summer's day. I'd swear it was about 3 centigrade. I was frozen to the core. Henry was lean-looking, but I was 15kg lighter and petite by comparison. Chris Caisley, the Bradford chairman, was waiting with David McKnight, our manager. Goodness knows what Chris thought when he saw this little shivering figure emerge. All he had glimpsed of me up until then was four televised edits of me scoring a try for Te Atatu and a few runs in one game. Maybe he had spotted some potential from those brief flashes on a video, possibly he had seen a bit of Henry's talent in me, who knows? In the flesh standing before him was a wide-eyed 11 stone stripling.

Chris had taken a punt. It was hardly a bank-breaking contract, but he had taken a risk nonetheless in signing someone on the basis of his brother's say so and a few grainy television shots. I hadn't a clue what he was thinking, other than probably what on earth he had done. It was not a conventional overseas signing, to say the least, but I was a Bradford Northern player now. The frightening bit was that we went straight off with Chris to Bradford and Henry jumped into another car with David to go to Wigan. We were now on our own on the last leg of a marathon journey to the land of *Rita, Sue and Bob Too*. The M62 motorway climbed and climbed the backbone of the Pennines, a drive across a beautiful, rugged landscape that still impresses me now. The road eventually flattened out, with a huge reservoir on the left and, if my jet-lagged eyes did not deceive me, a farmhouse in the middle of the motorway to the right. That just blew my mind and still does. I spent the rest of the trip to Odsal wondering just how the people living there got any sleep.

As we approached the ground, the stadium itself was not exactly obvious. In fact I couldn't see it before it eventually opened up to me in all its glory, a giant hole in a hillside; what used to be a rubbish tip. There was no rugby on that Saturday night but a speedway event, and what struck me – apart from the showers of shale being kicked half way up the terraces – was a lack of people watching. In that moment I began thinking whether I had bitten off more than I could chew. I was taken into the clubhouse and introduced to a few people, including the kit man Freddie Robinson, who was an awesome guy. I was then led to a back room, which was described to me as the gym. All I could see was a bench press with a barbell on it. The weight next to it on the floor could not fit it because the hole was too small. The only other piece of equipment was a deflated boxing speed ball. I had come 12,000 miles to this? Dad's garage gym was ten times better – for one thing, the weights worked – and I had been getting cutting edge advice from the Australian Institute of Sport as part of the cream of a new New Zealand generation of players. This was no better than my amateur club at home. To say I had been expecting more was putting it mildly.

The place we were going to move into was a club house where Darrell Shelford was still living before moving to join Huddersfield, so we spent the first three days in a hotel on an industrial estate next to the M606. The following day I went to watch to the A team, or second team, who got flogged. I was taken afterwards to the Fire Brigade pub in the city which, I discovered, was to be my personal sponsor. The landlord and his wife were fantastic, although a little disappointed that I declined a pint for a Coca-Cola, something I drank a lot of in my early days at Bradford.

My debut in the reserves came the following Wednesday against Wakefield at stand off outside Neil Holding, a former Great Britain international nearly twice my age. It chucked it down and I couldn't hold the ball all night. I put myself into space on numerous occasions but each time the slippery pill bobbled from my grasp. It was an inauspicious start. Neil did a lot of the reserve team coaching alongside Nigel Stephenson. They put me in two days later against Halifax. It was freezing and miserable again but I had a storming game, scoring a hat-trick of tries and setting up two or three more. The Halifax defensive shuffled from sideline to sideline and there were gaps galore for me to put on some footwork. It was a pattern that continued over the following weeks. I was tearing teams apart at a time when the first XIII began to do badly, despite a strong opening to the 1994-95 championship.

In the November of that first season the Bradford board started putting pressure on Peter Fox, the coach, to pick me in the first team. Peter had coached Bradford from 1977-85 and was three years into his second stint at Odsal. To say he was something of a legend in rugby league is an understatement. Peter was a true blue Yorkshireman who called it as he saw it. If you were crap, he told you that you were crap. Peter was direct and honest, occasionally brutally so. When he first clapped eyes on me, he said: "I'm not picking thee because thy's not big enough." It was an accurate enough assessment of my physical attributes, so I was hardly in a position to argue otherwise, especially as Peter had asked Chris Caisley to buy him a world class front rower from Australia, not a Kiwi whippersnapper.

He called a spade a spade but I ended up loving him for it. I liked listening to Peter's wonderfully broad Wakefield accent, even though I had no idea most of the time what on earth he was on about. I would turn to one of the others. "What did he say?" Peter came along to a reserve team game and turned to me as we got off the bus. "Has thee got a woolly coit?" He repeated it three or four times before one of the lads stepped in with the translation that he wanted to know where my woollen coat was. "No, no, I'll be all right," I said, to which he stared at me as if I was quite mad. Five minutes into the game at Castleford, I was freezing my proverbials off on the sidelines.

One day at training on the asphalt pitch over the road from Odsal, Peter looked up to the skies and said, as bold as brass, that it was going to snow. Sure enough, it began snowing five minutes later. I looked over at the old sage and thought, man, that is impressive. Peter remained concerned about my size, although there was little doubting my speed, which even he acknowledged. However, as much as I was living the dream of a professional rugby league player, there were a couple of occasions when I asked myself what I was doing here. Frustration got the better of me in the second team, but the reality was that both Peter and Nigel Stephenson were nurturing me and possibly waiting for me to develop physically a little quicker.

My first team chance finally arrived on November 27, 1994. Neil Summers, our regular stand off, was injured and Dave Heron filled in, with me on the bench. I had been on five minutes in the first half when Deryck Fox, our Great Britain scrum half, put up a bomb. I hared after it and outjumped the Wakefield full back. I came down with the ball over the goal-line, so that wasn't a bad start for my senior debut. Bradford dominated that day and I bagged a second try in a 34-0 win from another astute kick by Deryck. Dave Bailey was playing at scrum half for Wakefield and I had played alongside him in the Waitakere team earlier in the year. As Dave came towards me, the ball cannoned off his leg, bobbled and I toed it on in winning the race to touch it down. A brace of tries in my first real taste of a Yorkshire derby and I enjoyed my first headline in the *Bradford Telegraph & Argus* the next day.

Peter Fox was very much his own man and didn't like anyone telling him what to do, especially as he was the heart and soul of Bradford Northern. But he had seen enough to convince him to start me the following week against the French club St Esteve in a Regal Trophy second round tie. We won 32-6, I scored a hat-trick and got the man of the match award. I still possess the framed photograph showing a scrawny kid with a ridiculous gold hooped earring receiving his first ever trophy. The first few months were never warm and by January the place felt like an icicle. I was on the bench for a match at Doncaster thinking to myself, why on earth are all the guys playing so soft and so slowly? No-one seemed to want to get caught with the ball. I came on at a million miles an hour, went into my first tackle, slid across the icy surface and left half my skin on the ground.

It was one of 13 first team games I played that first season, including against Henry's Wigan. Henry got a try in a 14-10 win for them and I got knocked out. It was the first time we had come face to face on opposite sides although, in truth, we had done that all our lives in baseball, volleyball, touch rugby, you name it. The biggie, though, was against big, bad neighbours Leeds, to whom Bradford were very much the poor relations then. Leeds had great players such as Kevin Iro, Craig Innes, Garry Schofield and Ellery Hanley in their side, and Alan Tait. Most full backs would stand their ground when I got one-on-one on them, I'd do a bit of nifty footwork and they would not be able to stop me. Not Taity. He did something I'd never seen a full back do before. Rather than stand up to me, he began running backwards. I was coming out of my 22 and got to Alan at the 40 metre mark. Rather than wait for me, though, he jogged backwards. It completely bamboozled me. I was unable to do anything to him because he was shepherding me to the sideline. He always had the angle on me for the tackle. Alan, of course, had unsuccessfully tried to do the same to Martin Offiah in the 1994 Challenge Cup final against Wigan, except that I didn't quite possess the pace that Martin famously demonstrated at Wembley that day.

At one stage during that first season I was playing in both the reserve and first teams. Sometimes I would turn up to watch the reserves, someone would drop out, they would chuck me a shirt and cry, "Robbie, get on". One week I played matches on Saturday, Monday, Wednesday and Friday, and I loved every minute of it. Nigel Stephenson pulled me aside at the A team awards evening and said the club had big plans for me but not for another two or three years. I remember thinking that I was good enough right then, but when I see what we do with kids now, Nigel was right. I was not big enough. Rather than wait for youngsters to mature physically at nature's fickle pace, we nowadays try to turn boys into men by putting muscle on them. In 1994 no-one in the British game did weights properly; some players not at all.

Bradford was not professional in the contemporary sense, nor was it alone in the British game then. The word professional merely related to the money the players received. As a sporting organisation there was no active marketing other than the traditional methods of a big sign outside the ground and some work with the local media. Not that it mattered to an 18-year-old, who was concerned only with what was happening on the pitch. Bradford Northern were hardly a glamour side. We gloried in the name of the Steam Pigs. We loved to get dirty on heavy, muddy fields and belt the opposition. Those were the club's values.

With the big boys flying at one another, I had what every natural animal has built into them – fright and flight. Growing up with huge Maori and Polynesian boys, you had to come up with something and my quick feet were my saviour. After that first glimpse of the so-called gym at Odsal, I knew I could not work there. Mostly I trained on my own and I joined a gym in Wibsey, doing the sort of weights that make you look good on the beach but not much else. Most gym instructors did not have a lot of qualifications then and I was following what everyone else was doing there in building up big muscle groups, basically to look like Arnold Schwarzenegger. I did not appreciate then than it was pretty hopeless in terms of your rugby and explosive power, however ripped you looked in the mirror. There was no science then regarding energy retention and the importance of hydration. Crazily, I was lifting weights on the morning of a game.

I made up my training from frameworks I had brought over with me. A lot of the other guys were in their 30s and in jobs, whereas I would turn up at Odsal on my own every day and run up and down the hundreds of steps. Up and down the bleak terrain I would go. The office staff who were there thought I was bonkers. In the cold and wet on your own there were times when it was difficult to get motivated and it took a call to Henry, who would berate me for being a softie and get me going. I did sprint training on a daily basis and joined in with the Tuesday, Thursday and Friday sessions with the rest of the players. As for nutrition advice, forget it. In the house Antonia and I did not even know how to switch the oven on for the first two months. We just grilled everything, although she was very health conscious and a great cook. I also hit on Creatine – tubs of sand that tasted of sand too. Our hooker, Trevor Clark, who was doing a sport science degree, was testing it out for his academic studies. It was a natural nutrient but attracted plenty of controversy at the time.

Nothing about our approach was particularly sophisticated but typified the pre-Super League age. Peter was not one of those coaches who mucked in with you. He would stand at the top at Odsal watching Nigel run us through our set patterns. Peter had also built a side of players who pretty much coached themselves, who knew their roles inside out, with Deryck Fox as our on-field general. I learned so much from players of vast experience like Deryck and Neil Holding, who also taught me British humour. The first thing you learned was the ability to laugh at yourself. Nothing is sacred in dressing room culture. If you got too big for yourself you wound your neck back in. The beauty of Bradford was that there were no big stars. If you were not part of that close-knit family you did not last long.

A lot of the lads were brickies, labourers, farmers, police officers, all massive men, who no-one messed with. They were awe-inspiring to me. Karl Fairbank and Paul Dixon did not bother with weights because they were throwing bullocks around on their farms. Karl had hands as big as trucks and then there was Paul Medley, the human bowling ball. The Kiwis in the squad were all natural athletes through their blood lines. Paul Newlove, an established Great Britain international, was an individual blessed with fantastic abilities, grace and balance, while Roy Powell was a machine who would do all the hard yards and grind it out on the field. I had never seen a man so unaffected by alcohol. On the end of season trip to Tenerife, he would be the same at 3am as he was at 3pm. It was like he was carved from granite. He was built like a Greek god but with a weak heart, which we tragically discovered a few years later, with Roy's sudden death at the age of 33.

Running up and down the steep inclines at Odsal, the only player I would bump into was Roger Simpson, who was also the groundsman and a guy who could move on a dime. Without Roger's encouragement, I would not have been able to sidestep as well as I did. Brian McDermott was six years older than me, a painter and decorator who was not long back from service with the Royal Marines and was the skinniest forward I had ever clapped eyes on. He was raw but a heck of an athlete with a great engine on him. The point was that on the field these gnarled, wise old guys looked after you.

Trevor Clark was an early mentor and the dual-code Wales international Gerald Cordle took me under his wing. Like me, he regarded himself as a foreigner coming from rugby union in Wales and we both shared a love of rap music. We had another thing in common in that Gerald wasn't a drinker either. There was a big New Zealand contingent with Trevor, Dave Watson, and Eugene Bourneville and later Carl Hall, who had both played for Mount Albert when I was cutting my teeth in the New Zealand premiers. These guys were much older than me and could party hard. That wasn't for me at the time. I was too driven by my goals to bother with alcohol. At that time I was further inspired playing in a Regal Trophy tie at Whitehaven against one of my great New Zealand heroes growing up, Clayton Friend. I lasted 10 minutes against him after he tripped me up.

Due to the big age difference with most of the other players, sometimes I just stuck to myself. Only Phil Hepworth and Gary Christie were anywhere near my age, apart from the under-19s team, who also asked me to play with them. Despite being a glutton for punishment, I really did have enough on with both the first team and reserves, even though I wasn't doing a day job like the vast majority. A lot of the lads ended up in management positions or owning their own companies. There is a lot to be said for the semi-professional game, as it was then, with the singular exception of the fully professional Wigan club. Rugby provided decent income for players on top of earnings from the day job that they just continued with on retirement from playing. Now we drag kids out of school at 16, make them live, breathe, eat and sleep rugby, get them to 30 or so, if they are very lucky, and bid them farewell, without providing them with the necessary skills to take them into a non-rugby future.

As I was the baby of the Bradford team, the older players did their best to protect me. I like to think that they saw a young fella with a young family who had potential and some ambitions to achieve. We went to the pub once, with me on my usual pints of Coca-Cola, and every one of the lads pulled me aside to give advice or warnings to watch this or that. They never sought to lure me into the drinking culture or ask me to join in. Mum and dad were a long way away, but their moral underpinning stood me in good stead in my formative years. They taught me right from wrong and left it up to me to choose. The lifestyle of a sports professional can be a seductive one at times, if you bow down to primal desires, but I had none of those distractions then.

We lived two streets across from Odsal, a stone's throw from training. I was a teenager with a partner, baby and a hunter gatherer's instinct, yet with one serious flaw. I had no idea about finance or budgeting. My parents had taken care of all that in the past. All I knew was that if I worked hard at achieving my goals then money would probably look after itself. It was a much tougher life for Antonia, who started beauty school at Bradford College but found that the chemicals intensified her eczema. She eventually qualified as a nail technician and began in business on her own, but the early days were no picnic for her in a foreign land and before long we had another mouth to feed. When Mia was born, she looked a tiny scrap but was a beautiful bundle of joy. I could not have been prouder in this foreign land.

Bradford was like no other place I had visited, although the city and Yorkshire itself quickly came to feel like home. Antonia and I would go into town in just t-shirts and shorts and in bare feet. People would stare at us. I put it down to me grabbing the odd headline in the local newspapers, until someone pointed out: "Where are your shoes?" It was only then that I looked around and noticed that everyone had footwear on except us, even little kids. That was unheard of in New Zealand. You went out in your bare feet and thought nothing of it. I immediately went out and bought some canvas shoes and flip flops. Culturally, I conformed in that respect, to the point that on a trip back to Auckland I saw a guy walking up Queen Street in his bare feet. Look at the state of him, I thought. I didn't think I'd be assimilated as a Brit so quickly. I must have been, though, because I could not go barefoot now. My feet are far too soft.

My A.R.S.E

Or attitude, responsibility, sacrifice and education.

"Talent is overrated". It's a term you've no doubt heard before – and it's true. Talent will only get you so far.

Throughout my career I have been constantly asked by parents and youngsters what it was I did that separated myself from other talented youngsters and allowed me to move into the professional and then international ranks.

I would hear myself time and time again give the simple, obvious answers that we've all heard regurgitated by most sportsmen and women, governing bodies or health experts – eat healthily and train hard.

That used to be my stock response, then one day, after another bout of interrogation from a couple of parents, I sat down and had a really long think about what it was that really did separate me from other talented youngsters? I spent days turning myself inside out, wrestling with the different notions, then bit by bit I started to realise my four factors of differentiation.

It starts with:

Education
What I mean by education is having the ability to open your mind up to absorb as many ideas as possible and never feel like you ever know it all. Life has this funny thing of continually evolving and if you ever decide to stand still, you'll get into trouble, because it will fly past you and you'll be playing catch up for a long time. Embrace tradition but only as the foundations to move your life forward. Never let tradition stand in the way of positive innovation. Rugby changes season on season, industry changes year on year. This quote sums it up for me: "To learn and never be filled is true wisdom" (Anon)

Sacrifice

This is one of the tough ones for a young person. But it is also one of the most important, providing mum and dad have blessed you with the tools to do something special. At some point in your young life you are going to have to make self sacrifices to achieve your goals. This may mean missing a best friend's party, if you have training or a game the next day, or deciding to concentrate on important things like school work and training and sacrifice time socialising with boyfriends or girlfriends. Remember, if they are really your friends, they will support your dream rather than trying to distract you. The "Big Fella" above only gave us so many hours in the day, so something's probably going to have to give.

Responsibility

Accepting responsibility for all that happens to you will allow you to embrace what you will become. Once you learn to accept responsibility for things that go wrong, where you could have affected a better outcome, you will search for excellence within yourself. Don't get down on yourself for failing to achieve something. If you pull yourself down you will start to fear failure and that fear will stop you from going outside your comfort zone, learning and growing. Many of my best lessons learnt came through the mistakes I made and continue to make. Responsibility was thrust upon me at a young age as a father and team captain with Bradford Bulls. It is something that I embrace as part of my life's pathways.

Attitude

I look at this factor as the daddy of them all. The correct attitude will also drive education, sacrifice and responsibility. My attitude to achieve my goals was relentless. I searched high and low for a way to grow and be better. I kept my mind open, made sacrifices and enjoyed the responsibilities laid at my feet. At times it needed adjusting and also a good kick up the backside as the world started to spin differently and evolve, but it was always at the forefront of my personality and I was aggressive in applying it to all of the things positive in my life. As Albert Einstein said: "Weakness of attitude becomes weakness of character."

As you can see, none of these four factors take into account athletic ability. Of course, to be a professional you're going to need the right mix of mum and dad's gene pool, but that will only take you so far. Applying these factors, plus others you develop yourself, will create the psychological advantage all athletes need to reach High Performance Peak, and not leave you among the thousands of athletes kicking stones and thinking, "if only". The best athletes are psychologically really strong.

To make this easy to remember, I decided to make an acronym out of the first letters of these four factors in reverse order and that's how I came up with my A.R.S.E (or sear if you're young).

The A.R.S.E Tetrahedron

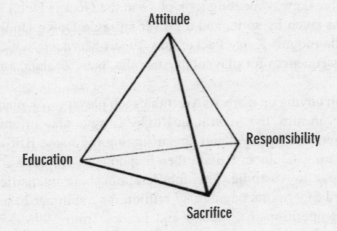

Chapter 5

Brave New World

Rugby league was never the same after 1995, thank goodness some would say. It was the year the sport's world turned on its axis. Not that I fully appreciated it at the time. I was a young player making my way in a vastly experienced Bradford Northern team and viewed very much as Henry Paul's kid brother. The centenary year of the sport, 100 years after the historic breakaway meeting took place at the George Hotel in Huddersfield, was riven by splits and a power struggle Down Under between the media moguls Kerry Packer and Rupert Murdoch, which had dramatic consequences for players in Australia, New Zealand and Britain.

Murdoch began buying up many of Australia's top players with plans for a new league. In turn, the Australian Rugby League also offered payments to players to stay loyal and began signing big name British players for vast sums. Clubs in Britain then responded with deals for players not to move to Australia. This febrile atmosphere intensified with Murdoch and Sky Sports paying £87 million for a summer-based Super League competition in England and France from 1996. Not knowing anything about money, of course, I never thought I would be offered anything. The Wigan players were targeted first – Henry was offered X, Y and Z – but the only player of any genuine value in the Bradford side at that time was Paul Newlove, who subsequently transferred to St Helens in a combined record £500,000 deal, with Paul Loughlin, Sonny Nickle and Bernard Dwyer joining us from Knowsley Road in exchange.

All I knew was that for four or five months I had been running in arrears in terms of my personal finances. This had forced me to ask Bradford for my monthly payments early. It was towards the back of the 1994-95 season when I got a call from Chris Caisley asking me to come to his office in Leeds for a word. I wondered whether he was going to cut me or sell me on to another club. I rang David McKnight, my agent, in something of a panic. All sorts of things were whizzing through my head. David was heading down the M6 at the time, but told me to wait and that he would be turning the car around to pick me up. He said that there were lots of deals going around and was confident it was to do with that.

I received the smallest loyalty fee of anyone, to my knowledge. To me, though, I was suddenly rich. I got a £50,000 sign-on fee, a year's extension to my contract and stepped payments boosted by £10,000 each year, all basically locking me in for three years at Bradford. At 19, after just a dozen or so games, no wonder David whispered in my ear: "Get in there, son." It was the sign-on fee being twice what I got for the whole of my first season that blew me away. We had outstanding bills and no money in the bank, then all this. I could not quite comprehend it, because I was in Britain to fulfill the dream I had as a youngster. However, here I was with a stack of money for basically having done nothing.

However weird that sensation, I knew where to go. Direct to River Island, where I bought four pairs of different coloured jeans, a leather jacket and Antonia a new wardrobe. It was not quite on the scale of the £500,000 I heard some players in Britain received, but it was okay by me. Of course, it did not last long. It wasn't the cars or bling I went for. I blew a load of it on going to the movies, seeing as many as three films in one day. We were sensible enough to put a deposit on a house, but that meeting with the Bradford chairman was far from the only change to my life.

We all went home a week later and I had not been back in New Zealand long when Chris telephoned. All he would say was that there were big things happening at Bradford and that I was really going to enjoy it. The atmosphere in the city was scarred by the riots in Manningham in the summer of 1995. However, a phenomenon known as the Bulls was emerging that would transform Odsal and rugby league in general. When I got back, Antonia was pregnant with Mia and the club I had left a short while previously had all but disappeared. Odsal did not look that different but there was a new coach in Matthew Elliott, a media guy called Peter Deakin, who was just a bundle of energy, and a whole new raft of staff. Rather than pay off debts, as some clubs did with their Super League cash injection, the new-look Bulls had decided to build the club's infrastructure.

Players were coming, others were going. It seemed that everything was up for grabs in this pre-Super League dawn. It perhaps explained why I marched into Matty Elliott's office, not even knowing him, and threw my cards on the table. "I want to be the stand off," I demanded. "This is who I am, this is what I want to do, and I'll do everything it takes to achieve it." The look he shot me left me momentarily regretting my machine gun mouth. I think he secretly liked my attitude, but with Deryck Fox and Neil Summers still in the halves, he saw me as a bit of a future project. "You're not the biggest lad in the world, are you?" he said, passing me what turned out to be the St George club under-19 weight training programme and nutrition plan.

Matty was the advance coaching party from St George, with Brian Smith a few months away from arriving and taking over. Matty saw in me someone a little different. He came round to the house one day when I was carving bone with a special set of knives that I had brought back from New Zealand, in the days when airport security was not quite so jumpy. I had got some beef bones from a farm shop, bleached them and was doing intricate manaia carving. I could almost read Matty's mind that here was a strange little creature, not your average rugby league player. For the first four weeks of the training programme he gave me, he trained with me and taught me lifting technique. I believe that he, in turn, fed off my enthusiasm.

The first training session in preparation for the curious shortened 1995-96 season, before the switch to summer and advent of Super League, was incredible for me. We hit the tackle bags like missiles. Matty stepped in and said that our technique was all wrong, at which point my heart leaped. At last we were going to be properly trained. Small things, such as how to put your hands up and spread you fingers to catch the ball, which would enable you to do this and that. Basic stuff nowadays but it was a revelation to us then. I absorbed everything like a sponge, even more so when Brian Smith finally began coaching us towards the end of the four-month centenary campaign.

Brian's involvement until then was basically acting as chief executive officer in pulling the Bulls structure together. He and Matt were buying players and ejecting others at such a rate that he had no idea from week to week what the team would be. Karl Fairbank had the captaincy over the centenary season but when he got injured, Brian asked whether I would take over for a game against Sheffield Eagles. Perhaps it was because I was one of the few players left that supporters recognised from the not-so-distant Bradford Northern days, although Brian sidling up to me for a word five minutes before a game became almost a tradition. "You're captain again," he'd say. "We'll see how you go for next week."

He liked it when no-one felt safe. Brian hated comfort zones. By making every player feel just a little uncomfortable he reckoned that they would push their bodies that little bit further. He was spot on. The guy knew what you were thinking before you did. At video sessions, he could pick your leg out of the corner of the television picture. "What are you doing there? That's not your position, you should be supporting here." He would hammer me in those sessions, but I listened to every word he uttered and I knew he was always correct. If we played his system we would be all right, but everyone had to buy into it. That fear of being caught out by him motivated you to do the right thing.

There was never a time when I did not understand what he was on about, perhaps explained by his background as a school teacher. You could never argue with his impeccable logic. If I did not always have Brian's voice at the back of my head, I would never have changed, improved and gone on to fulfil my ultimate goal of playing internationally. If there is a better way of doing something, find it. On one occasion he put four front rowers directly in front of me with a simple instruction to put some footwork on them. He made me do this time and again. I felt I was trying to survive more than anything, but by spinning out of tackles and sidestepping into little gaps, I was making half breaks. "See," he said. "You're still alive. You don't need to pass all the time, take them on." As a scrum half, I had got into my head that my job was to distribute and not get caught in possession. The point he made, most effectively, was that we could get quick play-the-balls from me engaging the opposition line. It not only altered my mindset, it changed my game.

Having done the St George programme for four months, I could feel the physical change. I was eating like a machine, doing all the right things and loving the new Bulls environment. I was a bit anal in following it to the letter but I wanted that edge, even if it meant setting the alarm for 6am, downing a yoghurt, banana and bowl of cereal, then going back to bed, just to fulfil the instruction to eat six meals a day. The gym was no longer the sad little place it had been. The equipment actually worked, but perhaps the biggest indicator of change was the car park. Rather than players' work trucks and white vans, there were sports cars. The Bradford Northern drinking culture was no longer prevalent and players were more finely tuned. But just as I thought it couldn't get much better than this, my worst nightmare turned up.

Brian Smith was bringing the best out of me and then he went and signed Graeme Bradley from St George. Brian would question why I trained harder than I played. In games, I would wait for an opportunity rather than go looking for one, so he sent out Bradley to ride my back. I honestly thought that the guy hated my guts. "You little Kiwi runt," he would bellow. I would look up at this long streak of something and utter every swear word under my breath. This went on for six or seven games until it clicked. The key was to keep moving all the time and sniff out chances, combined with the fact that I had got faster with Matty's St George programme. If he saw me walking, Penguin would bite my head off. You looked, learned and even grew to love Mr Bradley who, in truth, was our on-field leader and the player we turned to, despite me wearing the captain's armband.

The captaincy was more of a marketing tool. I was the one comfortable talking to people in any situation, never afraid of the cameras, as well as being able to play a bit of footy. I was uncomfortable initially with the Bulls brand, which as a fan of Michael Jordan I associated with the Chicago Bulls. But the brand identity that the club developed and what the Bulls stood for had nothing to do with Chicago. In the whirl at Odsal, I found myself promoted as the Bulls' marquee player – basically defined as a player with the skill and popularity factor. Most players went for their traditional number when the squad numbering system was introduced for Super League. I went for number one, not because I saw myself as a full back but because that was the number I had worn playing touch rugby as a kid. The fact that it happened to fit perfectly into the marketing strategy was merely a happy coincidence.

Publicity spin in rugby league was not new to me, having seen the Auckland Warriors' ferocious promotional drive up close and the impact of the Australian competition on television in New Zealand. Peter Deakin was a force of nature in driving the Bulls forward and his passion for using the club and rugby league as a means to communicate rubbed off on me. I lived in his pocket and loved every minute of it. When I finished training, I would go to Peter's office and say: "Hey, what have you got next?" As much as Brian stretched me as a player, Peter stretched me as a marquee player. It was a case of more outside the comfort zone for me the better, whether it was running a healthy living classroom at Odsal and talking about eating and exercise, or going into a recording studio to create a new club song.

Bradford's anthem 'Run with the Bulls' had been a tape that went on for about five minutes, with no music and just a depressing monotone cry of "Northern, Northern." I was asked to help Dave King and singer Anita Madigan, who together formed the Bulls Experience, and told them that I could write a rap. All the players went into the studio and we sold 2,000 copies, for which I actually received a plaque. We took the song into schools and even created mini concerts. The point was that Peter positioned the Bulls at the very heart of the community, and our crowds, which had averaged 5,654 in the last full winter season, quickly doubled.

The word spread. Bradford were the first big club to understand that match day was not just about the rugby. There were big name music acts, fairground rides, face painting, everything imaginable. Importantly, it provided value for money. Odsal was a place to go and be seen. The emphasis was on fun, but we engaged with our supporters and the community. As players, we had a vital part to play in that two-way process, all of which stimulated the energy about the place. Bradford quickly became industry leaders in the sports entertainment business. Other clubs and sports were quick to try and understand what we were doing and how we were getting it right.

Everything in that short centenary season, in other words, was building towards the brave new world of Super League. Brian drove around the country signing up players and Matt made do with what we had got while at the same time developing our core skills: simple things such as standing a metre away from one another and passing. We could do 1,000 passes a time, learning to use our wrists and elbows to be more accurate and create clean ball. We finished the championship in seventh place, which was not that much of a surprise considering a staggering 44 of us played first team rugby that year. There was little consistency or continuity as Brian manoeuvred the club in readiness for the spring of 1996. When that historic inaugural season arrived, though, the wind of change had transformed Odsal.

I no longer recognised the place or my team-mates. I was among just a handful left from our Bradford Northern incarnation, along with Brian McDermott, Karl Fairbank and Paul Medley. Not that it felt much different in terms of the calendar. As one season ended, the next began two weeks later with the early rounds of the Challenge Cup. We thrashed Batley and I got sin-binned for the first time in my career in the round afterwards at Leigh. Their Aussie scrum half slapped me, I slapped him and we scuffled about like extras from a bad 1950s movie. After beating Wakefield, there was a month gap before meeting Leeds in the semi-finals. Already the differences in us were manifest under Brian's tutelage.

We had a proper defensive structure for the first time and a co-ordinated attack with a straightforward premise. If someone was carrying the ball, we all started to move. That way you were always playing on the front foot and a lot flatter and more direct. When our line came under pressure, rather than man marking and shifting from sideline to sideline, we worked in small defensive units or pods. It was so much harder for opponents to break down. Then there was Brian's three point play-the-ball: leveraging your knees from underneath where you're strong, then snapping your legs in using the power from your backside, in order to give you the bridge to play the ball on the front foot.

No-one in the English game before had really thought about shaving time off the most basic component of the game and the impact that would have. The skills Brian introduced reduced an eighth of a second off a play-the-ball, the difference of a metre in movement and, consequently, catching out a team as they were trying to get onside. It was about exposing defences too slow to react. We would spend hours perfecting the technique. Brian's philosophy, one that holds good in so many walks of life, is to ask yourself where you are now and what you need to do to improve.

He developed the ethos of Bradford Bulls being the hardest working team. Basic skills were at the heart of this. It was not about making the biggest hit but tackle technique, getting your feet in the right place, dominating the tackle by grabbing levers, catching defences out through our ruck speed. It was energy conserving as well and far removed from the days charging up and down the steep inclines at Odsal on my lonesome. We would run resistance drills on bungee cords and do hurdles as part of Brian's appliance of science from the Australian

Institute of Sport. Other clubs learned eventually but Bradford were early pioneers with, on the face of it, a rag tag outfit of youngsters with potential, old-style championship players and some old guys from St Helens and Down Under.

Our team came of age in the semi-final against a Leeds side who had reached the previous two Wembley finals and were red hot favourites. Jon Scales had signed from Leeds and grabbed a hat-trick as we won 28-6 against the odds. Even Ray French, the BBC commentator, had felt that I had got across the line after a run from half way only for Stuart Cummings, the referee, to rule a knock-on. Nothing, however, could wipe the smile off my face that day. I joined Brian at the after-match press conference, at which a reporter asked what it would feel like to be the youngest captain in a Challenge Cup final. I went off on one, saying that it would be absolutely amazing and a wonderful honour, to which Brian sagely added: "It looks like Robbie's chosen himself. I may have a say in that." That translated as 'wind your neck in son'. He was right, as usual.

Everything changed with that semi-final victory. Bradford had not been to Wembley since 1973 and Peter Deakin was not going to miss out on the opportunity that presented the Bulls on the marketing front. He must have had a hot line to every sports editor. Blanket coverage extended through to Super League's kick off a week later amid glitz and fireworks in Paris. There was an equally glamorous launch for the new competition at the Landmark Hotel in London, for which I caught the train with a couple of old lags in Karl Harrison and Lee Crooks, captains of Halifax and Castleford.

They patently saw a naive young fella and took him under their wing. In the hotel bar, every time they ordered a beer they got me one. I did not really drink, but all the club captains were there and I was anxious not to lose face. They put me to bed after half-a-dozen beers, a complete mess. When I checked out the next morning, I was presented with a bar bill for £890, with a load of big blokes cracking up behind me. They were heady days money-wise patently, because the Rugby Football League picked up the tab. I had also bought my first suit for the launch event, a big baggy one like I had seen in hip hop American teenage movies, although what I looked like as a little Kiwi boy, not much more than 11 stones in a suit two sizes too big and nursing a hangover, I dread to think.

After a heady opening night in Paris, summer Super League began at Odsal just under 48 hours later in a snowstorm. It was the last day of March and all four seasons were crammed into 80 minutes, during which we managed to beat Castleford and began to ride the Wembley tiger. Brian also brought in an Irish sports psychologist. I read a lot of books on new age thinking and was especially struck by Dan Millman's spiritual *Way of the Peaceful Warrior*. So I was keen to tap into the psychologist's messages. Before our next Super League game at Sheffield, he gave me a Walkman cassette player with an instruction to press play five minutes before I ran out for the warm-up. I could not wait for this pearl of wisdom: a poem by Vince Lombardi, a sentiment to carry with me the rest of my life? I went into a toilet cubicle, sat down and pressed play. M People's 'Search for the Hero' began. Was this a mistake, was the guy kidding? I was a rap fan, for goodness sake. I decided to kick the Irish psychologist into touch.

We won only one more game before Wembley. That final, in many respects, represented the end of one professionalism – players simply receiving payment to play – and a new professionalism – the advent of the professional rugby league player and all the values that entailed. Henry and I got into an argument about this, with big brother coming from the standpoint of the Wigan club where you were conditioned into thinking that you were the best, especially with such a legacy of success there. On the other hand, I saw what we were doing at Bradford and knew that our training techniques were well in advance of those at Wigan. The BBC got the pair of us to go head-to-head in a discussion as part of their build-up coverage for Wembley. We began talking about catching the ball in two hands. At Bradford we were being taught to raise our hands in order to catch the ball earlier and speed up our decision process, whereas Henry was arguing from the Wigan perspective that it was safer to catch the ball in the breadbasket. I was arguing that it wasn't the right method. It was a ding-dong that made good television. As always, we agreed to disagree, although, funnily, Henry began teaching that exact same hands high skill to kids once he came to the Bulls. My own profile snowballed, with Bradford reaching the final. "There is more to the elfin-featured Robbie Paul than meets the eye," *The Times* wrote. "He cut his first record recently, writes songs, paints, is a student of fine art, teaches children about healthy living and will lead Bradford Bulls as the youngest captain at Wembley in a Challenge Cup final. Everything, it seems, but sit on a mushroom, where he looks to belong."

The game itself went down as one of the greatest at Wembley. Writing in *The Observer*, the rugby league-loving actor Colin Welland said: "When Paul did a family pirouette to slam down another try, the game seemed over. Then 'Adolf' Goulding released his V2s, putting up bombs which descended vertically, impossible to detect or collect. And in a twinkling, Saints had scored thrice and this marvellous match apparently was theirs. Paul thought otherwise. With pace off the mark, which one only hears about in tales of heroes gone by, he broke through a cloying St Helens line and, leaving the full back gasping for explanations, dived under the posts for the finest try I have ever seen at Wembley. He was awarded the Lance Todd Trophy and £10,000 for the first Wembley hat-trick. But it wasn't enough. Saints held on to win an unforgettable game after which victors and vanquished received the same acclaim."

I was not properly aware of the stir my Wembley hat-trick had created until a few months later. All I knew was that, even in defeat, the Bulls had momentum. Although it took us until 2000 to learn how to win a final, the 1996 loss to St Helens was the springboard for our eventual dominance. A week later, we pumped Warrington at home in winning 36-14. I scored an easy try, raised the ball with one hand and waved to the crowd, for which I paid a heavy price at Brian's video session. "Here he is, the hat-trick hero," he said, disparagingly. Don't get above yourself was the Smith mantra and I never stopped following it from that moment, although I nearly came a cropper a short while later against Paris Saint Germain, the impossibly glamorous new team in the fledgling Super League. We had been scoring tries for fun and letting them in at nearly the same rate. I was having a diabolical game but managed to score a try. As I rose up over the line, I had this daft idea of celebrating with a big karate-style kick. Fortunately, I imagined Brian's voice in my ear and pulled out of it. He still ripped into every one of us afterwards. "You look like a fish flopping on the Sunshine Coast," he barked at Glen Tomlinson, before turning on Bernard Dwyer. "You look like a fat old man from St Helens," before he finally reached me. "And you, you're all talk, you missed four frigging tackles." It was the first time I had seen him like that and you could not wipe the smile afterwards from Graeme Bradley's face. "Well," Peng grinned. "I've been waiting all season for that."

Ultimately, we paid for the pre-Wembley losses in that first summer Super League, but only lost twice in the league after the Challenge Cup final. We finished third but did affect the eventual outcome by beating Wigan to effectively put St Helens back on top. It was a match in which we had Jeremy Donougher sent off and a certain Wigan stand off tried to pull my head off, one Henry Paul. "Not since lamb has New Zealand had an export success quite like the Paul brothers," one newspaper reported, but that 20-12 victory was especially sweet, considering that Henry had emerged the victor in all four previous encounters between us.

We also learned that week that Brian Smith was to return to Australia at the end of the season to take over Parramatta Eels. He rated that win over Wigan as one of the finest of his coaching career and his leaving came as a shock to everyone, especially me. It coincided with huge flux in the sport and consequent opportunities. Wigan winning the 1996 Middlesex Sevens and the impact of the two Wigan-Bath cross-code games at Maine Road and Twickenham that year had created a market for league players with now fully professional union clubs. David McKnight was talking to several of them about me, Henry, Jason Robinson and Gary Connolly crossing codes for the duration of the off season. The three cup final tries had been the catalyst for the interest in me, whereas the Wigan trio were established players. The financial carrot being dangled could not be ignored.

My original thought in going to England had been to play a couple of years and return Down Under but the goalposts had shifted. I was Bradford's pin-up player, their captain, and even though Brian was leaving, Matty Elliott was already in place to take full charge. So when Brian pulled me aside after a training session to go for a coffee, his question about whether Henry and I would fancy joining him at Parramatta came out of left field. Strangely, my first reaction was to laugh: how on earth would two blokes like Brian and Henry, who abided by their own rules and never backed down, possibly get on? Henry's a lot more diplomatic and obliging now but in those days he walked his own path. Having learned so much from Brian in such a short space of time, I could envisage myself developing so much further under him.

I cannot regret something when I enjoyed my career so much.

Nonetheless, there is a part of me intrigued as to where a move to Parramatta at that stage may have led. In seeing the conveyor belt of half backs developed by the Brian Smith stable over many years, I imagine that he would have developed the world class ball-playing skills that I definitely lacked. The Bradford chairman Chris Caisley was very astute. He knew that I worshipped Brian and we had a great affinity. By allowing me to go to rugby union for a few months and extending my Bulls contract, he knew any potential suitor would have to give more to Bradford to buy me out. As it turned out, Parramatta was not the only offer I had to turn down for a lucrative spell with Harlequins in London, and this one shook me to my core.

The rugby player as a brand

So what does this mean? I remember when I was a kid dreaming about becoming a professional rugby player. My aspirations were to represent my country and play for a high profile club.

I never in my life thought about who I would be important to and how I could be a talking point for people I'd never met before on Monday morning around an office water cooler. I also never dreamed that what happens in my private life could possibly be of any interest to anyone other than me and my immediate family, and why should it?

As a sportsman or woman, like it or loathe it, you represent certain things to society because sport elevates you to that position.

Take rugby. To me the values of rugby are split into two sections.

There are the obvious values related to performance and the team:
- Positive lifestyle management.
  - *Health and fitness.*
  - *Quality nutrition.*
- Mental toughness.

- Skill and ability.
- Sportsmanship.

Then there are the intangible aspects that make up the spirit of rugby:
- Family entertainment.
- Social inclusion.
- Community and cultural cohesion.
- Non gender or sexual orientation bias.
- Sportsmanship.

(Notice that I use sportsmanship twice, as I feel this value crosses both sets of values, both on the field of play and into the spirit of one's lifestyle).

The values that make up the 'spirit' of rugby are now just as important to an athlete as the first set that focuses on the performance side of the game. The reason for this is because it has to do with the market place of the supporters and their expectations of sporting role models.

It is important that you never take for granted the supporters. Remember, they are your life blood. Without them there would be no television rights deal and no media. Without the media, there would be no need for commercial partners or sponsors. No money, no professional sports, and no professional sports people.

So now you have to ask yourself, who are the supporters and what do they want from you? Well, in rugby it is the entire family, from grandparents, parents to children. We are not just talking male family members, as in some sports, but both genders.

Rugby engages so many different people. Parents and grandparents want their children to see and emulate athletes who uphold all of the values listed above. Their expectation should be honoured. I reckon it's pretty easy: if you don't want to represent these things, then don't become a sports professional.

As a pro you will gain attention and your world will become smaller and closely scrutinised. If you just enjoy the game and want to play rugby then there are a thousand amateur teams looking for talented players. If you want to live like a rock star, that type of lifestyle does not align itself well with rugby and you find yourself constantly annoying people, hurting people you don't mean to and ultimately hurting yourself (a lesson I learnt myself a couple of times).

Those who do fulfil sporting brand values and make them a part of their own values find themselves lifted to a high status by the sports industry and held in the highest regard. You can become what is known as a marquee player, user friendly and more marketable, opening you up to more clubs and making your value to your own club stronger. More money, in other words.

This can lead on to a life time of wonderful relationships and open up opportunities for your post playing career lives – jobs, networks and lucrative opportunities. Remember, you will be retired longer than you play and we all like the likeable people.

At the end of the next chapter I will explain how you can start creating your brand now.

Chapter 6
You Don't Get Me I'm Part of the Union

By the time Brian Smith mentioned that he would like both Henry and myself with him at Parramatta, the pair of us had almost worked out our rugby union deals over the winter break. Everything seemed to come at once towards the end of the 1996 season. It was not like Bradford had actually won anything, but Brian had taken a rag tag team and built a strong core. We had steamrollered opponents and enjoyed our brief time in the sun at Wembley. The other reason that the club was on the tip of everyone's tongues was the whole marketing drive, in which the players were swept along by the glorious, mad Bulls phenomenon. The Challenge Cup hat-trick had gilded my lily. I was young, marketable and Harlequins had seen someone who could play a bit with a rugby ball, albeit someone without the same affection I possessed for my native league code.

At that juncture, international rugby league was not on my radar. That was the purpose for playing, the very reason for being so far from my New Zealand homeland. I was a pup on the league scene and pulling on a Kiwi jumper seemed like a different world at that stage. The contract with Harlequins was put in my lap by David McKnight, who had a hand in Henry and Jason Robinson going to Bath and Gary Connolly joining me at Quins. It was a time when players who had crossed to league, such as Alan Tait, Scott Quinnell, Scott Gibbs and Jim Fallon, were moving back to a newly professional union code, with Martin Offiah committed to playing both league in the summer for London Broncos and union in the winter for Bedford. For all that league had supposedly been professional since 1895, league, too, was coming to terms with the modern concept of professionalism in how clubs promoted themselves and treated the players.

A week after I had signed the contract with Harlequins, I received the telephone call I had been waiting for all my life. It was Frank Endacott, the New Zealand head coach, who uttered the words I had dreamed about: "I would like to invite you to join the New Zealand team." Hearing Frank say what I had yearned to hear, I was caught up in the moment, briefly forgetting that I had made another commitment. It was not public knowledge then that I had signed to play rugby union for four months, with two or three weeks of the league season still to go.

Frank's call was both wonderful and terrible at the same time. Elation, euphoria and joy turned in a heartbeat to complete despair. I went from looking at achieving my ultimate goal to seeing it snatched away, ironically at my own hand in having put pen to paper with Quins. My whole focus had been that black and white jumper, but mum and dad had brought me up to be a man of my word. If you say that you are going to do something, you do it. I was only 20 and it was a call-up I never expected but it left me with one overriding emotion. I felt as sick as a dog.

Growing up, all the players around me, Henry included, had signed contracts with the Auckland Warriors. I had missed out on that chance very early in my career. Here I was on the other side of the world, getting the call I had always wanted and having to turn Frank down. In doing so, the window of opportunity for Test selection – small enough when you are plying your trade at 12,000 miles distance – narrowed a little further. Frank had wanted me to play in the Test match against Papua New Guinea. What could I say? As much as it pained me, I told him that I couldn't play for New Zealand. As the words formed in my mouth, I could feel a lump in my throat.

Unbeknown to me, Frank had already had a similar conversation with Henry, who was already an established international having featured in the 1995 World Cup. He explained that Henry was in the same situation, having committed himself to Bath, and that he fully understood our dilemma. To Frank's enormous credit, he calmed me down and said he was sure that there would be other opportunities to play for the Kiwis in the near future. As a still impressionable and vulnerable kid, however, you just do not think that you will get that sort of chance again. We were living in a new house in Bradford, which we had bought with money left over from the loyalty bonus I had been paid. I replaced the receiver and sat down. Antonia was at work and the girls were at play group. I was home alone and just broke down in floods of tears. It was the first time I had cried since the last time Henry had beaten me up as a kid. As it turned out, I had no regrets about signing to play rugby union that winter. However, in that moment on my own, basically having denied myself a lifetime ambition, I did despair at what I'd done. Had I played just once for New Zealand, that would have been good enough for me. Would I get another chance?

The last few weeks of the league season before my temporary union switch were difficult. St Helens finished a point ahead of Wigan in clinching the inaugural Super League title, deservedly so on the basis of their consistency throughout the year, while any chance Bradford had disappeared with a 27-26 loss at home to a resurgent Halifax Blue Sox. The last game was another Paul v Paul clash at Wigan in the end of season Premiership competition, with Henry coming out on top in a 78-point minor classic. Graeme Bradley and I managed to score five tries between us in the halves and still lost a game in which Great Britain scrum half Shaun Edwards demonstrated the class he still had in scoring four tries.

Harlequins were really accommodating and gave me the time to join the boys in Tenerife for the season end bash. I had never been on a lads trip before, and not being a big drinker at the time, it came as something of a shock. We were there for seven days. I drank the first three and called a halt. I simply could not take any more. I spent one day recovering and the next three days training, knowing that in a week or two I would be playing rugby union. The boys thought I was mad, running all over the island, but I could not let my new temporary employers down, especially as they were paying my Bradford wages for four months.

The agreement was that I again extended my Bulls contract by another year. It was smart thinking by Chris Caisley, Bradford's solicitor chairman. If anyone wanted to buy me out, the Bulls would be significant beneficiaries, especially with talk early in my union spell of Harlequins considering a £500,000 offer to retain me, although none of that bothered me at the time. Harlequins picked up my wages with a further slice on top. Naturally, the extra cash was a nice bonus, but having turned Frank and New Zealand down, my mindset was very much on making the most of this extraordinary opportunity at an exciting time for both rugby codes. The money was of secondary importance, however much that might have been perceived as the prime motivating factor. People sometimes do not appreciate that it is the chance to move somewhere new and try something different that can inspire and excite a player.

As an athlete I was also conscious of opening myself up to a new marketplace. Rugby union has a bigger market appeal than rugby league, but when I joined Harlequins the sport was only just coming to terms with professionalism. In fact, Quins were not even fully professional. It was still a semi-pro environment, with half-a-dozen full time players who came in to do weights and sprint training each day and the rest who trained on Tuesday and Thursday nights before a Saturday morning team run through. It felt like the clock being turned back two years to my first experience at Odsal. There were times, I admit, when I questioned why on earth they had signed me.

I got selected to play at full back. I had featured there a few times for Bradford at the back end of the 1994-95 season, but as I discovered then, I was not exactly the epitome of calm and confidence under the high ball. It was the same in rugby union, coupled with the fact that every time I got the ball, I had run it back; I did not do any of the kicking that they went in for. Andy Keast, the coach, complained at half time that I was all over the place. "You don't look too comfortable back there," he said, to which I replied, "That's right. To be honest, I'm a half back." "What do you mean, you're a half back. You wear the number one shirt in rugby league. That's full back, isn't it?" Keast said. It took a bit to convince him that it was simply my squad number.

Dick Best, the Harlequins director of rugby, barely spoke to me at first. There had been big play made of the club signing myself and Gary Connolly, plus the Rugby Football League's stipulation that all of us having a partial winter season in union should be back with our league employers by the January. Gary gave a prescient interview before he joined up at the Stoop, in which he said: "In the short-term, rugby league players may not be good enough [to play for England], but if we have a couple of years' experience it may be that we can make ourselves into international union players."

I was this little Kiwi runt thing to Besty, a bundle of energy bouncing off the walls. The game at full back followed my first experience at Harlequins on the wing where I was equally baffled. In rugby league you looked for space. Naturally, I kept putting myself into gaps, except that the ball would never come my way. It was only screaming for it that I got a chance against a Welsh team who were pretty poor. The ball popped out of a maul and I was away for a try. Not many people could catch me at that time, least of all a few huffing and puffing forwards. I always looked to promote the ball. I would pop it up to a forward who would promptly knock it on. I kept thinking what was wrong with these guys, but it was not until a month of basically following an edict of just get in there and go for it that Dick Best began to teach me the small stuff.

We played some terrible teams, though. We beat Orrell 89-18 in a home league match. Both Gary and I scored two tries. There were a few games like that, featuring guys who not only did not know how to tackle but looked like they had just emerged from the pub. This was the position rugby union found itself in at the time, with a widening gulf between those teams getting their professional acts together and others falling by the wayside. One of the Harlequins trainers pulled me aside, explaining that he wanted to learn as much from Gary and myself as possible. I went through a typical league pre-season with him and what we would do training-wise throughout the season. He was blown away by the sheer amount of work we would do by comparison. Union was only then starting to grasp the concept of professionalism, simply because it had no historic reference point. That is where league's expertise came in. It was not so much the athletes that union needed to learn from but league's systems. Phil Larder, Joe Lydon and later Shaun Edwards moved across to focus on defensive structures. They were league's trailblazers for union, whereas in league we had a system that had a major input from the Australian competition which, in turn, had borrowed a lot from the professionalism of American Football.

Harlequins and what they represented did not mean much to me at all. I was ignorant of their history. I had heard of them and knew of their multi-coloured shirt, which at first glance looked the ugliest jumper in the world. Once you wore it, though, you looked good as a group. It was all part of the learning experience in a part of the world that I did not really know. The first place the club got us to stay looked a bit rough, so we ended up at a property closer to the Stoop. You drove down a long avenue of big fancy houses to three smaller town houses at the end. Ours was the middle one and a lovely spot it was, too, with the River Thames on our doorstep, Twickenham, Richmond and Kingston Upon Thames all close at hand and with the school next door. It was perfect for a young family and we quickly settled in.

The great thing about rugby as a culture is that it does not matter where you are or whether you are playing league or union, the locker room humour is exactly the same, and Harlequins were a team packed with great characters: Jason Leonard, Keith Wood, Welsh brothers Glyn and Gareth Llewellyn, a couple of big ugly American forwards Luke Gross and Tom Billups, a trio of enigmatic, smooth Frenchmen in Laurent Cabannes, Laurent Benezech and Thierry Lacroix, plus – and begging his pardon – royal bum chin himself, England captain Will Carling. There were three great hubs of energy at the club with Jason, Keith and Will, who was famous for delivering killer one-liners and just exiting the room. He was a funny man and a professional before his time in the context of rugby union.

I learned a lot in my short time there from Carling, a man who took so much crap on that chin of his, yet just let it roll off him. That time was not so far removed from false press allegations about a romantic relationship between him and Princess Diana. We would get off the team bus and paparazzi were waiting for him. Some people would shout out the most disgraceful insults, yet nothing fazed him. It would boil my blood, but I could not help but admire his handling of the situation, as well as his intelligence and quick wit. He seemed the unlikeliest of jokers but had an obvious foil in Keith Wood, who loved to pick on people and take the piss but was just an amazing athlete. Bradford asked me to inquire with Keith whether he would be interested in playing rugby league. It did not come to anything, but he would have been a fantastic league convert. Then there was Jason Leonard, a guy as wide as he is tall, built like a nugget. It was not always what Jason had to say but his physical presence that spoke volumes.

They were all great guys to be around, though they saw me as just a cocky little Kiwi who had some talent about him but some odd ideas. My interest in the arts was not shared in the Bradford dressing room and it was the same at Quins. I was also green and ignorant of so many things, being fearless of my standing. I had no idea that I stuck out as a bit of a loudmouth at times. I like to think that a bit of my charm also came across in my sometimes crass approach. I am not a malicious person and always wish the best for people, so they found me harmless enough. Gary Connolly, though, was a different beast altogether, an established player who knew the rules of society better. The trouble with Gary was that he was rarely there. It was a bit of a holiday for him. He was in Wigan most of the time and would just turn up the two evenings for training.

I found him asleep in his car at the ground once and asked whether he was coming in. "Nah," he said, and went back to sleep. Henry had introduced him to me as Gary Lager. The Quins lads just shortened the nickname to Lager. There was much amusement that Lager would sink a few pints and painstakingly go to the trouble of removing the skin before eating chicken as part of his healthy diet. He also happened to be blessed with natural talent, power, dense muscle and blistering athleticism. Gary was a good fella to be around and a formidable defender, as I found when I teamed up with him in the centre, where I was at my most comfortable in union. Gary was at outside centre, with me on his inside, and he would catch attackers out with a league-style up and in wedge tackle. Gary would see my man coming in on the crash ball, which for a league player is just the juiciest tackle. They wanted me to come in on the crash ball but, right at the last second, I would side step and catch defenders out, while Gary would come across and wipe others out. It probably seemed like we were making it up as we went along, but the pair of us knew exactly what we were doing.

The whole training set-up was so different to what I was used to. Backs and forwards would train on their own and only come together on the Saturday. Tactically, we would run through some set plays against the second XV. I cannot recall doing any specific defensive work. In four months I saw Will Carling train once. He spent almost all his time getting physio treatment. Jason Leonard would be in the middle of the park grunting it out, Keith was Mr Perpetual Motion and always first to the breakdown, but A-lister Carling was nowhere to be seen much of the time. He would be having massages on his old joints and I would be thinking, is this guy just some sort of a star in a bar? That was until my first game alongside him. The guy played like a demon. He was everywhere and blew my mind with the way he went head-first into everything, like an Exocet missile. He was down and dirty, utterly fearless, even when a blood vessel in his eye exploded. I presumed that was him done for the day. Not a bit of it. He played straight through, and I thought to myself, this fella is as good as his reputation.

Training at Harlequins was my biggest bugbear. There was simply not enough of it. Our forwards had dominated early in the season, but as the weather changed and the pitches became heavier, the pack was no longer on top of opponents. We slowed down as a consequence and it strangled the life out of our attacking game. In my position in league you got the ball a lot, less so in union. But if that ball is slow and messy, that is when union can become hard to play. The few occasions that you do get your hands on the ball, it is incumbent on you to do something with it. It explained the repetition in training of set plays, although it became monotonous and one-dimensional for someone used to learning every skill conceivable as a half back in league. The power weights we did were never enough for a small guy like myself trying to put on timber, so I would do my own additional weights training. The occasions when Dick Best came on to the training pitch with us, we knew that we were in for a flogging. Those sessions were akin to the toughest league sessions.

The biggest learning curve for me came on a trip to Ulster in the Heineken Cup pool stages. It was freezing, miserable and a kickathon. Gary and I glanced across at one another thinking, what do we do here? In rainy, bitter, heavy conditions you had to play the percentages. It was all about staying in your opponents' half. It was a kicking and lineout duel, with us jogging forwards and backwards for an interminable 80 minutes. There were a few games like that, but none I played in a Harlequins shirt, in my position at centre, that ever really compared with a league match in physically taxing you. The closest came against Brive in France. We went there quietly confident, but on a warm afternoon met a red-hot French side. This team – it was no coincidence they went on and beat Leicester in the Heineken Cup final that season – possessed genuine talent, pace and power. They played a game the like of which I had not encountered before in my brief union sojourn.

It was coming home from that trip that I got buttonholed for an interview by a rugby union reporter. He wrote that I said that union was a better sport than league, which was a complete fabrication. It was a distortion of my comment to him that union was a better sport than I had thought it was. I rang the editor of the newspaper and the reporter himself in complaining about an obvious anti-league agenda with the story, but too late to prevent a hue and cry about what I had supposedly said. Dean Bell, a huge hero of mine, said that I needed to be grateful for what league had given me. That really affected me, because anyone who really knows me appreciates my passion and love for league would never lead me to knock it.

Harlequins was a different world to Bradford. The guys I was used to were brickies and builders but a dozen of the Quins squad worked in the City of London as stockbrokers. It seemed pretty impressive to me, but they said that their day job mainly consisted of picking up the phone. The point was that they were looked after, paid handsomely for their day job and got to play rugby at weekends for another pay cheque. Those of us at the club called in to do marketing for the likes of Vodafone and Royal Bank of Scotland would be picked up by stretch limo. It was all very nice and curiously in contrast with the sponsorships at Bradford. Quins were good in respect of me regularly going back to the Bulls for autograph sessions at Burger King, with whom the club had a relationship, and meet-the-players days.

Those of us coming from league were portrayed as pioneers and a new hybrid breed of year-round codebreakers in this brave new professional world. Unlike some, though, I did not see it as part of a long-term project. Once my commitment had ended, I was champing at the bit to get back north, although Antonia completing a nail technology course in London delayed our return a week after my last appearance against Bath, for whom Henry and Jason Robinson had been making lots of headlines with their try scoring feats. An intriguing union encounter with big brother unfortunately did not come to pass after Henry had injured his back.

Of the league converts that winter, Jason made the greatest impact with his bold running from deep, whether at wing, centre or full back. He had destroyed Quins at the Recreation Ground before Christmas, which is perhaps why I was asked to mark him in the return league fixture at the Stoop. If you did not know how to defend Jason – and I am not saying that even if you did, it would make that much difference – you were in a whole heap of trouble. Players not used to him would try and rush Jason. That was their first mistake, because he would put on his soft shoe shuffle footwork and they would be left in his slipstream. With his speed and twinkling feet, the trick was in showing him the touchline, just not too much of it. Rather than go up and try and grab him – the equivalent of nailing down a grasshopper – the best way to blunt his sidestep was let him come at you. Twice I managed to collar him and twice he got up with a rueful grin on his face. That was humbling from someone of Jason's quality, a glorious freak of nature born with exceptional gifts.

I never got to play against Martin Offiah in his prime and arguably a bigger name than Jason for the spectacular nature of some of his tries for Widnes, Wigan and Great Britain. Personally, I believe Jason was the more gifted player in terms of the number of weapons in his armoury, whose success spanned both codes with Wigan and Great Britain in league and Sale, England and the British Lions in union. Whereas Martin wreaked havoc against poor defences at times, Jason bamboozled the best defensive structures. I grew up watching Martin scoring tries for fun in Wembley Challenge Cup finals, but the reality is that rugby league defensive structures can deal a lot with speed now. What's tougher is dealing with someone with a low centre of gravity, who moves on a dime with ability, power and speed to kick off both feet. That is what made Jason so exceptional.

Bradford were under no illusions from me that the spell at Harlequins was a one-off. Andy Keast said: "We'd love to keep you, but we can tell you want to go back, so we aren't going to try and convince you otherwise." He was right. Even though I had loved playing rugby union, I had a burning desire to return to Bradford to fulfil my dreams of winning silverware. David McKnight asked a couple more times over the years whether I would be interested in another go at union but the answer was the same. I did not want to hear about the money potentially on offer, so as not to put temptation in my path, but, in truth, I was happy with the money and my life in league. It got to the stage also that this particular dog was too old to learn new tricks.

During the 1999 Tri-Nations series in the southern hemisphere, Henry and I were taken out by Auckland Warriors officials for a slap-up lobster meal on the Auckland waterfront. They had wanted us as a package, but even at this point Henry had his eyes on going to union eventually. Notwithstanding a big financial improvement for him, the competitor in Henry was driving him towards a different goal to mine. It was all about positioning himself for the big global stage of the Rugby World Cup in Australia in 2003. As an athlete you want to test yourself and that was the ultimate for Henry, who was never going to make it as an All Black, because that would have meant going back to New Zealand to start all over again. Sir Clive Woodward was in charge of England and Henry was in his sights along with Jason Robinson and Kris Radlinski at Wigan. Before crossing to union at Gloucester at the end of the 2001 Super League season, he was one of the best league players in the world, if not THE best.

When I think of Henry, Shontayne Hape and Lesley Vainikolo, two more Bradford and New Zealand team-mates, wearing the England rugby union jumper, part of me does laugh. The eligibility rules are a joke. From an athlete's perspective, if the opportunity presents itself, you will take it. It is about competing at the highest level and testing yourself. The athlete in me would think exactly the same: try your hand, stretch your boundaries, expand your comfort zone. Like Henry, I knew how I felt living in England after a few years. I had become part of the culture. A big part of me is British, for all that I remain a proud New Zealander. Henry was caught in the middle of that dilemma playing for England against New Zealand on the sevens circuit at the "Cake Tin" in Wellington. He scored an amazing try and was roundly jeered. It is an argument that he could never win, being qualified for England under the grandparent rule but being born and brought up in New Zealand.

If rugby union was not for me after my Harlequins experience, I was fully supportive of Henry's decision to represent England in the code. It did not work out in terms of his World Cup ambition, but he was chucked in at the deep end and fast tracked into the England side before being taught how to play the important bits and pieces. If you are not au fait with these things, you can get exposed. The last of his half-dozen England appearances came against Australia in 2004 when Andy Robinson, the coach, hooked him off after half-an-hour. Henry was not the only one left perplexed. "At the time I was confused and didn't really know what was going on," he said in an interview later. "I wish it had been handled differently. I went out there to attack as I'd been told to do, and wasn't given much time."

England's traditional style is to keep it tight and grind out the wins. Henry played the game more like an All Black, an entertainer and a maverick. But he never got to play for England again, apart from at sevens – with a lot of distinction, I might add – after that Australia match. Towards the end of his career at Leeds Carnegie, he was still head and shoulders above everyone else. The problem was that people did not know how to play alongside him or coach him. Henry had peripheral vision, so he would put a ball behind his back into a team-mate's breadbasket and the player would knock-on. He loved to play an open game, but rugby union in England generally is not like that. Henry's other problem, a little like me, was a runaway mouth at times.

He was a bit too honest on occasions. He did not play the political game or keep his head down. He got into a few scrapes, too, which reflected unhappiness at times.

When Henry left Bradford after the 2001 season for Gloucester, David McKnight still had contacts interested in other players switching codes. I did not want to move across myself, but I was not going to prevent others taking the opportunity if they wished to pursue it. It was my relationship with Shontayne, Leslie and Karl Pryce at the Bulls, and David and his network, that in part led to them trying their hand at union. It was a great move in some cases and not in others, but how can you know until you try? Rugby union is a different game and environment now to the one I briefly entered in 1996 – a sport that set its sights on younger league talent once it saw the likes of Chris Ashton, a wonder kid at Wigan – but at that point in time it was not for me. There were bigger fish to fry at home in Yorkshire.

Your brand and social media

Since the social media revolution it has never been easier to communicate to huge numbers of people so quickly and at no cost other than time. I absolutely love these media platforms, they provide us all with a means to cross boundaries and tear down barriers to innovation.

I remember the days when I first arrived in England and purchased my first fax machine so I could communicate with my family in New Zealand. It was a long-winded affair hand-writing a letter, then feeding it through the machine and waiting days for a reply. Now all I do is send a text, turn on the computer or switch on the smart phone.

This technology explosion can be a real strength for the modern day athlete as you get to have direct control over the information you communicate, especially as you can "speak" to a large number of people at the press of a button. I use Twitter (@rhunterpaul) and Facebook (facebook.com/pages/Robbie-Hunter-Paul). These are really simple social media platforms and a great way to engage with supporters.

Once your page is set up you need to start thinking about what it is you post/write. If I can refer back to the previous chapter, when I mentioned the rugby audience, you should understand that it is this same audience that you want to be thinking about when making your postings. This audience will be the ones interested in you when you make it, or potentially are already interested in you right now. This audience generally comprises children and their parents.

What is your brand about?

When posting/communicating with this audience you should, again as in the previous chapter, refer to the values of sport.

Spirit
- Family entertainment.
- Social inclusion.
- Community and cultural cohesion.
- Non gender or sexual orientation bias.

Performance
- Positive lifestyle management.
  - *Health and fitness.*
  - *Quality nutrition.*
- Mental toughness.
- Skill and ability.
- Sportsmanship.

Did you notice that I have put the "performance" values below the "spirit" values in this case? I do this because even though you will be engaging and entertaining supporters, you are not actually playing sport, so they will not measure you by these "performance" values at this time. However, you will be measured on how you conduct yourself in public and whether or not it is in the spirit of sports values. Remember, social media is a very PUBLIC place. So in this regard the "spirit" values are more important and relevant.

So, keeping these values in mind, make sure your posts or messages align with these values.

Offering value
- Grow your brand and your following by offering:
  - Value (No-one really wants to know how your bowel movements are, so be a source of quality information. Follow people who also offer value and share the information they share with you. Remember, once information is posted it can be seen by all).
    - Follow your favourite club, rugby journalists, players, etc. All things to do with the sport, let them be the original source, then add your own ideas or thoughts.
  - Listen to people who follow you and ask you questions (encourage them to engage with you).
  - Reply to them (make the engagement a two-way process).
- Align your brand with your followers' interest.
  - Your followers will be interested in rugby.

Protect your brand (Be aware of the pitfalls).
 The most amount of damage to your brand will come from yourself. Remember, children and their parents will be your main market place because they are the sports market place.

So don't:
- Post compromising pictures of yourself (imagine flying into Australia for your first ever Test series, walking through customs and being greeted by The Sydney Morning Herald and a front page picture of you in a mankini and looking a little worse for wear. All of this because your pal took a photo of you three years earlier when you were messing around. You may think it's funny now, but with the focus you will need to prepare yourself for the biggest game of your career, that kind of distraction will potentially tear you apart. Believe me, I have seen it happen).
- Do not re-tweet or re-post something you wouldn't say yourself. When you do this you validate what someone else is saying, so it's just as if you said it yourself. Best avoid all together.
- Swear words with symbols in them are still swear words. A seven-year-old knows what you are saying. Avoid using that type of language.

The easiest way to control what you post is to run through this list and communicate accordingly.

Post as if you are talking to:
- Your boss (or potential boss).
- Your coach.
- Your mum.
- Or a member of the press.

What's in it for you?
- You become a marquee player (opportunities).
- You'll grow your following.
  - Commercial opportunities may come your way.
  - Your network will grow (again more opportunities).
- Increased income.

Follow this simple guide and you shouldn't go far wrong. Educate yourself. The more you take in the better prepared you'll be. It does not matter how old or young you are, becoming a marquee player starts now and these values will never be wasted. They will stay with you and set you well for the rest of your life.

Chapter 7

Grunt and Glory

Before I got back to Bradford after my adventure at Harlequins, I found myself in Townsville in hot and steamy northern Queensland for the World Nines. It was not quite a Test jumper, but pulling the New Zealand jersey on for the first time at senior level felt good, knowing also that I would be back at the Bulls for a new season under a coach I respected and admired in Matty Elliott following Brian Smith's departure for Parramatta. Moreover, we won the Nines competition, although I did not celebrate that much with my fellow Kiwis. Joe Tamani, my Bradford team-mate and good buddy, was in town with the Fijians. It was also my 21st birthday the day we were going back. But I was in no mood for a celebratory hangover on the return trip and kept it quiet with Scott Naylor and Stuart Spruce, who had been in the England Nines squad, also on the flight. All I knew was that it was a happy trip back to England, Bradford and, unknown to me then, a force of nature by the name of Carl Jennings.

Carl was the 1987 British shot-putt champion and I can honestly say that I had never met anyone quite like him. He had quite a few theories about power and rugby league. After a chance meeting with Matty, he was keen to put them into practice. Carl was born in Hull, so he was not unfamiliar with the sport. His father had been a competitive bodybuilder. I loved the guy because he was such a ball of energy and enthusiasm. He was all about power, power and more power. If you were slacking, you could always rely on Jenno to give you a boot up the backside. You would walk in for training dragging your knuckles along the ground and Jenno would swiftly have you ripping in. I learned from him just the positive impact that some people can have on you. I have been with some coaches and trainers who can drain you of energy with their negative attitude. Not Jenno. He was always feeding into the Bulls' power grid. He had to do some fine tuning, of course, because he had some lads harnessed up to cars and pulling them in pre-season. A few players' knees and other things blew up, so the car pulling stopped, but we were at the start at Bradford under Carl of the power era – one that was going to carry us to glory later that season.

If 1996 was the set up year, 1997 was the season that we at Bradford really nailed our colours to the mast. To those who saw fun as heretical in sport, Peter Deakin, our great marketing wizard, was unapologetic. "We epitomise what Super League is all about – vibrant, young, glitzy," Peter, in typically ebullient form, said in an interview. "It is what some critics pompously think sport shouldn't be about. Why then have we doubled our crowds? We're as serious as any sports club in this country, but there has to be a sense of style." Peter successfully addressed Bradford's problem – a dying audience – and attracted families in droves. After a five-year spell in the United States marketing different sports, he held up the Chicago Bulls basketball team as an example to follow. Club merchandise sales in the first Super League season went from £70,000 to £500,000; we were reaching out to 27,000 local schoolchildren through our community development scheme. "Chicago Bulls have Michael Jordan, Manchester United have Ryan Giggs and we've Robbie Paul. The kid has got film star status in this city," he said.

Odsal, though, was no glamorous film set. Peter, quite rightly, was rather embarrassed that three Portakabins above the great bowl formed the nerve centre of the Bulls' operation, to which he would invite reporters from London. "We are now the biggest rugby club in Europe. Not just in league but across the codes," which was no idle boast, as the *Sunday Telegraph* noted. The 15,000 attendances at the start of 1997 outstripped all those in Super League and rugby union in England, Wales and France at the time. The club had big renovation plans, but its hands were tied by Bradford council, the stadium's owners, and fanciful talk of a £300m Superdome project, which never came to pass.

Decrepit as the stadium remained in some parts, there were a few new faces about the place in Danny Peacock and Tahi Reihana and, later that season, Jeff Wittenberg, Abi Ekoku and Paul Anderson from Halifax, and Mike Forshaw following his time in rugby union at Saracens. All I knew was that it was great to be back. I gave an interview on talk at the time of a hybrid code: "The two sports are worlds apart. The best thing would be to get rid of the word rugby. Union is a winter sport, we are a summer sport now and both should just get on with what they do best. I wouldn't want to see them join up. Rugby league now has the opportunity to go in its own direction." After my own time in union, I had my rugby passion back for what turned out to be an arduous, agonising, bewildering but ultimately rewarding season. Just as the year before, it began with another good run in the Challenge Cup.

We began an unstoppable roll to Wembley again. In between cup rounds, we steamrollered all-comers in Super League and, again like 1996, we came up against Leeds in the semi-finals. It is still referred to as the "Mac, Bang, Wallop" semi, which one supporter had embossed on the back of his replica shirt. Brian McDermott stood up that day as our enforcer. He had come out of the Marines as a raw talent but with an ability also to box. He got permission from Brian Smith to have a professional fight at Norfolk Gardens Hotel in Bradford, which he won. However, Smith told him that he must decide between boxing and rugby league. Once he did, Macca went from strength to strength. He was the skinniest front rower I had ever seen, but his sustainability was extraordinary. He would just go and go like the battery bunny. He had an engine that enabled him to be the first player to get in, get smashed and play the ball. He eventually got stronger and developed a great pass for a prop, but in 1997 his job was to take no prisoners. Macca took three Leeds men with him that day.

It was a vitriolic derby that ended with Macca sent off five minutes before the end for chucking a couple of rights and a left hook. As one reporter observed, had Don King wandered into the stadium at Huddersfield that day he could not fail to have been impressed by Macca's pugilism. What annoyed me was that I had made a half break and set Paul Medley up on one of his great bowling ball runs for a try that got ruled out, because Macca was back on the half way line with flattened Rhinos all around him. Matty Elliott had a go in the press about Russell Smith, the referee. He compared our dressing room to a M.A.S.H unit and said that the Bradford players had been put at huge risk of injury in incidents that went unchecked or penalised. There was plenty of bad blood that afternoon but, wonderfully, a second chance at Wembley to beat St Helens and lift that lovely old silver trophy.

The build-up to the final could not have been more different than 12 months earlier. Similar to ourselves, Saints rolled through to Wembley pretty much unbeaten, but partly because of our agonised loss the year before and Bradford's transformation on and off the field, we found ourselves in a new position as favourites. After arguably the best final in 99 years for sustained excitement, the centenary Challenge Cup final was partly built up as my revenge after the hat-trick in a beaten cause. "The old saying that there's some that think they can and some that think they can't is right. We can't think we are going to lose," I told one interviewer. "This is the pinnacle of rugby league. It doesn't come better. You've one shot at the Challenge Cup. The only person remembered is the one who lifts the trophy."

As part of their final preview, *The Times* wrote: "As a master of the soundbite, Paul could be a politician. Painter, song writer, fine art student, he is no ordinary league player. Not only is he a fabulous playing talent, he is generous, genuine and as a father of two at 21, pretty humble except when it comes to winning." There was certainly a hole in my psyche that I needed to fill and why wouldn't we be confident? Jenno's power game was coming to the fore. We were bulldozing teams and physically dominating them. This time at Wembley we knew what was coming. There was no wide-eyed bus trip to the famous twin towers. Our problem, however, was that we knew how to win games, not yet how to win a final.

Rather than the suffocating heat at Wembley the year before, it was a cool and overcast day. There was also the disruption of a suspect package being found and the game having to kick off 20 minutes late. Maybe that is why the game never really took off. Danny Peacock was sensational for us early on in the centre. Danny never really did weights, yet he was as hard as rock, with a body that he could slide through a keyhole. He would come on at a good line, get belted but keep going. He would break down teams because he never stopped. It is why the Bulls fans loved him and we loved him as players. Danny got an early try in a fairly dominant first half but another eluded him. When he was denied an equalising try by an ankle tap from Tommy Martyn, the Lance Todd Trophy winner that day, it was almost as if we were doomed.

Within a minute of that happening, I dislocated my foot when someone stood on me. Some of the metatarsals sprang out. As I limped off for treatment, the game got away from us with further tries by Chris Joynt and Anthony Sullivan in building on Saints' 16-10 lead at the break. It did not help much that Sullivan's try would have been ruled out in Super League by the video referee spotting that he had not grounded the ball, but the BBC was a bit behind the times technology-wise at that time. I had painkilling injections and got back on with 15 minutes to go, although the foot was already blowing up. The game ended up 32-22 and I dragged myself to the press conference. By the time I got to the team hotel I could not put any weight on it. The disappointment was acute, as was the pain in my foot. "For last year's Lance Todd winner Robbie Paul the afternoon stood in stark contrast," Paul Fitzpatrick wrote in *The Guardian*. "He produced some dazzling moments but never threatened to score three tries this time and at the end the hobbling Kiwi was wincing with a foot injury."

In the *Yorkshire Post*, correspondent John Ledger summed up Bradford's plight: "It is 49 long years since Bradford won at Wembley. On Saturday they completed an unwanted hat-trick of defeats at the stadium which brings out the worst in the club. In 1973 they were swept away by a Featherstone Rovers side which showed greater hunger for victory; in 1996, Bradford's hopes were bombed out of existence by a St Helens team which had the greater tactical know-how to secure victory; and on Saturday they conspired to concede defeat to a St Helens side which could hardly believe its luck."

Bobbie Goulding's slide-rule kicks for Martyn to pounce twice undid us. St Helens possessed too many fine players to let it slip. We were hesitant in defence, failed to convert our chances and learned a harsh lesson. We were a powerhouse team and favourites to win. It was almost as if we waited for victory to happen instead of making it happen. In our pain and misery we appreciated then that you have to take your game to another level in finals. That means all 17 players being willing to go that extra yard. You can go through league games, even semi-finals, with half the team turning up to play, but in finals everyone needs to be keyed in. It took some great battles with St Helens for that penny to drop. Once it did, the Bulls exploded as a force from 2000 to 2005.

Eight days after the final, we beat St Helens 38-18 in Super League in front of the biggest Odsal crowd for 24 years, at the start of a 12-match winning league run. My immediate focus was my first experience of hyperbaric chambers after the foot dislocation, to assist the recovery process. It was a bitter-sweet feeling after Wembley watching that match, a conclusive victory accurately portrayed as a tribute to the motivational qualities of Matty. Still, losing a second successive cup final was the kick up the backside we needed. It was my first long injury and it took me a while to get back up to speed when I returned, partly because the team had worked out some really good combinations without me.

Graeme Bradley and Glen Tomlinson were working really well together in the halves, Jimmy Lowes was on fire at hooker, Stuart Spruce was going from strength to strength at full back and Danny Peacock was running amazing lines. Tevita Vaikona was scoring tries for fun on the wing and Steve McNamara directing the team from loose forward. Everything was gelling together without me at that stage. A lot of what we had been doing as a side had previously been directed through me. Now we had strike weapons across the park. I also felt that I had lost something with having played rugby union over the winter and missed out on Bradford's pre-season. Everyone had been working on little rhythms and partnerships, to which I had not been privy. When I came back I felt somewhat of a bit-part player in a group who were really motoring and it took me some time to get back into the groove.

1997 was also the year of the hopelessly ambitious and ill-fated World Club Championship, for which Bradford, as Super League leaders, were cast as the great white hopes for European rugby league. The scale of the competition was mind-boggling: 22 clubs criss-crossing the equator for short tours over a couple of months before a last eight knockout. An idea arising from the split in the sport Down Under, which had started out as end-of-season play-offs between the top teams in each hemisphere, had turned into a monster mid-season competition and logistical nightmare, however inviting the fixtures might have looked from the outside. It was a vision of rugby league's vaulting global ambition, but one that the organisers were somewhat reluctant to share and discuss with the actual protagonists. As players, we simply got overlooked, which was inexcusable.

Had the players bought in to the concept it might have worked. But we were not consulted, just instructed to play in an additional competition with a minimum of six matches per club. Not only was it disruptive, the venture just wasn't taken seriously by the players. It was trialed and failed because it was regarded by us as a gimmick. It provided a lesson for all those administrators in the sport that, without player support and understanding of a concept, some things might be best not pursuing. It was the strength of the Exiles' introduction in 2011, as a means of the best overseas players in Super League combining to play England, that players supported and bought into as a well conceived idea. At no point in 1997 did the Rugby Football League or

Super League authorities in Australia and New Zealand consult the players.

There is far more engagement with players nowadays. Players have a lot of spare time on their hands and can make waves. Let's be honest, who do the supporters listen to? Players' own brands remain strong while they are putting the ball over the line or putting in the big tackles, so they need to be recognised and heard by the sport's authorities. The power of the GMB trade union behind the Rugby League Players' Association is significant, while there is strength in numbers with the formation in 2012 of the 1eague3 organisation by such high-profile players as Jon Wilkin and Jamie Peacock. With no such engagement in 1997, there was no idea what the authorities wanted delivering. Within a week of it kicking off, the World Club Championship already looked a thoroughly bad idea.

The portents had not looked good at the start of the year when the Australian Super League asked the Rugby Football League whether they could send out two players to help launch the competition there. I had permission from Harlequins to join Paul Sculthorpe on a whistle-stop promotional trip to Sydney. With two global corporations burning money on the sport Down Under, it wasn't a surprise to learn that we would be travelling business class and staying in a fancy hotel. When we got to the airport we found that we had been booked economy. On arrival in Australia, Super League officials said they were aghast at the mistake and promised that it would all be sorted out for our return trip. We did the big press conference the next day and an official came to us to promise again that our business return flights had been arranged. Thoroughly jet-lagged, we turned up at the airport check-in the next morning at least thinking that we would get a good kip on the flight back. Once again we were checked into economy. I phoned the official who had promised us business seats and extracted an admission that they had actually sold out. "We've had about four hours sleep in three days, we're in bits. Put us in first class then," I said, to which I heard the sound of laughter at the end of the phone. "First class," she said. "We don't even send Laurie Daley first class."

A month after my foot injury, I was back in the side for Bradford's first World Club Championship game at home to Penrith Panthers. Far too soon, as it turned out. The foot simply was not right. I winced every time I tried to explode off it. The game was close enough and we had

15,000 Bulls fans behind us at Odsal, but we let slip a 16-6 lead and Sid Domic got us with a last-minute try for Penrith in what turned out to be a pretty disastrous opening round of matches for the European teams. Of the 12, only Wigan recorded a win at Canterbury Bulldogs. It was the theme for the tournament, the odd gutsy British win amid a tidal wave of southern hemisphere victories. Bradford, alas, were no exception to this rule. Next up were Auckland Warriors and some very familiar faces in the likes of Stacey Jones and Joe Vagana. But as Andy Wilson noted in *The Observer*: "Bradford are unbeaten in the domestic competition, Auckland bottom in Australasia, and yet the Warriors played with 12 men for 43 minutes and still had too much for the Yorkshire side." Even with Syd Eru's red card, the Warriors had our number. Things just went from bad to worse against Cronulla Sharks in the last of the home legs, a game I missed because the foot was still playing up. In a perverse way, though, it was good to get those losses. It was a reminder of our vulnerability at a time when we were still storming through Super League, for which we did have the right psychological approach.

Leeds, Castleford, St Helens and Salford were all summarily dispatched before our extended Australasian break, otherwise known as the World Club Championship round two. If we thought round one was bad, the defeats Down Under were of nightmarish proportions. The first of the return fixtures was against Auckland. I was back home and in demand to talk the game up which, naturally, I did. I went on radio, television and in the press explaining how Bradford were one of the most dominant teams. To then get thrashed 64-14 was, to say the least, painful and embarrassing. We got flogged in training, yet still it felt like a mid-season break with some rugby in between. We rolled from there to a 54-point hammering by Penrith and a 40-point drubbing by Cronulla, with our Australian players taking the opportunity to visit friends and family.

To say that our minds weren't on the job is something of an under-statement, while my misery was completed in the Cronulla game by popping my shoulder. Matty felt I should build up muscle and undergo a reconstruction at the end of the year, so showed me special exercises that lifeguards did to build up stabilisation in the shoulder joints. I worked up from 1kg weights and became so strong in the shoulders that, rather than a reconstruction, I just needed a clean out. The World

Why so serious
Henry?
Looking after
his little bro,
then aged nine
months.

Me at 8 in my
Te Atatu Roosters
kit with cousin
Jamie Nikora and
Henry in his
Auckland
representative top.

Gone fishing - catch of the day for the Paul brothers beside Auckland Harbour Bridge with good mate Ariki Sim.

Playing softball was a favourite pastime as kids ... and strangling the odd cousin.

Butter wouldn't melt - me at 11 at Te Atatu North intermediate school.

Boys and guns - Henry and I playing outside Auckland Museum.

Shipshape - grandfather Bill Allen cuts a dash on deck.

Pictured at a new year's eve dinner with my grandfather Bill Allen and Auntie Maria, my mum's youngest sister.

Four generations of Pauls with Big Nan, Henry, cousins and nephews.

A couple of
Rodin thinkers
with mum and
dad.

A family shot in a rare
moment when Henry
and I were stood still.

Seeing Henry off on the 1993 Junior Kiwis tour with mum and grandparents Mary and Bill Allen.

Dad and mum in Auckland Warriors and Te Atatu Roosters gear.

At my Bradford testimonial dinner in 2004 with mum, dad and Henry.

Dad with Mia and Iesha in the playground next to the family home where Henry and I kicked about as kids.

School picture of elder daughter Iesha.

Daughter Mia in her Huddersfield Town Football Club cheerleader outfit.

Mr and Mrs Hunter-Paul walking down the aisle after tying the knot.

The Paul and Hunter clans together after the marriage of Mr and Mrs Hunter-Paul.

A line up of legends on our wedding day (left to right): Joe Vagana, Henry Paul, the new Mr and Mrs Hunter-Paul, Stacey Jones and Phil Leuluai.

Wedding top table line up of lifelong mates and family (left to right): Theo (Henry's son), Wendell Sisnett, Henry Paul, Warwick Aspin, Ueta Siteine, Dean Hilliard, Robbie and Natalie Hunter-Paul, Milan (Henry's daughter), Lucy (Natalie's sister), my daughters Mia and Iesha and Helena and Annabel, Natalie's sisters.

Our favourite wedding shot on an idyllic day at
a picturesque vineyard in west Auckland.

The artist in me was there at an early age and art has been a lifelong passion.
(Yorkshire Post Newspapers)

My real life red phase - with a piece of my figurative art.

Say it with flowers - a publicity shot of Henry and I for Marie Curie Cancer Care.

Band of brothers - Massey's line-up: Robbie Paul, Glenn Simons (aka Lazrus) and Henry Paul.

Henry and I boxing clever at a dinner with "Marvelous" Marvin Hagler, former world middleweight champion.

Looking good but smelling even better! (Yorkshire Post Newspapers)

Move over Jamie Oliver! To say that I'm a wow in the kitchen would be lying.
(Yorkshire Post Newspapers)

Working with schoolchildren has been a key part of
my life in rugby. (Yorkshire Post Newspapers)

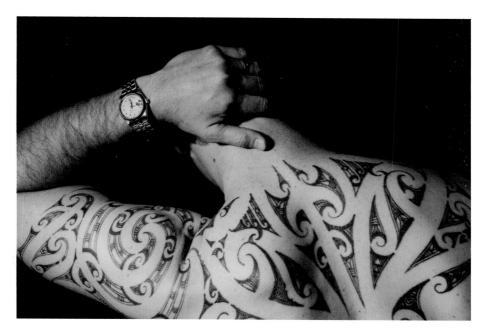

The traditional
ta moko (tattoos)
I have basically
tell the story of
my life so far.
I will add to them
on life's journey.
(Matt Johnson)

Tongue-lashing - the wahaika is a traditional Maori hand weapon, made of wood or whalebone, and ideal for hand-to-hand fighting. It's purely ceremonial in my case, honest. (Matt Johnson)

Club Championship was not so easily cured. Bizarrely, in losing six games we qualified for the quarter-finals. We were drawn away at Auckland, which involved a second trip home. Wise after the last event, I did not shoot my mouth off this time, which was sensible because the Warriors flogged us again 62-14. One of my mates said: "Man, you guys lost me a bet – I bet you'd lose by 50 and you only lost by 48." That was only because Sean Hoppe stepped forward to take the final shot in front of goal and missed. Rarely, though, have I been as glad to leave New Zealand after that debacle.

If the World Club Championship was a low in leaving its ugly stain on the season, raising the Super League trophy was the high point of the 1997 rollercoaster ride. A 22-8 win at home to the old enemy Leeds set up the title match on a hot and steamy Saturday night at Don Valley Stadium against Sheffield Eagles. By that point Peter Deakin had left the club to market rugby union at Saracens and Brian Smith had been back in Australia ten months. Nevertheless, their twin visions were fulfilled that evening. It was not the prettiest game, some players were low on energy and the Australasia trip had taken its toll during a long season. Physically you can always refuel your body – and Carl Jennings' power philosophy sustained us – but mentally we were just about done after that game, which clinched Bradford's first league title since Peter Fox's championship-winning sides in 1980 and 1981.

Moreover, we had won the title without dropping a point, a triumph for so-called "Bull Power". "Bradford have shown the way, first off the field and now as champions of Super League," Chris Irvine wrote in *The Times*. "Two years after the name change from Bradford Northern, the Bulls have completed the transformation. The sport as a whole should learn from this one example of a rugby league club that is a picture of health. An average of 6,100 attended home matches when the championship last ended up at Odsal; support today numbers more than 15,000. The fact that the M1, north and south, was choked with jubilant supporters after the 32-12 victory at Sheffield Eagles that secured the title indicates the widening radius of Bradford's appeal."

All our focus had been on going through Super League unbeaten – that did not quite happen, as we lost our last two games to Wigan and London Broncos after the title had been won – and the World Club Championship had failed to dent that ambition. In a way it fuelled it. We turned up at Sheffield just wanting to get the job done and were tip-toeing on glass at times before I finally got my hands on the trophy. The party the following Friday was when it really sank in when beating Paris by 68 points. Not that anyone knew then that it would be the last time the Super League title would be decided under the first-past-the-post system.

The play-offs route was the one I had grown up with Down Under, so its introduction for the 1998 season was not the shock it was to some people. The same people, I might add, who said that summer rugby league would never work. Well, that little theory had been proved wrong, and I loved the thought of a winner-takes-all Grand Final determining the champions. Just as your body works better in warmer conditions with proper hydration and the emphasis is on skill on dry pitches compared with the mud of winter, so the play-offs determine who is the best team at the right time. Players have to lift themselves for that part of the season and intensity and excellence levels go through the roof. Then there is the excitement it provides for crowds. It was a case, yet again, of rugby league being pioneering rather than just a stick-in-the-mud sport. Exciting times were in store, although 1998 didn't quite work out as everyone at Bradford hoped.

The big signing for the season by Matty was certainly a big enough name, indeed the most decorated player in rugby league history. But Shaun Edwards was a square peg in a round hole at Bradford. He enjoyed 14 gilt-edged years at Wigan, before a season at London Broncos, and his arrival at Odsal for his 16th league campaign at the age of 31 was seen as a somewhat unlikely move. The club had let Glen Tomlinson go and Giz and I were viewed as a creative half back pairing. He began the season on the bench with Graeme Bradley still at stand off. It was when we lost at Castleford in the fifth round of the Challenge Cup that Giz broke cover, so to speak. "At Wigan, I was the organiser, but I didn't want to storm into Bradford saying we should do this and that," he said in an interview. "The trouble in the Castleford match was that there were too many chiefs and not enough indians. I felt afterwards that the coaching staff wanted me to take more responsibility on the field." There was disgruntlement among Bulls supporters over stories about Wigan wanting Edwards back, which he addressed in the interview: "Bradford fans are quite rightly sick of people going on about me and Wigan. I'm committed to the club. I've everything to prove here. A big attraction of joining the Bulls was the atmosphere their fans created at the Broncos last season."

At the same time Shaun made it clear that he would still have been at Wigan had Eric Hughes, their coach at the time, allowed his request for a second day off each week to be in London with his former girlfriend, Heather Small, the singer, and their baby son. Wigan had got their act together under John Monie, with whom Shaun had achieved so many of his triumphs during Monie's first stint at Central Park. Whether Bradford was the right club or not, Shaun did not fit the mould at Odsal. I got on fine with him but many others didn't. All our guys were generally working class and he was seen as something of a glamour boy of a bygone Wigan era. It took the club a dozen games to work out that he had a really disruptive influence on the team. Not purposely, but simply because he was chalk to our cheese. He did not really train with us because his joints played up. When we were doing Carl's power weights and sessions, he would be limited in the gym to doing his own programme. That was just the way Giz was. Probably out of everyone I chatted to him the most, although I was just a forest boy from New Zealand and he was a worldly individual. He came from a different world to us, from the golden Wigan days. He had played with and against the world's best. I just felt that he did not fit. He did not see the game as the team did.

Our brand value was the hardest-working team in Super League. That was what we were known as internally. We had some descriptive values: brutal, uncompromising, loyal, lethal, superior (BULLS), and those words were plastered everywhere. As a club, we were about grunt, not glory. We just wanted to roll our sleeves up, but Shaun was not a grafter in that sense. He was a finisher, who would move the team around. It must have driven him crazy that he was not the dominant force he was playing behind a great Wigan pack. Whereas everyone in the team worked together, Shaun operated in isolation. On quite a few occasions a player would make a break, he would do a support run, then someone would dummy him and hold on to the ball. Shaun would throw his hands in the air in frustration. Our culture was that you were simply expected to reload and go again.

Following conversations with some of the other senior players, I went to see the coach to explain that things were not working out for us with Shaun. To be fair, he was not losing us games but the mix wasn't right. Nor was he missing tackles or dropping the ball; it was just that his style of play and training methods did not gel with the team. One player, perhaps, but there was a separation in a unified group. He was a fish out of water unsettling our pond. Quite a few players went in to see Matty before a game at Salford, to the extent that I was surprised he selected Shaun. He got taken off at half-time, we lost that game and within a month Edwards had re-signed for the Broncos.

It was around then that Henry and I first began talking about the possibility of him moving over from Wigan, but overall 1998 was a horrid year for the Bulls. We were blighted by injuries, including a cartilage injury which I sustained. The invincibility of 1997 was long gone and we scraped a fifth place finish in just about qualifying for the new top five play-offs system, 18 points behind league leaders Wigan. It meant a trip to our old nemesis St Helens for Graeme Bradley's last game. Trust Penguin to go out with a bang by being sent off one final time. The nickname came from the stiff way he walked. He was intelligent, quick-witted and the nastiest piece of work I've seen on a rugby field. Defending outside him, I'd think 'I'm just glad I'm in your team because you really are a horrible thing'. He was nasty in tackles and a past master at winding up opponents. I'd swear there was no flesh on his body, just raw skin and bone. He was a tough guy who backed up everything he said and was an inspirational presence.

I was sad to see him go, because he was such a fine player, although I never liked the way he tested the mental toughness of some young fellas. He broke a couple of them in the Bradford team; the ones he didn't break, turned out to be world class. That was Peng. He tested everyone. He intimidated, mocked and exploited every weakness he could in people psychologically. If they were not able to take it, they were not able to play with him. Those who passed the test flourished. I was the captain but he was the one who would question referees, often because he knew the rules better than them. When he elbowed Chris Smith in the face we were 12-6 up after 16 minutes. We lost 46-24.

The professional has rights (the pay-off)

Now that you hopefully have aligned your brand, let's think how you can use it to your advantage.

A lot of the time athletes will wait for their managers to source them low level sponsorship opportunities. The problem with this approach is that managers in low-paying professional sports have a lot of players on their books. To make any returns the main source of income will come from athletes' playing-contracts.

Any extra deals are usually shelved, as they don't pay well and require a lot of time to source. The cut for managers means it's not worth the work, unless you are a sports marquee player/individual.

The concept of this HP section is to show you some simple ways in which you can source yourself some deals, or help your manager out by offering more for them to "sell".

All athletes have "rights"
No, I don't mean "rights" in the sense of human rights, but in terms of sponsorship rights. It's a luxury for all professional athletes that they have a natural market place interested in them and thrust upon them. This fact is due to the club that they play for (the club's supporters), sport that they play in (the sport's supporters) and industry that they work in (sport supporters in general). As this market place is interested in you, it means there is interest in what you say, think, support and even look like. This makes you interesting to potential sponsors/partners interested in all of these supporters.

So what is it you have to offer?

- **Social Media followers**
  - If you have followed the messages from the last two HP sections, you will start to grow a strong, complete sport-friendly social media following. You can now show a marketplace directly to a potential sponsor/partner. Here you can now prove that you can communicate

directly with this marketplace in which you can mention a partner's brand, services or product.

WARNING! You could drive your following by being controversial, in which case people probably won't be following you because they admire you. It's more likely they're waiting for the next stupid thing you do or say. So this will mean you have a big following but with negative brand equity and partners don't want to align their products with anything negative. This is a strong reason for living up to sports values.

- **Image rights**
  - Easily explained, this is your image and it can be used as part of an advertising campaign for someone interested in your following and support base.

- **Intellectual rights**
  - As a professional athlete you will be perceived as an expert in your industry because you've achieved a level of success most can only dream of. This fact will allow you to make comment, so an easy way to earn from this is to offer your services as a journalist. This could mean a local, regional or even national newspaper, a blog, social media, a sports industry paper or magazine. I suggest doing a journalism course at a local college because editors will be more welcoming to athletes who can produce "copy ready" articles (writing that is ready to go straight to print or online) than ones that editors have to rewrite themselves.
    - HP tip – editors are overworked and don't have time for rewrites.

- **Timing rights**
  - Turning out for a signing session for a company is something you see many athletes do in all regions and the fact that they get news coverage should be seen as another tool in the armoury. Your image will sell papers, it's newsworthy and all you have to do is give up an hour or two.

- **Physical rights**
  - Create your own events.
    - Unlike your club you don't have a stadium that can be renamed or perimeter boards, but as you are perceived as an expert in your field you could consider creating your own events, such as former England captain Jamie Peacock's and former Great Britain captain Paul Sculthorpe's coaching academies. You can create physical properties to put partners' branding on: banners, flyers, handouts, T shirts etc., all integrated into your event. Imagine a training camp for 16-20-year-olds sponsored by a nutrition company. They could offer free samples of their products to young players who are their targeted growth marketplace, as well as have their branding positioned as part of your camp's title and promotional offers to drive sales.

WARNING! Make sure that your new partnerships do not conflict with your employers. The standard deals with your club will give them access to your rights also, so it is always important to work with them and not against them. If you're worried then ask the question to the people who are best positioned. Remember, you want to be known as an industry "marquee" athlete not a problem "star in a bar". Also if you're lucky to have more than one extra partner never get partners that are in competition with one another (that's just bad form).

You will notice that I have stopped using the word sponsor for partner, because this is what it should be – a partnership where what you do offers benefit for yourself, your partner and the supporters that your partners are trying to engage with. By having something in it for supporters, it will allow them to enjoy the partnerships you have on a physical and emotional level. As sponsorship expert Kim Skildum-Reid suggests: Win (for you) Win (for partner) **WIN** (supporter).

Now you know what you have to offer, you can approach a potential partner. Don't say this is what I have, ask what do you need? When they tell you, look at your list of rights. If you have something that ticks their box, which may be just one of your "rights" or part of your rights, whatever balance suits, then you can negotiate a price (I'll leave that up to you as it will differ depending on budget from your sponsors, your reach as an athlete and the impact your partnership will make on the targeted audience). I suggest starting slowly and getting a feel for it all.

HP tip
This whole approach can be used if you decide to undertake charity work also. It may be completely selfless but it will always be well received.

Chapter 8
Band of Brothers

Only the overwhelming experience of walking out at Wembley in 1996 for the Challenge Cup final compared with the euphoria I felt one night in a Japanese restaurant in Sydney as a fully paid-up member of the New Zealand rugby league squad. I had not yet played in my first Test match but here I was among my heroes. As a 21-year-old who had dreamed about this, I had reached my heaven, my Utopia; the Tepanyaki was quite something, too. It was funny to think just a few months earlier that this had appeared the impossible dream, having had to turn down coach Frank Endacott's invitation, due to my rugby union commitment at Harlequins. How lucky was I right now?

Look at me Wally Lewis, you are the one who gave me this goal. I still get excited seeing the great man fronting Australian television coverage and interviewing players. It is a job I do myself for the BBC, but Wally is incomparable, even with a mic in hand. I have him on such a pedestal, I think he should be living in a golden castle somewhere. And, yes, I know he was the great Kangaroo. For this Kiwi, he is a sort of honorary New Zealander. Whenever I pulled on the New Zealand jumper, part of me thought back to the kid running on to the pitch – "Mr Lewis, Mr Lewis" – for his autograph, even though he had just destroyed us. He remains the definitive rugby league talent. King Wally.

Having missed my New Zealand Test chance against Papua New Guinea in October 1996, the World Nines the following January in Australia were a testing ground for me. It was all a bit of a mad rush playing my last game for Harlequins and flying out to Townsville less than two weeks before the start of the rugby league season, for which I had not been part of Bradford's preparations. I travelled with Nigel Vagana and Tony Tutupo via Cairns. We barely had any sleep and within a few hours of arriving in remote northern Queensland, I was whisked, bizarrely, to a wet T-shirt competition. It was all a little surreal, the heady excitement of representing New Zealand at senior level for the first time, mixed with far too many bourbon and cokes – the Kiwis' drink of choice for many of the players. That particular hangover set the drinking tone for the rest of my life, in that I'm no good at it. When you are a lot smaller than the big guys and try to drink at their speed, the laws of physics take over. As I got older I found that the best thing for me was not to get into rounds of drinks. Not before I learned the hard way, however.

Henry was familiar with the New Zealand set-up, having been part and parcel of it since the 1995 World Cup. It was not until 1998 that I got to play alongside Henry for New Zealand, due first to nerve damage in his back, then a broken arm and a knee injury. But the Kiwis were keen to test out Henry's little brother, both on the field and in the drinking stakes off it, which I was not really used to. We beat Western Samoa 16-0 in the final at Stockland Stadium to win the World Nines, which was a good enough start to life with the Kiwis. When Frank next called me he said: "You're not playing rugby union are you?" It was the call-up for the Super League Test match against Australia at Sydney Football Stadium, eight days before the 1997 Challenge Cup final.

I had just got back from France where I had scored a couple of tries in a league win over Paris Saint Germain. Bradford were pretty much unstoppable at that point, I was bagging tries for fun and we had another Wembley appearance on the horizon. On that wave came the call I was so anxious for – and this time, thank goodness, I was able to say yes. I did not sleep at all the night before boarding the plane. I have always been something of an insomniac, with my mind constantly ticking over, and now it was in overdrive. Henry knew them but these were guys I hero-worshipped. Naturally, I did not sleep on the flight. I arrived on the Tuesday to be told I was rooming with Tea Ropati, one of the old heads, who was great to have as a roomie. The game was on the Friday and I was green about everything. I entered the breakfast room with my jaw hanging.

These were the band of brothers forged by Frank, players I had grown up with, such as Stacey Jones and Joe Vagana, who were part of the set-up already. Legends like Tony Iro and Tawera Nikau were gods to me. Ruben Wiki was coming into his own at that time and I knew Rubes through family. Our mums were friends. But this was not just a team of athletes. They were members of a tight-knit family, a band of brothers. I got sucked into it. These guys drank hard and played hard. To be part of the unit you did what everyone else did. One or two senior players, including Kevin Iro, walked their own path, but to be in the gang you had to fit in. The team did everything together to build that camaraderie. The reality was that we were going into battle and you had to trust one another. This is what Frank propagated and he was a master of it. With such a short time span there was no need to be technical. He grabbed us by our hearts and minds and we loved him for it.

The night in the Japanese restaurant was a magical one for a wide-eyed new boy on the scene. Two chefs were flinging bowls of rice 20ft or more. They would almost float the rice bowls on the air and it was your job to catch yours. If you did not catch it smoothly, the rice would fly up. These guys knew that we had pretty good hand-eye co-ordination, so when it came to Frank's turn to catch his bowl they sent it high. As Frank rocked back to catch it he fell off his chair. He was literally wearing the rice. Everyone, Frank included, cracked up. We laughed together, drank together and played together.

My first Kiwis training session was like nothing I had experienced before. I had been selected on the bench along with Tea, Joe and Tyran Smith. We were asked to run against some of the other players, with me instructed to mark Richie Barnett, the full back. Richie was in his prime but I was confident in terms of my speed, footwork and physical ability. Basically, no-one at Bradford could catch me. The ball emerged from a scrum, I moved up to Richie who put a side step on me, accelerated and disappeared into the distance. It took my breath away. In that moment I appreciated what level of athlete I was dealing with here. You have got to be good at club level but this was another level and I had to seriously raise my game. It was daunting, challenging but, above all, exciting.

It was a life lesson, too, in the value of taking say four or five junior stars away on a senior international tour. The Kiwis took Lesley Vainikolo and Ali Lauitiiti on the 1998 Great Britain tour. They were never going to play. They were there to learn. What you have on a tour are 25 of the most developed athletes with different skills and techniques and if you are smart enough you will ask questions of the experienced guys. The young players, especially, should always be inquisitive and open to being educated. It keeps you growing. As soon as you think you know it all, life will leave you behind. With the Kiwis, I like to think that I made what I term as an ARSE of myself – Attitude, Sacrifice, Responsibility, Education.

That first week was bliss. Jarrod McCracken had taken a bit of a shine to me. At least I think he did. Maybe I just got on his nerves, kicking around in his shadow. But he was one of my all-time favourite players. He was big, powerful, aggressive, the epitome of a man's man, rather like Quentin Pongia. The two of them were tougher than tough. McCracken was aptly named Crackers. As tough as he was, he was as mad as a hatter and played up to that image as well. I had so many of these guys on pedestals that when it came to entering the dressing room at Sydney Football Stadium that night I had to catch my breath. I took a moment to stare at my number 14 shirt hanging on the peg. It was mind blowing, enough to make you cry. I was in shock really. My heart was pumping. I could feel the blood throbbing through me.

All the jovial nature of the past few days had disappeared. Everyone was focused. All the fun and togetherness were honed to this sharp point, game time. I was swept along by it. By the time I came on in the second half to partner Stacey after Gene Ngamu had come off, we were 20-0 down. Frank said to me at half-time: "You're going to come on and win this game for us." Even with that deficit to an Australia side on their favourite home patch in Sydney, I sort of believed Frank. He filled me with positive energy. It also nearly did the trick. We pulled a try back while still under the cosh before I set up another for Daryl Halligan with one of my first touches. I snuck down the blind side, drew the cover and passed to Daryl who got over. Rodney Howe, a brute of a prop for the Kangaroos, kept picking me out on the edge. He was running over the top of everyone. "Get into him, you little pussy," Quentin shouted at me. Easier said than done because Howe was killing it at the time, although this Aussie monster underlined for me that as much as you have to run the ball at international level, you cannot possibly compete if you are not going to tackle properly.

Then it happened, a Test debut try. It was late in the game and, yes, we were chasing a hopeless cause, but Richie, just as I had seen him do in training, displayed brilliant footwork in coming off his right. He had seen something on, so I started heading up. The art of the support player is to get the feel for what your team-mate is going to do. I could see that Richie was working towards space and David Peachey, the full back, was coming to meet him. I knew, too, just how wicked Richie's step was. He cleverly drew Peachey and there I was perfectly placed to take his pass for the try. It wasn't a win – we lost 34-22 – but, in that moment, I was thinking, yes, I'm here!

I rode the crest of euphoria all the way back to Bradford. I had in my mind that I could play on the Sunday against Sheffield Eagles. The lads won easily enough without me, although that had not stopped me putting a call in to Matty to say that I wanted to be picked, that I had only played 25 minutes of the Test match for New Zealand and had plenty of energy left in the tank. I had only had four hours' sleep but Matty was adamant in ordering me back to bed with a reminder that there was a cup final to play in less than a week's time. The foot dislocation that I subsequently suffered at Wembley was, perhaps, some kind of warning that my body needed a rest. Up until then I had felt pretty much indestructible, as if I was made of rubber and springs rather than vulnerable flesh and bone.

The injury was a foretaste of agonised spells out of the game to come, but if I could have played seven games a week I would have done. The next Kiwis call up was for another Test against Australia but at North Harbour Stadium in Auckland, a week before Bradford were due in the city to play the Warriors in the World Club Championship quarter-finals. Frank had come up with some crazy notion about me sticking my head in the front row by putting me at hooker. I had not figured in the pack since my back row days in the under 10s. What he wanted was someone to get out of acting half quickly, although when he saw the blood drain from my face, he said not to worry about it. I knew then, though, that Frank was looking for me to switch there some time down the track. He went with Syd Eru at No 9 for that game, which turned out to be a pretty inspired move as he claimed two of our six tries in a sensational match.

It was not cold but wet, a typical Auckland day you might say, with a young guy playing his first game for Australia at full back by the name of Darren Lockyer. We kicked off long and the new kid dropped the ball. On two occasions Lockyer ran the ball out, got chopped down and lost possession. It was an invidious start for a true great of the game who still scored two tries on his debut and was still cursing himself afterwards. We had Matthew Ridge back at full back and captaining the side. He was possibly not the most physically talented players I had come across. In terms of mental toughness and psychological aggression, though, he was in a league of his own. He also had a massive mouth on him. Ridgey did not make tackles because he would fill in all the gaps by directing you. Even though the guy was skinny and not the tallest, I was a bit scared of him. He could not fight his way out of a paper bag but he knew how to direct the team and the bloke had ice in his veins when it came to goal-kicking. He quite liked me, probably because I was gobby like him. In a subsequent international match at North Harbour, I had got back and he just said to run the ball in. I had two markers there with baseball bats and thought, I'm not going to make two feet here, so I flung the ball at Ridgey, who promptly got smashed.

We were 12 points up with five minutes to go when I made a break, burned off one of the Australia front rowers and came one-on-one with Lockyer. There wasn't a full back in England who I could not leave for dead. Not this guy. I was 20 metres out, came off my left foot, then off my right and somehow he got me. His mistake was in continuing to hold me down in giving away a penalty in front of the Kangaroos' posts. This is where I learned from Ridgey about psychological warfare. A kickable penalty, two points and surely the game in the bag? Ridgey slapped my arm down. "Who are you to say we're going to take two," he said. "What we're going to do is rub it in."

At international level, it is all about ruthlessness. So many teams will take the two points to eat up time, but a winning psychology is that you continue to push down when you have got your opponents by the throat. We were in the ascendancy with a full stadium of screaming New Zealanders behind us. We ran the ball, drove the nail in Australia's coffin and prevailed 30-12. I recalled Joe Vagana when we were playing together for the Junior Kiwis saying that there is no better feeling than beating Australia – and he was right. Not because of antipathy necessarily but purely because you have beaten the best. It is a joyous feeling. Auckland Warriors quickly brought me back down to earth with their thrashing of Bradford in the World Club Championship last eight, but we had sensed something special with the New Zealand side that year.

Henry was finally fit for the 1998 ANZAC Test, again at North Harbour Stadium. Brothers in arms at last representing New Zealand, the 29th set of siblings to play for the Kiwis in a rich history of Sorensens, Ropatis, Tamatis, Shelfords, Manns and Iros. I think it was always a little bit more special for me playing alongside Henry than it was for him. Maybe it is a younger brother thing, but that first Test together was also a pretty special time for Henry, with him jetting back to play for Wigan in the 1998 Challenge Cup final. Sheffield Eagles proceeded to pull off the shock of all time at Wembley, but for those few days in Auckland the two of us were in clover. We did not get into camp until the Wednesday, two days before the match, with the pair of us to finally link up in the same side since our Te Atatu and Waitakere days some five years previously.

The thing about me playing hooker was still buzzing around Frank's head. He mentioned it again and had me passing a few balls off the ground. I did not let on to anyone but I pulled something in my lower back, went off for a massage and kept quiet. Understandably after our last win against Australia in Auckland, there was a lot of media interest in the game. I would do a lot of tongue-in-cheek stuff in England and no-one took it that seriously, so when one reporter asked about the hooking role, I said: "I've never played there before. The reality is, though, I'm too pretty to play hooker." I thought nothing more about it until I got on the bus to training the next morning.

Ridgey was at the back of the bus in fits of laughter reading the paper. "Boy, you are gold, you crack me up," he chortled. My flippant comment had been read out to John Lang, the Australia coach, who had retorted on television: "We'll see how pretty Robbie is after 80 minutes. I'll have a special word to my front rowers about that." Frank, though, was still playing mind games. The Paul he actually had in mind for hooker was Henry, who went out and killed the Kangaroos. Partly because we came from the English competition, Australia did not know how to read us. There was a headline the next day that said, "Fabulous Paul boys". Henry told one interviewer: "I didn't see it as playing with my brother, but him as another player who I relied on. It was only afterwards that you thought, 'yes, we did that together'. Robbie's another mate to rely upon."

A 22-16 win set us up nicely for the rigours of that autumn, although Australia had their revenge in two Tests – games in which the nonsense of unlimited substitutions meant everything went way too fast – before the relative sanity of the 1998 Great Britain tour and a curious sort of homecoming. Much of the publicity appeared to hinge on the two of us, rather than the Great Britain players, partly because Henry had already confirmed his departure from Wigan to Bradford. It was the start of a beautiful three-year relationship on the field.

"The ties that bind the Pauls will tighten further next season when Henry joins Robbie at Bradford Bulls after four years at Wigan Warriors," *The Times* said in a feature on the eve of the first Test at Huddersfield. "There were parallels drawn with Sherlock Holmes and Mycroft when Henry, first to arrive in England, insisted that he had a kid brother back home more talented than himself. Bradford took Henry at his word, but Robbie was mainly kept hidden before Brian Smith took over as coach from Peter Fox in 1995 and created a side around the extravagantly gifted Paul. In the intervening years, one of the brothers has usually stood out, but rarely together at the same time. For two seasons, Henry was the fulcrum and pivot in Wigan's domination of the last two winter seasons. Last year belonged to Robbie and the Bulls. This year, Henry inspired Wigan to their first Super League championship. For Great Britain's sake, it is important to keep both of them quiet, a near-impossible task as they can pop up just about anywhere."

We both fitted around Stacey Jones because he ran the show. I slotted in at stand off, with Henry and Syd Eru interchanging at hooker. The two of us always felt it was tougher to play Great Britain than Australia on the basis that their players knew us inside out. There were no tricks they hadn't seen. The only novelty was that we had not been seen in tandem before. Fortunately for us, the opening game plan worked a treat for New Zealand's first victory in England for nine years. Great Britain probably should have won with the amount of possession they had, but we were direct, positive and rode our good fortune on occasions, not least when Great Britain turned their backs on a play-the-ball that was deemed by referee Bill Harrigan still to be in progress as the hooter for half-time sounded. Joe Vagana could scarcely believe his luck in sauntering over from 30 metres for a try that, by the end of that night, had been turned by the big fella into a length-of-the-field spectacular.

Henry came on after half-an-hour for Syd, and Frank kept him there because he was playing that well in the front row alongside Quentin, who put in a magnificent 80-minute stint. Henry got a superb pass away to Stacey for a crucial try and Stephen Kearney slipped an equally good ball away for me to go over. Great Britain fought back to within six points through a late try by Jason Robinson, and there were just a few seconds remaining when Andy Farrell put up a crossfield kick. As I watched the ball arc across and down towards our goal-line, Keith Senior jumped, just as I reacted in tackling him. Boom, I took him over the sideline in one motion. It certainly felt like I had tackled him in mid-air, which would probably have meant a penalty try – and a draw for Great Britain with a conversion from under the posts – but Harrigan was having none of it. It was the year that Super League outlawed tackling players off the ground, but international rules were – and remain – a frustrating grey area. My body had reacted purely on muscle memory. Here was a guy about to snatch away our victory and I was going to do everything in my power to prevent him scoring. It worked out for us but I was far from the only person that night thinking, how was that not a penalty try for Great Britain?

From 16-8 down at Bolton in the second Test, we rattled up 28 unanswered points and secured New Zealand's first series victory in Britain since 1971. The incident that stuck out for me, though, was big Joe and Keith Senior swinging handbags after Keith had a go at Henry. Joe came flying in at Keith and the pair of them threw the worst punches I had ever seen. No technique, just haymakers missing their mark. But that is the thing I loved about Joe. Not only was he always first to wade in, he was the best front rower I played with, possibly because he had the mind of a half back. He would tear into the teeth of any team and never be bent backwards in defence. When I did eventually convert to being a hooker, having Joe beside me meant that we were always going to be on the front foot and sure of a quick play-the-ball. He had twinkling feet for a huge lump of humanity and the most amazing pass in his armoury. I would shout for him, he would get the ball, take a couple of steps, draw the defence and hit me with an on-the-money pass of up to 40 metres. He attracted defenders like flies, three or four at a time, because he was that hard to bring down. However, as for that fight with Keith, it was not the finest hour for either of them.

Great Britain and Andy Goodway, their coach, got berated in the press, but the truth was that we were on fire. "We would have taken Australia apart with our second half performance," Frank said in the media conference. "We were eight points down at half-time, but considering the amount of ball we had given away, we were reasonably happy. All our talk was about composure. We knew if we held on to some ball we would crack them." Crack them we did, with Henry getting in on the try scoring act. We were the only two English-based players in the side. Much was rightly made of the roots in the series win stemming from the Auckland Warriors' four-year exposure to the Australian competition. We proceeded to Watford intent on completing a series whitewash, but although Henry and I each had one of our best outings for the Kiwis, I blame myself for allowing Britain to salvage some pride by drawing the third Test.

I scored two tries, Henry one and Stacey was pretty much unstoppable, but Great Britain clawed their way level through a converted try by Tony Smith, their scrum half, after I had wedged out of the line in allowing Sean Long to draw Ruben Wiki and put Smith over. The difference between us was a drop goal by Stacey, which is probably how it would have stayed had they not succeeded with a short kick off and reclaimed possession. With the clock run down but the ball still in play, Smith had the last say. "Not only had Smith never dropped a goal in his life, the joke is he has two wooden legs, yet the Wigan scrum half's hand-eye co-ordination and right foot were inch-perfect," *The Times* noted. It spared them the ultimate embarrassment. In fact, the Great Britain boys were so relieved that they were shouting and punching the air as if they had won the game. Not that it dampened our enthusiasm. We did some serious socialising on the tour and the mic was passed around everyone on the bus for a final sing-song. A lot of the boys were heading back off to New Zealand at 6am, though it did not stop us celebrating. Henry was rooming with Stacey, who had gone off in Henry's jacket with his car keys. Nursing the world's worst hangover on a Sunday afternoon, the two of us got a tow truck to take us from London back to Henry's house in Wigan.

Another rush trip half way across the world for us nearly paid dividends in the 1999 ANZAC Test. Henry played Australia off the park until a nasty injury, and I grabbed the first of our three tries, including one by Lesley Vainikolo on his international debut. The Kangaroos snatched the win, but my immediate concern was for Henry. I collected the man of the match award on his behalf after he had landed on his neck in a tackle. We went to hospital together, still in our kit. Somehow two Bradford fans in their Bulls gear managed to get into the hospital to wish Henry well. They were a little worse for wear and were alarmed, as I was, to see Henry lying there in traction. He was okay, though, because a short while later he was in the bar.

The next time we met Australia, they were building a team around the likes of Brett Kimmorley, with the great Allan Langer having retired at international level. The 1999 Tri-Nations tournament was when New Zealand matured greatly as a team, starting with a 24-22 opening win over the Aussies at Ericsson Stadium in Auckland, during which Stacey ran the Kangaroos ragged. Willie Talau offered a new dimension in the centre, Ruben Wiki was our talisman and Henry again had a field day. I turned my ankle in the match and was given the week off, which meant I skipped an exhibition match against Tonga, the same weekend that Great Britain got a 46-6 hiding off Australia in Brisbane. In the Tonga match, Stacey went to make a tackle, just as big Joe was coming through on the same opponent from the blindside. The only thing between them was Stacey's arm as Joe cleaned out the Tongan. His arm just shattered. I ran on to Carlaw Park and he looked green. An ambulance came on to the pitch to take Stacey away. Two rods had to be inserted into the bone, meaning that I had to get healthy straight away.

For the first time, the Paul brothers were the half back combination for the Kiwis. One newspaper described us as running the New Zealand rugby union publicity machine a close second in the week that the All Blacks were gearing up to play France in the Rugby World Cup semi-finals. We had already been filling the half back roles for a season at Bradford, so we just did what came naturally. We were the devils that a Great Britain side, mainly composed of players from Wigan, Leeds and St Helens, knew well enough, although nothing was going to stop us that day. Henry, in particular, was on fire outside me. There would be times when Henry would just do what he had to. With a player of his natural talent, that would amount to more than the vast majority of players. But with the bit between his teeth, Henry would blow everyone away and the Great Britain game at Ericsson Stadium was one of those occasions. The pair of us routinely settled into our Bradford roles, Henry landing an early penalty and sending Matt Rua charging over for the first of our four tries. Big Joe, Craig Smith and Jason Lowrie destroyed Great Britain up front and we played off the back of their strongarm work. Nigel Vagana intercepted a pass by Iestyn Harris and Henry put him over for a second before Joe joined in the scoring act with his cousin. "There was no unity at all in the Britain team," I was quoted afterwards. "Three or four of them were running the show and the rest were running in different directions."

There was even more of an emphasis on the Tri-Nations final with Australia once the All Blacks crashed out early in the Rugby World Cup. "The biggest beneficiaries are the New Zealand rugby league team," one newspaper wrote. "Win what is being called the unofficial world championship and watch Henry and Robbie Paul displace Christian Cullen and Jeff Wilson in the popularity stakes." No pressure then. Henry told reporters: "It hurt [the All Blacks losing the semi-final], but the fact is that rugby union is ingrained in New Zealand's blood, like football is in England. This is our chance to show off our sport, try to do New Zealand proud and get a few more people along to watch us." We succeeded in all aspects bar the result, a 22-20 thriller won by Australia, in which Frank Endacott came close to seeing his Kiwis side winning, unlike John Hart, his badly-beaten All Blacks counterpart, on a night when Lesley Vainikolo was justly compared to Jonah Lomu and the so-called "Bulls brothers" pushed ourselves to the limit.

I was denied one try by Darren Lockyer but scored on the back of reading Henry. I instinctively knew what he was going to do once he had isolated an opponent. I headed after him, broke straight through Australia's line, drew Lockyer and was away. It was an epic encounter, with Australia taking control, us chipping away and scrapping in defence for our lives, them losing their heads with Lockyer and Darren Britt sin-binned, and Henry punishing them with his goal kicks, six in all. We were 20-18 ahead with five minutes to go after Joe had offloaded for Nigel to score, despite having half the Kangaroos' pack on his back, when up popped Wendell Sailor with a heartbreaker try. Mat Rogers converted for the win. Henry nearly stole it at the death with a kick for Logan Swann but the Kangaroos muscled up in defence. According to Brad Fittler, their captain, pride got them home, but New Zealand were tantalisingly close to them at that stage.

Australia obviously saw Henry and I as a big threat, because when we arrived at Sydney for the 2000 ANZAC Test there was a posse of photographers waiting. The next morning we were on the front pages of the newspapers, pictures of us pushing our luggage emerging from the airport. That blew me away; you don't get that in England. Unfortunately, Australia blew us away that time in a match in which Frank finally delivered on his dread promise to put me in the front row.

Despite it not being the greatest of introductions to the hooking role, that is what ruined me with coaches for the rest of my career. If he can play in the front row against Australia, they thought, where else can he play?

For the World Cup in Great Britain and France later that year, I still considered myself as one of the babies of the New Zealand team. A baby, however, without a fixed position, with Frank seeing Stacey and Henry as his first-choice half backs and with Richard Swain starting to make a big impact at hooker. It was a surreal start to the tournament in freezing conditions at Kingsholm, the home of Gloucester rugby union club, against a Lebanon team mainly made up of Australians. Richard got hypothermia along with four of the Lebanese players, who I just remember shivering away in the bath together. There were not many people there to see us win 64-0, nor were there many at Reading for our 84-10 demolition of the Cook Islands, in which I partnered Tasesa Lavea, who had returned from rugby union. We then walloped Wales in a tournament bogged down in appalling weather and critical headlines about the organisation.

It certainly was not the most auspicious of starts and there were just 5,000 to see our quarter-final against France at Castleford, in which I teamed up again with Henry in the halves. In Stacey's absence, I scored a hat-trick, which left Frank with something of a dilemma for the semi-final with England at Bolton. It was the question the press kept asking, but Frank was always minded to go with Stacey and Henry as his halves, with me as his plan B. Regarding myself as one of the young fellas, I was happy just to be there and, besides, Frank wanted me to rotate with Richard at hooker. "That's what I want from you Robbie," he said. "Run from acting half, quick play-the-balls, and off you go." It was not until five years later, under Brian Noble at Bradford, that I was taught properly to pass a ball off the ground, indeed any specialist acting half skills.

I improvised, a little like Andrew Johns did for Australia in the role. For all his massive and deserved reputation, I always seemed to play against Johns when he was at hooker. He would jump up and down in making an ass of himself before a game, getting all hyped up and pouring out nervous energy. I would think, mate, you are no hooker either. I came off the bench against England and, like much of that tournament, it was a non-event. We romped home 49-6 and into the final, for which a glorious 40 minutes or so it looked like it would be against Wales, as Lee Briers and Iestyn Harris ran rings around the Kangaroos. Order was eventually restored but, thanks to some Welsh wizardry, the tournament at last got a bit of momentum going into the final at Old Trafford. For all that it was a huge honour being part of a World Cup final team, a 40-12 result was a comprehensive triumph for Australia, one that I was never going to disturb in coming on after 58 minutes. It is hard enough at hooker having to put shots on players. In the halves, you might make one tackle per set, not two or three. They controlled it impeccably, turning us around and forcing us into errors. Wendell Sailor was again our tormentor with a brace of tries, as Frank bowed out of the Kiwis coaching job.

Australia were certainly in the ascendancy at that stage, as they again underlined in the last international match that Henry and I played together at the "Cake Tin" in Wellington in 2001. It was not one to write home to mum and dad about. By the time the 2002 Test series in Great Britain came around, Henry was in rugby union and Gary Freeman was in charge of New Zealand, with Frank the coach of Wigan. Another year brought another new position for me, this time full back, after David Vaealiki got injured in a game against England A at Brentford. I was put there for the subsequent match against Wales at the Millennium Stadium, Cardiff, and loved it. I looked at all the space in front of me and licked my lips. It was not like operating at a million miles an hour in the middle of the park. There was no need to do shuttle runs, you were just the window wiper at the back, able to pick your time when to chime into the attack. Stacey controlled everything with Lance Hohaia at six and seven and Gary picked me at number one for the first Test against Great Britain at Ewood Park, Blackburn.

I got on well with Gary, perhaps too well at times. He told me that I reminded him of himself: a bit of a cocky so and so, never afraid to strut his stuff. The match at Ewood Park was notable for Henry Fa'afili, all mad dazzling footwork, coming up with three tries as he outleaped poor Karl Pratt that night for a first hat-trick by a Kiwi against Great Britain. My first experience under the high ball at full back also proved a particularly painful experience. As I jumped to catch it, Stuart Fielden smoked me with the most perfect tackle, the sort he executed for Bradford on a weekly basis. I lay dazed in a heap. "Are you all right," Stu asked. "Not exactly," I said, "you've just driven me 3ft into the ground." There was a lot of rival banter with seven Bradford Bulls playing for the Lions. Paul Anderson was getting treatment in back play when I set up a try for Nigel Vagana. Balloo actually tried to give chase but gave up after three steps.

The injury curse that struck during much of the remainder of my international career began in the closing stages of the second Test at Huddersfield. We were leading 14-12 when Great Britain kicked a ball through, which I went to kill in-goal, just as Leon Pryce was homing in on me. Francis Meli, in coming in over the top, managed to stand on my leg. His studs sliced into the flesh, I came off and Andy Farrell drew the game with a penalty. I could only watch the third Test from the sidelines as Great Britain ran at Stacey all night. He must have made more tackles that evening than during his entire career, with the upshot that Great Britain won the match and drew the series.

A broken arm ruled me out of Test involvement in 2003 and I was groggy for almost all of my next appearance in the 2004 ANZAC Test in Newcastle, in which I clashed heads with local hero Danny Buderus. I had supported a break by Tony Puletua when Danny ran me down and his jaw rattled my cranium – I swear I could feel my brain banging on the walls – further compounded by my ankle giving way at the same time. By the time the Tri-Nations series came along between ourselves, Australia and hosts Great Britain in autumn 2004, I was 28 and, suddenly it seemed, the elder statesman of the team. I certainly did not feel old and my mindset was that of a young player, but what pulled me up short was the attitude of a new breed of Kiwis. I came from a generation that paid homage to doing the right weights late on. These were not the hard-drinking Kiwis I grew up with. This generation were like robots and machines, true professional athletes in every sense.

In the gym these players warmed up on the 120kg weights that I maxed out on. This was a step beyond what Carl Jennings had first introduced at the Bulls. These guys were part of the evolutionary process of science transforming preparation. The likes of Brent Webb, Paul Whatuira, Vinnie and Louis Anderson and a spectacularly-skilled kid by the name of Sonny Bill Williams came from a different rugby planet. When I saw Brent bench pressing 160kg, I knew I had to up my game. After that season I appreciated that I had to get stronger in order to play more effectively at hooker. That series, I learned more off the young blokes in the squad than they did from me. Although immature in certain respects, the 2004 team under Daniel Anderson laid the foundations of the Kiwis beating Australia in the following year's Tri-Nations final and winning the World Cup for the first time in the country's history in Australia's backyard in 2008.

I had a stinker in the second match against Australia at Watford, this after the countries had drawn the opening game in Auckland, which clashed with the end of the Super League season. Great Britain followed up with two wins over us in qualifying for the final in what turned out to be my last tour, although, remarkably, I could have ended up playing in the 2005 Tri-Nations final had my phone been switched on. Peter Leach, the colourful team manager simply known as the Mad Butcher, had been trying to get in touch about my availability for the final at Elland Road after an injury to Lance Hohaia. Not that they needed me in one of the great Kiwi performances in a 24-0 shut out of the Kangaroos, with a masterly display by Stacey, who had flown 12,000 miles home after his wife Rochelle had given birth to their son, and who arrived back the day before the game. Stacey ruled the rugby league world that memorable evening.

My one taste of action on that tour came in a friendly international that we won in Warrington against England, when Ruben Wiki asked how I would feel about leading the haka. In New Zealand that honour is next to captaining the team. As a displaced Maori, it was a dream come true and provided me with one of my proudest moments in rugby league. The haka was part and parcel of my culture in New Zealand. I had practiced for that moment just about my whole life. I had a pretty good game, too, coming on at hooker in a 30-22 win. My subsequent 33rd and final appearance in the precious black and white jumper was not the greatest. I did get an award from Huddersfield Giants for being the club's first international player for many years, but Great Britain comfortably beat a New Zealand team mainly composed of British-based players. It was a game in which I began at hooker, switched to stand off and ended up at full back. It brought the curtain down on nine wonderful years, from a wide-eyed youngster to an old dog taught a few new tricks by the pups in the team. All thanks to the seed that Wally Lewis planted, for which I will always be grateful.

State of mind

One area of professional sports which has been under the media microscope has been the health and 'state of mind' of sportsmen and women, especially with the tragic suicides in rugby league of Terry Newton, the former Great Britain hooker, in 2010, and in football of Gary Speed, the Wales manager, in 2011. They sadly joined a lengthening list of sporting professionals who have taken their own lives.

As athletes we have a lot of investment and support in terms of our physical wellbeing, but an area that has been overlooked has been the psychological approach to sport and the pressures that come with the expectation.

In this HP section, I highlight areas that are common for professional rugby players, based on personal experience, and suggest how best to deal with these issues.

You start with a dream

When you set out to become a professional sportsperson you generally have the idea that it's going to be a lot easier and more fun than it actually is. You believe it's just like your amateur club, that you just train a little longer and get paid for doing it.

The dream isn't quite as you think it is

As a young rugby player you're taken into a strange, hyper-masculine environment where you confront aggression with aggression to survive. It's a never back down culture where emotion is considered a weakness. Every player and every coach feeds that culture and nurtures it because it's needed to band brothers together and bring out your best. You're taught and you teach each other to fight and scrap for every little millimetre, every little "win". You compete with one another in the gym, on the field and in the changing room. You take the daily grind of that competition into the games and it's second nature to you. You need it, it creates the desire to win, creates the desire to get up off the ground when it hurts and when it screams with pain.

This culture, this mentality, is what you will need to survive. It's what you will need to work within the team and perform to the best of your ability, because performing is what it is all about. This is what is expected of you: perform and win, perform and win at all cost. It's drilled into you by your team-mates and your coaches. It's an extreme way of processing thoughts and it comes with an immense amount of pressure. People depend on you to be tough and strong. You believe your family depend on you to pay the bills; your club, supporters, coaches, board members, agents and yourself are depending on you to win the games.

What happens?

When times are tough you feel that pressure rise and it can be immense. As you believe everyone is depending on you, you feel there's nowhere to turn. All your best mates are in the same boat and, of course, it's not the culture to talk about your fears. You don't want let down those you care about.

So what do you do?

You turn inwards, can get depressed, angry, you feel hurt, you relive every play of the game, you relive every tackle you missed, you think to yourself how could I have done this better, maybe I should have done this or that and you chase yourself around and around in circles inside your own mind. You can't escape and you can't sleep. You think everyone is talking behind your back, you think you've let down everyone who is close to you. It can be the loneliest place in the world.

What can happen next?

Without knowing it, you bring your worries and fears home, but without being able to share your emotions. You think sharing them will make you soft. Sadness, anger, fear. All this negative emotion has a way of manifesting itself in destructive patterns. You continue to be internal, shutting out your loved ones as you nurse a bruised ego and feel sorry for yourself. Someone close says the wrong thing and you lash out in ways that are harmful to yourself and those closest to you. You feel that no-one understands. How can they? They've not got the same expectation on them.

Still you can't explain it yourself because you either think you don't have to or you don't even know where to start. You say to yourself, "I wasn't brought up this way, why am I acting like this?" It feels wrong and you know it is, but don't know what to do about it. You start to hate yourself and you think that everyone who looks at you is disappointed in you. Fear builds on fear and the downward spiral continues.

Injuries will be a dark place
Athletes are paid to compete and when you get injured you will find yourself standing on the outside of this surrogate family (team) that yesterday you felt you were the centre of. The longer you are injured the further that family gets away from you. You look on from the sidelines and see the lads training and laughing. You feel left out, you feel life isn't fair, you feel frustrated and angry at your unlucky outcome. You start to think, do I deserve the money I am getting paid for work I can't do?

Life of an athlete is short
On average professional rugby careers last between eight and 12 years, a small part of your life. You start the journey focussed on the one dream and you are consumed by it. The bubble you are sucked into is seductive and fun and you start to set new goals: win a championship, get paid more, play for a better team, play internationally. The seasons tick by and you reach your goals, enjoy the euphoria of success, the toys your high wage now allows you to buy and the satisfaction of being adored by the supporters.

But one day you wake up and realise you are 33 and your agent tells you, "we're struggling to find you a club", or they say "the club want to go with someone younger, someone they can develop". People start to call you a veteran, over the hill, fans yell at you from the stands to retire and give it up. Every game gets harder and harder to recover from physically. You start to question your ability, question your worth to the team. You realise you know nothing other than rugby. There aren't necessarily any coaching jobs around. You worry how will you pay your mortgage, put food on the table, you start to panic while on the outside pretending everything is fine. You get angry with yourself for not getting a trade or other work skills earlier. You had so much spare time and only have yourself to blame.

These are some of the scenarios that I have faced throughout the course of my career or former team-mates have shared with me when they retired and came out of the hyper-masculine environment of professional rugby. Many of their stories were my inspiration to educate myself rather than wait for the rot and Father Time to catch up.

In 2011 rugby league saw the launch of the "State Of Mind" campaign supported by the sport's governing body, the Rugby Football League. The aim of the campaign was to bring to light some of the issues surrounding mental health, with the aim of improving the mental health, wellbeing and working life of rugby league players and communities.

On the STATE OF MIND website 10 ways are suggested to improve your mental wellbeing and help you stay on top of all issues and pressures.

1. Talk about your feelings.
2. Eat healthily.
3. Keep in touch (with friends and family).
4. Take a break.
5. Accept who you are.
6. Keep active.
7. Drink alcohol sensibly.
8. Ask for help.
9. Do something you're good at.
10. Care for others.

These are all good concepts, which I often refer to when things are getting a little tough, as life can.

The culture of rugby does not encourage open emotional conversation. Over my career, as I searched for constant improvement, I sought the support of sports psychologists, personal counsellors, doctors and even a hypnotist to deal with emotional issues. The easy way I thought of it was when I'm happy I play good rugby, so do whatever it takes to be happy. I've never been afraid to walk my own path or ask for help. Think of your brain as just another muscle that needs to be looked after.

The pay-off will be good athletic performances. If you're not mentally happy, your focus will come away from your job and you won't be able to deliver what's expected. By looking after your mind a little better, you'll be able to stop any downward spiral.

Web Link

www.stateofmindrugby.com

Chapter 9

Backyard Footy at the Bulls

Henry never boasted about his achievements, nor rubbed them in. But to say that I was envious of his 1998 Super League winner's ring was something of an under-statement. I had won the Super League championship under the first-past-the-post system the season before. However, the first Grand Final and concept of the rings captured the imagination of everyone in rugby league. I coveted his ring from Wigan's defeat of Leeds in the inaugural play-offs showdown at Old Trafford. We were playing the board game Risk and every time Henry rolled the dice, I could see the gold ring gleaming on his finger. My jealousy got me to the extent that I rushed upstairs, grabbed my 1997 championship winner's medal and Sellotaped it to my finger. "You bloody cheapskate," was Henry's only reaction. But the race for that ring was on for me and, not so very long afterwards, for the two of us at Bradford.

We had played together a few times for New Zealand in 1998, although it was not until after we teamed up at Bradford that the Kiwis genuinely saw us as a dual strike weapon. Until then we were just siblings in the same team, very much like Andrew and Matthew Johns were for Newcastle Knights. Bradford brought together our respective strengths and moulded us as a twin force. Just as the Johns possessed, we had a sixth sense in that each of us knew instinctively what the other was going to do. Even though I did not follow up Brian Smith's interest in the pair of us moving to Parramatta Eels when he left Bradford at the end of the 1996 season, the thought of playing in the same club team together continued to buzz in my head. A "what if" scenario became a reality at the Bulls at a time when Henry was becoming restless at Wigan, despite their 1998 Grand Final success. Indeed, the deal that brought him to Odsal was completed several weeks before that match.

As soon as Shaun Edwards left Bradford to return to London Broncos midway through the 1998 season, I began talking to Henry about the possibility of him moving to the Bulls. He felt frustrated at Wigan and restricted in not being able to play much at stand off, with

Andy Farrell there and also kicking the goals. Not only did Bradford see us jointly as a marketing dream, we would get to play together in the halves. Henry was one of many stars at Wigan, but at Bradford he could be a star in his own right. I occasionally got frustrated with some of the players outside me, simply because they were not as supremely gifted as Henry. Now I would get to play alongside the guy I grew up with, who I looked up to and knew just from his body language what he was going to do next. Not that we had played too often in the same team. For Te Atatu, I featured on the wing and Henry at stand off, while his move to England in 1993 had limited our appearances together.

Henry had seen the things I had been doing at Bradford: the music, the publicity drummed up by Peter Deakin and his successor, Debbie Charlton, and the innovative marketing ploys that no other Super League club was conducting at that time. In turn, I got to play each week with someone who thought and reacted the way I did. Every attacking chance, every try scoring opportunity, it was on. There was no need for us to settle into a rhythm, it was genetically there from the start. He was the best half back partner I ever had because he also knew me inside out. I remained the marquee player, but Henry was the go-to man and Jimmy Lowes the point of a dynamic triangle, on the back of a gigantic forward pack. Nonetheless, the different requirements at Bradford did come as a culture shock to Henry initially. The Bulls were about engaging with fans, the same people I grew up with while playing for the club. Henry came along to a big supporters' day and disco during the 1998 Kiwis tour after he had signed for the club. I was in my element. To be honest, Henry did not quite know what had hit him or what he had let himself in for. It was not the Wigan way that he was familiar with.

The 1999 season was one of explosive growth for the Bulls. Henry joined a team with strength and ambition, with talent bursting through across the park. Stuart Fielden was a little kid – hard to think of considering what he grew to become – who had all his strength in the right places. Stu's introduction came in a Super League "on the road" fixture the year before at Hearts Football Club in Edinburgh, when a few London Broncos players ran at him and wished they hadn't. Paul Deacon also emerged that season to the nickname of "Little Hitler" because he could be a nasty little fella on the field, one blessed with outstanding rugby intelligence. Power was the overriding feature, from a massive back line of Stuart Spruce, Scott Naylor, Nathan McAvoy, Tevita Vaikona, Mick Withers, who was brought in from Balmain Tigers, and the emerging Leon Pryce, to the powerhouses of Brian McDermott and Paul Anderson – two members of the "Awesome Foursome" prop rotation with Fielden and Joe Vagana, eventually – Steve McNamara and, increasingly, Lee Radford up front.

Jamie Peacock became part of that potent mix in 1999, yet he could so easily have been lost to the Bulls and rugby league, which would have been a tragedy. It is strange to think that a long-serving England and Great Britain captain, one of the best leaders and rugby role models that this country has produced, a Man of Steel and multi-winner with Bradford and Leeds, was in danger of being shipped out of Odsal. Incredibly he was not seen as physically strong enough. He could so easily have joined the chronic waste of players in England picked up at 16, then dumped at 18 or 19 because they are deemed not fit for purpose. Thank goodness for Matty Elliott's intuition in sending him first to Wollongong for some bush rugby in Australia, then on loan to Featherstone Rovers. Like so many young players, it was not until 20 or 21 that Jamie began naturally developing the muscles in the right places, namely the backside and sternum, from where power derives. The great thing about Jamie was that his power increased as he developed further. I recall him in a pre-season friendly, his skinny legs pumping as he launched himself with every carry, never quite envisaging his rags to riches story.

I was so pleased that the club decided to give Jamie a go. I had him down as a good, average Super League player. But JP blew me away with his progress to superstar. As good as he was as a wide running back rower for Bradford, after a first year in the wilderness at Leeds learning to become a front rower, he emerged as a world-beater. I had urged Leeds fans to be patient. He thickened out that first year and everyone saw his incredible quality. It was a brilliant transformation into a prop who drives into the teeth of opponents with a wonderful offload, an engine that goes all day and who has never taken a backward step in his life.

In this land of giants, Henry and I were the Lilliputians, who at times lived in our own little world. We knew how to laugh with each other and at ourselves. At times we were an enigma to the rest of the players. We would hang out with Scott Naylor, who was bamboozled by the fact that Henry and I could have a conversation without saying a word. Everything would be conducted through facial expressions. It would drive poor Scott crazy. Our greatest joy, though, was the chance to compete against each other, just like we had done as kids. I was able to sharpen my tools against him, although it killed him having to take orders from his kid brother as the captain. Of course, he rarely did anything I asked.

To some extent he had to bow down. They were not my rules, though the trick with Henry is making him believe that ideas are his in the first place. He is so driven that he always believes he is right. Get him to buy into the message, though, and he's the messiah or great deliverer. It was about being diplomatic, though sometimes diplomacy went completely out the window and we were back to brothers scrapping as kids. We would give it to each other, on and off the field. We both knew when the other was not playing well or being lazy. We simply would not tolerate that from each other. On the field, I represented him and he represented me. Do not let one another down – that was the family motto. There were things that you could say as brothers that you could never get away with in respect of other team-mates. During a Challenge Cup tie against Halifax, I told him straight: "You're playing like a goose, pull your finger out." Coming off the field at half-time, we were in each other's faces. Spectators' jaws were dropping at the sight of us going at each other hammer and tongs. As soon as we got into the dressing room, we were trying to kick lumps out of one another. Scott Naylor pulled us apart, not for the first time, I should add. "Look at the two sisters," he'd say, "going at it again."

Henry came to live with us with his then wife and son Theo. We had some mates staying with us as well. There were 13 of us living at the house at one stage. That wasn't peculiar to me or Henry, having grown up in an open house environment in New Zealand, where people came and went and we were used to living in each other's pockets. It was how we were brought up, although Antonia struggled with it. Henry and I lived as adults as we had done as kids, and with the Bulls now treating us as a marketing twosome, we were up for anything. With Dave King, who did all the entertainment for the Bulls, we did a rap cover of 'Ain't No Stoppin' Us Now'. That led to concerts where the two of us would come out on stage rapping, the Bulls cheerleaders would join in, Nathan McAvoy and Neil Harmon would lip sync and

Paul Deacon, hilariously, would rock out with his air guitar. Half the time in those situations we didn't know whether we were rugby players or pop stars, though pretty average pop stars, it has to be said.

Few teams could live with us during the 1999 regular season. We finished five points above St Helens after 28 rounds and annihilated them in the qualifying semi-final in reaching Old Trafford with ease; perhaps too easily. In turn, Saints thrashed Castleford in the final eliminator in setting up our third final encounter with them in four years after the Wembley losses in 1996 and 1997. Surely this time? We were heavy favourites to make it third time lucky but found, once again, that it is one thing reaching a final and quite another winning it. Our problem was that we had played that game in our minds so many times, we were mentally spent. Two years later we turned up at Old Trafford in jeans and t-shirts but in 1999 we were far too wound up.

Just as I had experienced in 1996, Henry was man of the match in a beaten cause. But it was a fellow Kiwi who won the game for St Helens, as *The Times* noted: "Kevin Iro, known as 'The Beast', carved open opponents with the surgical precision that Bradford so pitifully lacked at Old Trafford. The Bulls, quite simply, bodged it, the brittleness of their big-match temperament again exposed." Iro's try and Sean Long's touchline conversion won the game 8-6. Henry showed off his backside in slithering over in the rain for the opening try as Sonny Nickle hunted him down. We were the more dominant team, but never had our foot on Saints' throat or looked like finishing the job despite what went down in folklore as the "Hand of Mick" incident. Mick Withers still swears that he did not touch the ball in flight as it was shifted wide to Leon Pryce for an apparent try which the video official ruled a knock-on. But the fact was that everyone in the team had enough experience of finals to set that and other missed opportunities aside and get on with the job. We failed to kick on and all Saints' big name players stood up that night. Finals are about being at your best when you really do need to be at your best. It was not until the 2000 Challenge Cup final that we finally got not just one monkey, but a barrel-load of primates off our back.

Once again we went into a final as heavy favourites against a Leeds side who had lifted the cup the previous year in the last final at the old Wembley. The 2000 final broke new ground at Murrayfield, the home of Scottish rugby union in Edinburgh. We steamed through to the final and were also killing it at the start of that Super League season. The methods that Carl Jennings, Bradford's very own Mr Power, had brought were now properly refined. The emphasis was on technique and competition within the group. It was not just Henry spurring me on but the rest of the lads. Whether it was weights or sprint speeds, we were so desperate and driven to not just outdo one another but push each other further. The lack of achievement hurt and the need to beat Leeds that day gripped us all. This time, too, Henry and I were heading back from an ANZAC Test the week before to play together in a final. The sense of anticipation on that flight was pretty acute, although what we returned to took everyone by surprise.

Flying from Leeds to Edinburgh I couldn't actually see the flood that people were talking about. Everyone was asking whether the game would be off but, in my mind's eye, I could see only a few puddles. I was wondering what all the fuss was about when I glanced at the front pages of the newspapers in the hotel lobby and pictures of the groundsman in a boat rowing across the pitch. "Will it take a stud or a stilt?" one journalist wit asked. The surface was under 3ft of water at that stage in the city's worst floods for 80 years. The Water of Leith burst its banks, inundating the playing area and car parks. How they got the game on was a minor miracle. There were still muddy water lines on the dressing room walls, but our big problem that weekend was finding somewhere to train. Everywhere was under water and we ended up going through our Challenge Cup final run at a council park. But no matter how bad the preparation, Bradford Bulls as a team reached maturity on April 29, 2000.

There was no shortage of confidence. We knew that if we all performed we could not be beaten, provided also that some players came up with some special plays. The emphasis here was on Henry targeting the Leeds wing Leroy Rivett, who had eclipsed my hat-trick feat in scoring four tries in the Rhinos' 1999 cup final rout of London Broncos. It is said that one game can make a career and one game can also break a career. That was Leroy's story in successive finals. Henry was starting to perfect the spiral bomb and had Leroy in his sights twice. The spiral kick is a nightmare for the poor soul underneath it, if the kicker hits the sweet spot. The arch exponent in Super League is Huddersfield's Danny Brough, who punts the ball so high that it turns at its peak and comes down like a rocket and can deviate up to 10 metres for those trying to catch it. You are not physically fast enough to get to it. Although the two that Henry aimed Leroy's way did not follow the smooth trajectory he wanted, they were still too much for Leroy to handle as they plummeted to earth. His hands were low in trying to take the catch. At that point the ball momentarily eludes your vision. We profited with two tries on the back of those dropped balls and Henry won the Lance Todd Trophy man of the match prize. We emulated what the Fox brothers, Neil and Don, had done in 1962 and 1968, although everyone in our dressing room agreed that our real hero that afternoon was Brian McDermott.

Nothing was going to prevent Brian Mac taking away a winner's medal that day. He rolled his sleeves up and slammed into the teeth of the Leeds pack time and again. By about an hour they had just had enough of him. The Rhinos brought on Dave Barnhill from their bench, another strapping forward, to have a go at me. However, inspired by what I saw Brian doing, I launched everything I had at Barnhill. It hurt because he was a big man, but I got up and yelled at him: "It's gonna happen all day!" He came at me again and I gave it him once more. "I'm not gonna stop. You're not going to come through me." Whether he heard me or not, he eventually stopped trying.

In their report, *The Times* said: "Never mind the neurotic tension that accompanied a disappointing final, Robbie Paul could write the sequel to Winning Ugly – Losing Gloriously. His three tries in the celebrated 1996 final came to mind as he was handed the trophy, erasing Bradford's tag as chokers after they had one hand clasped around their own throats. After the near-fatal error, at 14-2 ahead, of inviting Leeds Rhinos to come at them in the second half, the spectre of a fourth losing final in five years loomed. James Lowes, the Bradford hooker, said: 'After their second try I thought, gee, not again. But behind the sticks we agreed that it wouldn't happen, dug in and batted through. A relief, I can tell you.'"

The other outstanding figure was Bernard Dwyer, who two weeks before had torn his bicep, yet played his part at Murrayfield from the bench. Bernard had lost cup finals with St Helens in 1989 and 1991, as well as twice with the Bulls. Bernard had waited his entire career for that victory. He was a man amongst men, who was made of rocks, but there were tears in his eyes that day at the fulfilment of all he had worked for. "Bernard, do you want to lead the team up?" I said. "It's okay," he replied. "This is enough for me, but thanks for the sentiment." That was Bernard, modest to a fault.

A few days after winning the Challenge Cup, we played at Hull. We had all been on the drink, which is what it was like in those days, and Bernard was still operating with one arm. He went into a tackle and tore the other bicep. Both his arms hung limp, but like the Black Knight in Monty Python and the Holy Grail, there was a staunch refusal in him to give up. He got back into the defensive line and went to tackle with his head and shoulders. Matty Elliott showed us the footage the following day, which has resonated with me ever since. Bernard got back and did his job, despite effectively being without arms, minus the biceps to close them up. Matty put the video in slow motion mode, which showed the moment that Bernard tore his other bicep. "Watch what he does," Matty said. "He gets back and launches at them with his head. The guy's career has finished in that moment, but he didn't come off until we got the ball back." For everyone who witnessed that footage it became the stuff of legend. The only times I never made it back into the line were when I was in serious trouble. Broken hands, cuts, you get back in the line like Bernard Dwyer did. The bloke was an inspiration.

The 24-18 win over Leeds was my chance to finally put down that bag of bricks from 1996, along with Brian McDermott and Bernard, the only survivors of that side. That was a measure in itself of how far we had come. Henry, of course, was a key part of that in bringing with him the experience of having won both a Challenge Cup and Grand Final. Matty led the way in nodding his approval in the direction of Brian and Bernard before I got to lift a trophy so precious to Bradford. History can weigh heavily at times, but not when I raised the great silver cup aloft. I kissed it, turned to Henry and the pair of us lifted it together. Mum and dad loved it that we now played together. It drove mum crazy us being on opposite sides and dad loved it because he got to relive his sons playing footy in the backyard again. That picture of the two of us, then seeing my two girls and Henry's Theo on the lap of honour were special, although the overriding sense was one of relief. The euphoria came in the hotel that night and, as I said in the after-match press conference: "This isn't the end of the road. It's the first step in a greater picture. We've a two to three-year plan ahead of us."

Despite interest from Auckland Warriors, I was now on board at

Bradford until 2003 and Henry until 2001. It was a time, too, of opportunities for us. Like it or not, we generally came as a package. I had no trouble being the front man and shooting my mouth off, but Henry was a little more reserved when it came to the promotional and commercial work. I dressed up as Darth Maul from Star Wars, The Phantom Menace for one photoshoot with the Rugby Football League's official photographer Andrew Varley, a bit of an ideas man when it came to promotional work. If his props sometimes looked like they'd come from the nearest charity shop, he was spot on with his "Darth Paul" costume and make-up. I drove home in all the gear and terrified the girls when I got in.

Our profile was also on the rise after the Challenge Cup win. We fought out a draw with Halifax at Odsal in the August, in which I suffered broken ribs and a collapsed lung. Andy Hobson got slated in *The Sun* over that incident. It became big news because as I was coming out of hospital a few days later, a photographer fell out of the bushes in front of me. "Are you all right mate?" I asked. He explained that he needed a photograph, presumably of me emerging from the hospital grimacing. "All you needed to do was ask," I told him, putting on my best smile.

It was the summer when Henry and I decided to pursue our love of music by forming a band with our mate Glenn Simons, otherwise known as Lazrus. He had been cutting his teeth in the music industry, writing lyrics and was known on the rap scene. We all came from Te Atatu. That did not exactly roll off the tongue in terms of a band name. We eventually settled on Massey, a suburb of Auckland, where we all had girlfriends from some stage back in New Zealand. Skylark, then shirt sponsors of the Bulls, had their own label, Skylark Music, who gave Laz a contract to work for them. Within a short space of time the band was up and running, though I still cringe now at one of our first gigs. In order to promote one of the 2000 World Cup tournament games at Reading, the public relations people at the record agency and the Rugby Football League thought it would be a splendid idea for the band to play at half-time during a football match at the Madjeski Stadium. There were about 25,000 there to watch Reading FC, who were 4-0 up at the break. Three guys, two of them rugby league internationals, attempted to sing a ballad. You could sense everyone in the ground thinking, who on earth are these people and why don't they just get off?

We did, pretty rapidly.

The brief music side of my career is one that still leaves me feeling rather embarrassed, though there were some positive outcomes. One of them was working with our producer Menace, who came from a funk background in New York and who worked with the likes of Bootsy Collins and had a great reputation. He was also one of the friendliest blokes in the world, but everything he did was related to funk, which was not exactly our thing. House music and garage were massive at the time. The band brought out a double A-side featuring the tracks Sin in the City and Overkill. Frankly, they were rubbish. The release of that CD was followed by a concert in Bradford. People turned up, not for the music but to see me and Henry. When things went flat, which they did pretty quickly, the pair of us would whip our tops off. That had the girls yelling and screaming, which was all well and good, but the music patently was not the reason they were there. Notwithstanding the reality, a bigger 11-track concert was organised in the city and contracts were drawn up, at which point I declared that I did not really want anything to do with it.

I ended up going along with it, but the music business did not sit easily with me at a time when I was socialising and drinking rather too much. People would also introduce themselves by way of who they had worked with when they were nobodies most of the time – the ones fetching cups of tea for Madonna, not exactly producing her work. I was under no illusions that we were on the outskirts of the music industry, that it was a gimmick and our unique selling point was performing to a given market, specifically Bulls fans. We were not losing any money, as the record company was paying us, but I asked Henry and Laz whether they would honestly buy our music. The consensus was a resounding no. The trouble was that there was a momentum building. Skylark Music met with a promoter in New Zealand and arranged a gig for us to release the record there after the 2000 World Cup final, which we lost to Australia.

I did not want to go and not just because I felt that the record was weak. Laz had not been home for six years, so was all for it, while Henry was single again and did not give a damn. Besides, it was a trip being paid for by someone else. But I had a family and was struggling on a few fronts. There was some unhappiness with Antonia at home, my career had reached a peak and I was finding out about all life's ups and downs. However, the consensus was for us to go to New Zealand. It turned out to be 10 days of mayhem in Auckland. We appeared on television programmes still drunk from the night before. A couple of days I had a break from the booze but the other two were soldiers. The concert itself was at the Leftfield club, which was co-owned by the dual-code New Zealand international Marc Ellis, and also featured major hip hop artist King Kapisi as the opening act. I was just open-mouthed being in the same room as the guy. As for following him on stage, I could not think of anything more cringeworthy. It was a Sunday afternoon gig and my thoughts revolved around getting out of there as quickly as possible after our four tracks.

Long before going to New Zealand I knew that I had bitten off more than I could chew. Henry was the singer and had at least done some training in order to get himself to a reasonable standard. Laz's expertise merely highlighted my deficiencies as a rapper. My delivery and the way I breathed were fairly hopeless and the way I wrote was too old school. Laz would slice in verses and gel the whole thing as contemporary rappers did. I just did basic flat rhyming. I could not wait to exit right at Leftfield. People there knew us as rugby players, but the fact was that Henry and I were not going to save ourselves by getting our tops off in front of this audience. Some key music industry figures in New Zealand were there to check us out and realised instantly that we were no good as a band.

Once I stepped back, Henry and Laz began sampling their own music and Menace was brilliant at mixing. Henry had some money and Laz had the know-how, so they turned part of Henry's house into a studio. They added in beats and dressed the music up, but when Henry eventually departed for Gloucester and rugby union, it left Laz doing bits and pieces with me. I did subsequently learn so much from him about how to control my breathing, different delivery methods and using my vocal chords in the right way. I went from a poor rapper to an average one. I knew it was not for me, however much I enjoyed it. But there was the high point with Menace and the band of a gig at the Walkabout bar in Shepherd's Bush. There was a full house, we did a couple of songs, there was none of the Paul brothers hype as a distraction and I actually enjoyed it. We did two more concerts in Yorkshire before Skylark Music folded and Menace went off with his own band and Laz returned to carve out a successful niche for himself in New Zealand.

I am still left with the music which turns out, in retrospect, not to be quite as bad as I once thought, and the memory of a surreal episode of Laz and Henry coming to blows in a busy street in Bradford on our way to a photoshoot. Punches were thrown and I waded in between them just as a bus pulled up. I could see disbelieving faces watching the scene unfold. They knew who we were. "Guys, guys," I screamed at the other two. Laz had riled Henry with a remark about us living in a goldfish bowl world that was not real. As those in the bus pressed their noses to the glass, Laz's point was effectively made. It was time to leave the music behind.

Let's get physical

Rugby is not a contact sport, it is a collision sport. As such, it is important that athletes prepare themselves properly to make sure they have the tools to perform the activities that are required of them. Throughout the next seven HP sections, I will discuss a range of programmes and philosophies that deal with the physical side of the game. Throughout these sections I have also enlisted the help and support of some of rugby's best professionals and asked them to add technical support.

PREHABILITATION

Probably the most overlooked, yet most important parts of exercise preparation are the prehabilitation elements of training programmes. The unpredictable nature of rugby means that joints and muscles will come under an extraordinary amount of pressure in uncontrollable situations. By adding a daily routine of simple exercises to your programme, you will not only help build a foundation for strengthening your muscles and joints but help avoid injuries. You are no good to anyone sitting on the sidelines.

HP Tip: "Prehab" is a must. The importance of working on these core exercises should never be overlooked as they are the cornerstone to staying fit and healthy and on the field. I have decided to make this section first of all the performance-related HP pages as to position its importance to the training programme. I thought it best, too, that an expert in this field should explain and deliver a simple programme and its philosophy.

Introduction

My name is Nathan Mill and I work as head physiotherapist with the England rugby league team and Huddersfield Giants Super League club. Being involved in professional sport for eight years has given me a good understanding of key common problems that may go unnoticed until it's too late and an injury occurs.

I am going to give you some information about the importance of injury prevention and an example of some simple exercises. The exercises I will suggest are basic and address the common issues that lead to injury. In elite sport these are more commonly referred to as prehabilitation exercises. They are performed prior to the planned activity to prepare the body and are used to prevent injury before it becomes an issue.

You can prevent a whole range of different injuries by preparing yourself correctly for the activity you are planning to participate in.

In a sport such as rugby league there are contact injuries that are difficult to prevent. Then there are injuries without contact (non-contact). These are the injuries we can target with certain exercises and reduce the chance of them occurring. The main non-contact injury that affects any activity that uses your legs is a muscle injury, for example a tear/strain or pull. In my experience, muscle injuries account for 90 per cent of all non-contact related injuries.

Three key points to remember to maximise training and minimise chances of injury:

1. *Correct preparation (which includes hydration, nutrition and prehabilitation).*

2. *Effective recovery (includes rest, good sleep, use of hydrotherapy and stretching).*

3. *Technique (starting basic, progressing under guidance and control).*

Below is an example of a prehabilitation programme that includes exercises to target the upper body, lower body and trunk.

- **Upper body**

  - *Standing outward rotation shoulder.* Bend your elbows to 90 degrees keeping your palms facing up and elbows tucked into your body. Now rotate hands outwards away from your body and set your shoulder blades back and down. Repeat 10 times.

  - *Shoulder blade "I" holds.* Lying on your front set your shoulder blades back and down, lift your arms off the surface you are on to body level (this is the "I" position). Hold this for 5 seconds. Repeat 10 times.

- **Trunk**

  - *Front Plank.* Position yourself on your front on a firm surface. In this position push yourself up on your elbows. Your body should make a straight line from your feet to your shoulders. Ensure your lower back remains in neutral and does not sag downwards. Elbows should remain directly underneath your shoulders. Hold for 30 to 45 seconds.

  - *Side Plank.* Lying on your side, push up your body on the elbow closest to the ground. Keep your elbow under your shoulder. Maintain your body in a straight position and keep your lower back from falling forwards or down towards the floor. Hold for 30-45 seconds both sides.

- **Lower body**

  - *Side lying leg raise.* Lying on your side with the target leg on top, place your body in a straight position with your bottom leg. Bend the top knee and hip. Keeping your top foot behind your bottom knee, lift your knee towards the sky without moving your lower back. You should feel the work in the side of your buttock. Hold for 5 seconds. Repeat 10 times with each leg.

- *Double leg bridge.* Lying on your back with your knees bent to 90 degrees, keep your feet on the floor and push through your heels in lifting your bottom off the surface you are on. Focus on tightening your buttock muscles and keep your back straight so the movement comes from your hip and pelvis. Hold at the top for 5 seconds. Repeat 10 times.

The above exercises should be performed once a day. They should be used with a specific warm-up for the activity planned.

For further information or to contact Nathan follow him on Twitter @physiomill

Nathan Mill
Chartered Physiotherapist
BSc HONS MCSP SRP MMACP

Chapter 10

People in Glass Houses...

When Brian Noble stepped up from assistant to head coach at Bradford in 2001, his philosophy with Henry and myself was similar to Matty Elliott. As long as we were performing he did not care too much what else we did. The pair of us overstepped the mark on a pre-season trip to Florida. We had gone out drinking and I turned up for training the next morning still the worse for wear. Nobby pulled us aside. "You're my marquee players, the ones people look up to, but you can't be a distraction. You need to wind your necks in." It was a warning shot across the bows, but the fact was that the "play hard, party hard" mentality had, regrettably, become a part of my make-up.

I was not a drinker in my youth or as a young player at Bradford, simply because I wanted no distraction from the goals that I had set myself. Having achieved some of those, I trod a well-worn path in following some of my heroes. In the New Zealand squad, drinking was what you did, how you bonded, how you expressed yourself. If you wanted to be one of them you had to do what they did. Before I first played for the Kiwis I thought Jarrad McCracken was awesome, the epitome of rugby rock 'n' roll. Crackers fulfilled that image and more in real life. What he taught me was his ethos of "play hard, train hard, play harder, train harder". You burnt the candle at both ends and that was fine up to my mid 20s. Only Kevin Iro in the New Zealand squad did not drink. The rest partied. It was the generation of players who had got a lot of money from the Super League war Down Under, were now successful and had too much time on their hands.

It was a time when you could drink and get away with it, when the sport was still about metres, rather than the millimetres that can determine games nowadays. A drinking session with the Kiwis went on until late. If you had a day off the next day you could sleep it off. Whatever your state, though, you did not miss training just because you had been on the pop. If you were a dirt-tracker on tour, part of the non-playing team, it was a free-for-all in drinking terms, but again knowing that you were going to get flogged in training the next day. There was no compromise in that environment. It was my own mindset at the time but something that I came to detest.

Once in that sort of routine it becomes a case of how harder you can do it. When Nobby pulled Henry and I aside that day, I knew that I could end up having a bad influence on the younger players. It was fun and games at first as a whippersnapper in the international set-up. There was plenty of socialising on New Zealand's 1998 tour to Great Britain. One of the team's sponsors was Lion Red, so there was always a pallet of beer to hand. It was a lifestyle that walked hand in hand with the sort of professional player that existed then, well before the emergence of the professional athlete. To some extent we are still in that transition, although some players have been the epitome of athletic role models their entire careers, such as Kevin Sinfield, the Leeds captain, who led the Rhinos to five Super League titles between 2004 and 2011 and sums up the virtues of a professional sportsman to a tee.

Basically, I had socialised myself into thinking my drinking was acceptable behaviour. I did not know whether it was excessive, all I knew was that I came to realise it was too much for me. Compared to the capacities of some people, my drinking might have been seen as insignificant, but the way I was brought up it did not sit easily with me. Role models do not wake up with hangovers. At first the drinking was generally out of season, then it became the norm during the season. Some sessions would go into the small hours. Beer, whisky, nothing was off limits. I never handled it well. I suffered from memory blackouts. Instead of getting more tolerant I got less tolerant to it. That or I was drinking quicker. There are drinks now that I cannot touch because I got so sick on them. In the culture I was in at the time it was not seen as wrong. It was almost actively encouraged. It was part of the addictive competitive process. You egged each other on.

It was a lifestyle, though, that did not represent who I was or my values. I loved being a role model, accepted that responsibility and did not want to ruin my reputation. But the other of the two lives I was leading did not uphold the same good social morals. I did not drink all the time but enough to know that it was not right. I was not happy with who I was and matters began to come to a head in 2001. They were telling signals that eventually became a klaxon call. I knew I had not got a grip on all this when I got arrested and locked up in a police cell after a heavy session one night.

Friends had come from London and a few of us had gone to Leeds for an evening out. We were at a chicken takeaway restaurant grabbing something to eat on our way home when one of the girls came in and cried, "Robbie, someone's beating up Lance." I ran out of the door with my big Samoan mate Ueta to a scene of mayhem and pandemonium. There were pockets of fighting all around us. A bloke was having a go at two of the girls with us. I came up behind him, threw him on his back, stood on his collar and ordered him not to move. Not that he was going anywhere. I was still trying to figure out what on earth was going on when a taxi came along and I grabbed the girls. We were getting into the cab when a police officer approached and said: "Everyone here says it's your fault." I guess it was one of those things where people knew who I was and so had pointed me out. "I'm just taking these two home," I told the officer, who had accepted my explanation and was about to wave us on our way when Ueta intervened.

We have been best friends since we were six. He began to have a go at me about not chasing after a couple of other guys. It was basically two brothers having a drunken spat. That is probably how it would have ended had the police officer not stepped in between us. Unfortunately, in that moment I did not see someone in a police uniform. I pushed him, told him where to go and kept on arguing with Ueta. That is when I felt the adrenalin shock. I had been pepper sprayed on the side of my face. The effect sobered me up instantly. I just thought, no, no, I've pushed a policeman, what on earth have I done? Whether it was a chance to have a go at a rugby player or not, it was me in the wrong. I was immediately compliant, full of remorse and with my face blistering and on fire. I was handcuffed behind my back and chucked into the back of a paddy wagon. I could hear Ueta remonstrating with them, insisting that it was all his fault.

The police knew full well who they had arrested. I even signed an autograph in the station. They told me that they were not going to press charges but that I must sleep it off in a cell and I would be free to go in the morning. The pepper spray was horrible. It was as if I had liquid pouring from every orifice in my head. My eyes streamed, my head throbbed and the police took away my belt and laces from my shoes and put me in the cell. I was that intoxicated that they even had to wake me up in the morning. My first thought was how ashamed my mum would be of her son pushing a police officer, let alone swearing at one.

There were other drinking episodes of which I'm not proud but they ultimately motivated me to tackle the problem. I have always taken responsibility for my actions. I will always deal with them and look to improve. If there is a better way, find it yourself. That led me to Roger Brown, the club doctor at Bradford and confidant, who advised seeing a counsellor. My previous experience of counsellors had been those specialising in relationships, who Antonia and I had been to see. Personally, I had got nothing out of those sessions. I was embarrassed about the whole situation and resolved to roll my sleeves up and solve it on my own which, of course, was impossible. Not in the hyper masculine environment that I inhabited.

The dressing room was no place for talk about your personal issues, not even with Henry. I would not say he was the best influence at times, but I certainly would not have blamed him for my problems. He never said I should not be doing this or that. We were double trouble. At that time he was separated and a single professional sportsman with time on his hands and money in his pocket. I was in a fractured relationship. Henry and I were more of a couple in doing things together. We never dragged young players out with us. Then again, we did not stop them from joining us. When you are in that culture you think that this is what we are and this is what we do, yet burning inside me was something telling me that this was all wrong, that this behaviour was unacceptable. I saw this other person in me going out, being stupid on drink and acting like the star in a bar character who I'd always despised. In other words, everything I saw as misguided when a young player with great aspirations.

I could not figure all this out on my own, which is why I sought help from a counsellor in the end. They got me to see what was at the core of my problem: unhappiness at home and that something needed to happen on that front. Antonia and I split up a couple of times before we eventually called it quits in 2006. We gave it a go for the girls, but if you are not supposed to be together, you won't be. To deal with my unhappiness I would be destructive. Alcohol was my poison of choice, a tried and tested method. Inside my head, once we both decided that enough was enough, life began to improve for the pair of us. That journey took a long time, indeed it is an ongoing process, but I have socialised myself out of it. I am educated enough now to know how much you can hurt yourself in the public sphere. Meeting my wife

Natalie was the other leverage point in rediscovering my own brand values. Henry leaving for Gloucester and falling down a few times on my own had further motivated me to act. On reflection, knowing just how finely tuned you have to be as an athlete playing a high collision sport, abusing yourself to the extent I did seems the maddest thing in the world. When I drank to that extent, my appetite would go for a couple of days. For a small guy who trained the house down and had to recharge his batteries it was the worst thing possible. Proper hydration is everything now, not the beer and spirits some of us would pour down our throats.

It was not the only lesson I learned at that time. Henry and I decided to go into business together. It sounded a good idea at first, and it was until the bottom fell out of the pub business, perhaps a bitter irony considering my struggle with drink. We bought a third of the lease of The Turnstile, a sports bar and nightclub in Cleckheaton, with my former Bradford team-mate Neil Harmon taking a two-thirds share. The place made money at first but a combination of factors led to its eventual demise in 2008: changes in the regulation of alcohol sales, licensing hours, the smoking ban and the fact that two of the three companies which insured nightclubs folded. It was a perfect storm at a time when the economic recession was starting to bite.

Even though it made business sense at the time, I had not really wanted to get into it. Once Henry moved to Gloucester he had his social circles there and you cannot be in two places at once. We put down minimal money but had to insure our investment against our properties. When it folded, the breweries called their money in. That stung at a time also when an investment I had made in property in Spain also went belly up as the bottom fell out of the market there. I lost all the security I had built up outside my rugby earnings in the space of a year, although I am not a person to kick stones around and feel sorry for myself. You roll your sleeves up and go again, but bitter, painful and expensive lessons taught me not to invest in things that you are not really interested in. But I went in with my eyes wide open and it all contributed to making me the quintessential Yorkshireman that I am now. I'm frugal with money and proud of it.

My dad once gave me a sage piece of advice: do not chase the money, be good enough and the money will come to you. That is what I did through my life as a rugby league player, which is where my talents best resided. You can have as much money as you like, but it does not necessarily bring you happiness. In many respects that is why I chose to stay in league. It is what made me happy. It is laughable to think that there was not a big financial benefit to moving across to rugby union, but what prompted Henry to leave Bradford was the stimulus he always sought in higher level competition and playing on the biggest stage, which was then the 2003 Rugby World Cup, two years hence. That is what I love and admire about my brother, his ability to flick the switch on in the ultimate test, such is his inner drive.

It is sad that Henry did not get the support he needed with England in terms of the little skills in adapting to union. Maybe he was before his time. I suspect they would be far more welcoming now to a player with his abilities, but at the time there was still an entrenched attitude about the way they wanted to play. We had our scrapes and scraps in our three years together at the Bulls and certainly partied too hard on occasions. Possibly we needed that parting of the ways to thrive in our own right, but Henry's last season at Bradford proved fittingly memorable for both of us.

Staying active

A season can be a long, tiring affair. Top international players can play well in excess of 30 and 40 matches a season. To make it through a campaign you will need to prepare your body and mind. For most professional rugby players this starts in the gym lifting weights. To play top class professional rugby you will need to become efficient in the gym. To become the best you may also need to see the gym as another environment to compete in. Lifting weights will make you stronger. Again I have enlisted the support of an industry specialist, Greg Brown, to help shed light on the next three HP sections.

Introduction

My name is Greg Brown and I am Head of Strength and Conditioning at Huddersfield Giants and founding partner of a one-to-one personal training studio in Huddersfield called Extreme Conditioning. After graduating from university with a Bsc Hons in Sports Rehabilitation, I went on to become a rehabilitation conditioner with the Giants, a role I held for five years, before progressing to my present role with the Super League club.

Philosophy

Professional rugby is a collision sport where the constant impact takes an extreme toll on the body. The demands of how intense the game is dictates how intense the conditioners must make the training and for the players to be best prepared. At times we must push them further and harder in our sessions than in an actual game.

My own philosophy for rugby starts before pre-season and is actually during the off season. My approach is to plan ahead for the forthcoming season by focussing on the very end of the present season.

Athletes will normally get 4-6 weeks away from their clubs. As a conditioner my aim is to encourage them at first to rest. Recovery is important as it is a long hard year they have been through and it will also be a long hard year ahead of them. I will encourage them to have a period of 2-3 weeks when they just put their feet up.

Machines

Nowadays players are like machines. They love to train and sometimes you have to tell them to stop, that they need some time off and to relax. The human body isn't built to compete at that level non stop. To get the best out of the machine at the right times, you need to get the work/rest balance right. It's important because this way you will get the best out of your season and out of your career. Be under no illusions, pre-seasons are really tough. To get the best out of them, you must go into them on the front foot. The first message is to let the body and mind have a rest.

Active recovery

Rugby players are athletes. Athletes train and if you tell them to stop training, you'll find many players simply can't. The mind of an athlete is a crazy world. When we're in season they'll hate some of the gym sessions, they'll hate training and hate conditioning, but as soon as you take it away from them they want it back. It's what they do. Like it or loathe it, it's what their bodies want. You can give them a couple of weeks off but, believe me, they will be in the gym at some time because that's the athlete in them.

RH-P: I find this all interesting, as I can say from first-hand knowledge that come the end of every season I would force myself not to do anything for two weeks. I banned myself from the gym, from a road run, from anything, but I knew that by the start of the second week I was irritable, easily angered and frustrated. As soon as the second week was over and I had my first session back in the gym, I felt absolutely amazing.

So as the players go for their time away from the club, they'll be given what is called a home programme to encourage active recovery. This could be where the player comes into the gym for 2-3 sessions a week and undertakes some low level exercises. Light weights circuit, light swimming, boxing, etc, but in comparison to a pre-season it is really light work. Conditioners are looking to achieve a number of things with active recovery home programmes. The concept is to involve the athlete in sessions that are not intense and more about ticking the athlete over and helping them keep their minds on the job and focussed on their dreams and aspirations. This approach is to service both physiological and psychological needs.

It is also an opportunity to get the player to do some low level foundation training for the forthcoming pre-season. Done correctly it allows the player to roll into what will always be a tough pre-season and encourage them not to undermine previous work due to poor lifestyle management during their time off.

Examples of activities that can be undertaken:
- Golf, tennis, boxing, squash, swimming, basketball, indoor cricket.
- Anything that avoids moving at 100 per cent or any type of collision-based activity.

For further information on off-season training or to contact Greg follow him on Twitter at either his personal account @GregBrowny or at his business account @ExtremeCon

Chapter 11

The Perfect Match

Brian Noble was Mr Bradford. When Nobby succeeded Matty Elliott as head coach of the Bulls for the 2001 season, it was a seamless transition from the boot room. Even though match days had been shifted across the city to Valley Parade, the home of Bradford City Football Club, while Odsal underwent redevelopment, it just felt like business as normal. Another building block had gone with Carl Jennings following Matty to Australia, but Martin Clawson had been trained up by Jenno after coming in initially as a part-time conditioner. Carl's power philosophy of the Bulls was further developed under Clogger. Bradford were blessed not just by great players but a great support staff, who all contributed in Brian's first year in charge and Henry's last to the one perfect match of my career.

A lot was learned before the 2001 Super League Grand Final, not least losing the Challenge Cup final in depriving us of a double that season. I had been blessed by my time under Brian Smith and Matty. Brian Noble was another of my mentors, for whom I had the utmost respect. He was a Bradford Northern legend as a player and had captained Great Britain before he spent the 1994-95 season at Wakefield Trinity as a player/assistant coach. I sadly never got to play alongside Nobby, but he rejoined the club as part of Brian Smith's support staff for the centenary season and was integral to the birth that year of the Bulls and the plotting behind the scenes. He was a guy who I could really talk to and instantly bonded with. As a police officer in Bradford, Nobby was never short of stories from his beat cop days in the city. As I also discovered, we shared a particular love of reading.

This mutual interest later manifested itself in the Bradford Bulls Book Club, basically myself, Nobby, Tahi Reihana and Stuart Fielden, who would meet one lunchtime a week at the Waterstone's bookstore at the old Wool Exchange building in the city centre. It was an historic, convivial place to meet up, chat over a coffee and chew the fat about something other than rugby. The amount of down time you both require and receive as a full-time player would make any nine-to-five worker more than a touch envious, but it is essential to create a work-rest balance. The downside for a lot of players is just what to do with themselves. Reading and art were my distractions away from playing and training, but even that can be tough. I signed up at Dewsbury College to do an art course, but Brian Smith did not think it would fit in with my full-time routine. I managed to squeeze in part of a foundation year at Bradford Art and Design College, doing life drawings and sharpening up the skills I had, but the rugby ended up taking precedence. I am not one for doing things by half and so reluctantly dropped out of the course.

The book club was a less time-consuming diversion. It came about when Tahi and I would pop into the city for a coffee. We would blather away for an hour or two, talk books and chat some more with fans who would pop over to see us. It emerged that Stu Fielden was another big reader. The two of us went to a book reading by the British heroic fantasy novelist David Gemmell, of whom I was a big fan. I got Stu into Gemmell's books, while I was also into new age reading, thanks to Matty Elliott's influence. I particularly enjoyed the American author Dan Millman's *Way of the Peaceful Warrior*, a part-fictional and part-autobiographical account of his early life as a gymnast. It is a lesson in life balance, one that Matty tried to deliver once by getting five pint glasses and tipping water into and out of them to make some point that was utterly lost on the lads, probably even Matty himself. Matty was also responsible for the worst half-time speech ever during a Super League record 96-16 thrashing of Salford in 2000: we were 50 points up and Matty began a story of how he was bullied as a kid. I think he was trying to make a point about keeping the foot on Salford's throat but he got so tangled up that we all turned to one another and cracked up laughing. We had a T-shirt for "Tosser of the Week", which Matty was the proud recipient of that week.

Nobby's book reading habit stemmed from his love of British history, particularly the Anglo-Saxon era and the Norman Conquest. He got all of us in the book club little silver pins with symbols that represented speed and strength. Stu got them tattooed on his shoulder. Nobby was big into symbols and was an enthusiastic member of the book club until he got the head coaching position. He was too busy but he also needed to make the important distinction between being an assistant and the head coach. He did an awesome job during the Brian

Smith and Matty Elliott reigns of straddling the players' and coaching camps. Everyone loved him for it. When you are the top dog, though, and the buck stops with you, that is when you have to separate yourself. He took his responsibility very seriously. Naively, I got the lines confused at times, simply because I was so used to him being my mate. But the great thing was that he followed on in a system that worked. He was part of that system, steeped in its ways and was integral to the Bulls' culture. Crucially, he was one of us. We all bought into his appointment, we all supported him to the hilt. Brian took up the head coach's job and we were all on board and raring to go.

Nobby's greatest coaching strength lies in defence: slide systems, up and in systems, footwork, teaching all the little stuff. He has every angle covered. There was a great example of that when he took charge of Halifax's defence during the 2011 Championship season. Within a few days he had transformed them. He is also one of rugby league's great orators, a motivator who can stir you with his breadth of words and command of the English language. He could go from that big smile of his to delivering something serious and technical before you could so much as snap your fingers. Matty was possibly the better technical coach, but Nobby could express his point like no other. For all that he was the arch communicator, the 2001 Challenge Cup final at Twickenham was one that he and we all got badly wrong.

Card games were always part and parcel of the coach journey to any ground. It took the focus away from the game, simply because you can tire yourself out mentally in playing the game and everything surrounding it through your head. Nobby decided to clamp down on the card school for that one game. It was a bad idea, so much so that Henry and I decided to defy him by playing a game ourselves regardless of Nobby's specific instruction. We did not view it as outright defiance, more a case of keeping things light, going through the normal routine we had and not getting too tied up thinking about what was to come. Ignorance had blissfully rescued me that first Challenge Cup final at Wembley five years before. There were no worries that time. Thereafter, it was a case of knowing that there was a massive occasion coming up but not getting over-wrought. We did that by playing cards on the bus. It was more of a social occasion, but not on that strained bus ride to Twickenham.

Henry and I kept it quiet at the back but Joe Vagana joined in our game, while elsewhere there was just a deathly hush. The fact was that we always had a pack of cards handy. There was a big weekly poker school at the Bulls. It was always for money, although never all that seriously. It got a bit ridiculous with everyone owing each other so much that very few people actually paid each other out. We were all in debt. At one of the sessions, Lee Gilmour got stuck into Henry at the time that he was negotiating his rugby union deal and Clive Woodward, the England coach, was pursuing him. Henry chucked a brown envelope into the middle of the table because he owed the boys. "Yeah, here's Woody's money," Gilly taunted Henry, "and he's lost it all."

Nobby's single-minded purpose in banning the cards that day was to get everyone focussed and thinking in the right way for the game. What it had was the opposite effect in cranking up the tension. You could almost see the game whirring through everyone's minds. Play the thing over and again in your head and you burn up so much energy, you are never going to be able to perform. It was a lesson that was rammed home to us that day and we eventually absorbed. Train well but only at training time. The rest of the time, enjoy life, be relaxed. That way you stay fresh. The fact, too, was that as a collective we under-performed in another final against our nemesis St Helens. I did not feel I played that badly. However, Henry was first to stick his hand up and admit, "Bro, I let you down." Whether he did or didn't, Saints were too smart for us.

We were so used to blowing teams away physically that we did not have a recognisable plan B. Saints did a great job in tiring our big guys out by getting out of marker quickly and chasing them around the park for the first half-an-hour. That left the rest of us chasing shadows in Sean Long, Tommy Martyn and Keiron Cunningham all day. The three of them got out of acting half back like whippets, leaving us flailing on the back foot. Depressingly, it was an ugly game on a filthy day and on quite the worst pitch I had seen for a showpiece final. Twickenham was once a market garden and was known for many years as Billy Williams' "cabbage patch". Certainly, a potato or two would not have appeared out of place on a wretched playing surface that day. It was like no-one had given a damn. Not that the game, the 100th Challenge Cup final since St Helens beat Batley in the first in 1897, should have been played at the Rugby Football Union headquarters. It was a poor match in matching the lack of atmosphere there.

There was enormous media interest in Henry with him being on Clive Woodward's radar, likewise with Keiron Cunningham, who was a target then of the Wales rugby union coach Graham Henry. Much was made of the league invasion of union's headquarters, but as Eddie Butler wrote in *The Observer*, there was no class war. "There was one single note of revolution. [Prime Minister] Tony Blair was booed when announced to the crowd. Perhaps it was the Barbour brigade from the west car park, as curious to watch league as the league fans were to come to London. Perhaps the Bulls just feared a bovine cull. On the field it looked as if that was happening. The Bulls ran out as if they had just been released on to spring pastures slightly lusher than the worn patchwork of Twickenham. But soon they were hobbled by two kicks by the outstanding Sean Long. All eyes – and especially those union recruiters – had been on the Paul brothers and on Keiron Cunningham, but if ever a player declared himself master of the art of all-round rugby it was the Saints scrum half. Two little grubbers by him and Lancashire were two tries up, one by Tommy Martyn, the other by Cunningham. Long led the way for Saints, but he wasn't the only impressive individual. The Pauls went for trickery; Paul Anderson tried the bludgeon. But the kicking was more impressive than the running. The more the rain fell, the more the teams went through a complete repertoire of teasing, spinning defence-turners. In the end, the final went the way of most rugby games on which rain falls. It became submerged beneath error. Henry Paul kicked Bradford back into contention with penalties but the slime which settles over any make of ball in the rain meant that no great climax was reached. The PM did the honour for the Saints, handing over the trophy to Chris Joynt. The Bulls stayed on the sodden turf, bovine in their dejection, until it was Robbie Paul's turn to collect his third loser's medal."

A couple of days later, Nobby called Henry and I into his office as two of his on-field leaders to ask what we felt had gone wrong. I told him that our forwards were gone, they were flogged and that without them to set the platform we could not play off the back of them. That was the only answer I had for him. Significantly, though, the suits and ties at Twickenham were abandoned for Old Trafford and the Grand Final later that year. Nobby told us during our run through for that game that we would not be staying anywhere overnight and that we could turn up in anything we liked. The only club issue clothing we were instructed to have with us was a polo shirt. Other than that, anything went. The card school was back on the bus, too. We had all come to appreciate that normal routine was the best way, rather than expending energy through anxiety worrying about the game. Far from being stressed out, we rocked up at Old Trafford totally relaxed, yet fully prepared and mentally honed to play the game of our lives. We were in jeans, shorts, T-shirts and flip-flops, whereas Wigan rolled up looking very smart in their suits but visibly tense, much as we had been at Twickenham a few months previously. Incredibly, we sat on the stage in the middle of Old Trafford a couple of hours before the game kicked off playing poker, laughing and joking. Nobby had to drag us off to get changed.

The pre-match coverage had centred on Henry's departure to rugby union and our last game together. "I know some people have called me a rat," Henry told one interviewer. "But league has shown that the intensity of the domestic Super League is way above union's Premiership. The main reason I am going is because I have achieved everything I want to in the game. I am the sort of bloke who has to keep challenging himself. This is the way I have chosen to do it. It was not just about money. After three great years here, I felt it was time to move on. There were other possibilities in New Zealand and Australia, but I really like the idea of playing in a European competition ... I am sure a lot of eyebrows will be raised but it is not an issue for me. England has been my home for eight or nine years now. My son was born here. I am very proud of my dad's ancestry, but I am also proud of my mum's background and she still has her British passport. They were very proud when I played rugby league for New Zealand but they would be equally proud to see me play for England."

The Times wrote: "As a brilliantly polished double-act, there is no doubt that Robbie will miss Henry, as will rugby league in this country. Robbie summed up Henry's swaggering cool. 'I would hesitate to call him a genius, but his mind works on a different plateau to other players,' Robbie said. 'He can get very frustrated with those around him. He thinks he is never wrong, but that is because he thinks of the game in a different light. He doesn't say he is the best, he truly believes he is. He should have been a tennis player or a golfer, he is so within himself. But that is the very thing that makes him so special to have in your team.' Less flattering is Robbie's nickname for Henry – 'Nerd', a reference to his obsession with neatness and order, unlike Robbie's more chaotic alter-ego. Apart from training, Robbie has spent the week painting in his art studio, fulfilling the need to 'get more chilled and Kiwi' rather than winding himself up, which he feels has been his undoing in previous finals. That has not stopped him dreaming. 'I have scored three tries and we're 30 points up – the only problem is I have still to dream the second half,' he said."

The perfect dream became a wondrous reality. Maybe not the three tries, but at half-time we were 26-0 up and flying after an early score by Jimmy Lowes and a first half hat-trick, not by me but by Mick Withers, who perhaps I had been dreaming about. I never played in a game where everything had fallen into place quite so exquisitely. The first 40 minutes we tore Wigan apart, the second 40 we shut the game down. I gloried in the ebb and flow of it, seeing everyone do their job at their peak and Henry just turn it on at every point. I loved the way in which Scott Naylor just got into the head of Wigan's former Kangaroo Steve Renouf, one of the world's greatest centres. Psychologically, Scott ruined him. Scott was basically a front rower playing in the centre. Steve really did not want to know once Scott grabbed him, kneed him and told him, "This is going to happen for 80 minutes. You're mine!" Renouf had not signed up for this guy in his ear all night. Scott owned him and it was the same across the park.

To a man, the team was in sync and Wigan in retreat. The nature of a Grand Final is that you cannot hear a thing in the din, but there was no need for us to talk that night. We communicated with each other through our actions. I had never known anything quite like it. It is the game I measure everything else against, topped off by further tries by Stu Fielden and Graham Mackay after the break. Getting the preparation right is about 95 per cent of any success, and our preparation had been spot-on. It will not guarantee you a win but it will determine how you approach and how you play a game. If you do not prepare properly, you definitely will not win.

In his report of the 37-6 victory over Wigan, Andy Wilson wrote in *The Guardian*: "Robbie Paul was on his mobile phone on Saturday night when he wandered into the lecture theatre where press conferences are staged at Old Trafford. 'Henry? He's probably still on the field, looking at his ring,' said the Bradford captain. He was talking to his mum back in Auckland and, as he said, 'You don't hang up on your mother.' Robbie had been one of the first Bulls players to congratulate his big brother, who sank to his knees when the final hooter sounded to bring to an end his eight years in British rugby league. 'I was just so relieved and thanked whoever is upstairs,' explained the 27-year-old New Zealander, whose wonderful skills and engaging personality will now grace rugby union's Premiership. The Bulls' humiliation of Wigan, their closest rivals in Super League, was a hugely impressive team effort, and Michael Withers, their Australian full back, a worthy man of the match after scoring a hat-trick inside 20 first half minutes."

Elation was laced with sadness. It was the end of an era for the two of us – the so-called Brothers Grin. I was disappointed that Henry was leaving Bradford but I had known for a long time. My first thought was, am I going to play with this fella again? I knew in my heart of hearts that it would not happen. We did come up against one another a few years later when Henry had a season back in league at Harlequins, but I understood his reasons for leaving and was fully supportive of him. That did not diminish an initial sense of loss, although what we had to look back on was the perfect game of rugby league on the biggest of stages. For so long as kids we had spoken about such moments. We were able to celebrate an incredible success together. How many brothers get to do that?

The memories are contained for me in the 2001 winner's ring that I still wear. As much as the ring represents a season of toil ending in triumph, it is about the celebration of an era playing and winning with my best mate. There were days like beating Wigan in a league fixture at Valley Parade when everything clicked between us. Rather than being in front of 15,000 screaming Bulls fans, we felt like kids again in the backyard going through our spinning routines and trying every trick in the book. It was a joy. One of my other Grand Final rings was part exchanged for my wife Natalie's diamond wedding ring; I wanted it to mean that much to me. I had the money but I knew what the rings mean to me and she means to me, so it was a matter of making an even bigger investment. I will admit that I had been in two minds because I did not want to see it flogged. Each ring represents broken bones, passion, tears and everything good and bad of a year in your life. It was the 2005 ring and I was delighted that Maurice Willam, owner of the Gold Shop in Bradford, decided to frame and mount it, complete with a letter from me. I gave my 2003 ring to mum – dad has Henry's 1998 ring – but the pair of us wear our 2001 rings as symbols of the greatest match we played together.

Another symbol that night of an era ending and a new one beginning was Lesley Vainikolo coming on to the field at Old Trafford with us. Les had been signed for the 2002 season but Bradford wanted to make the most of his early arrival. Henry and I knew that Les could do a great job for the club, but part of me also felt that it was a bit of an iffy signing for us, which only goes to prove how wrong I can get some things. I had played some international matches with him, in which he did live up to an early "clumsy Lesley" reputation. He was unbelievably powerful and dynamic, yet lost a lot of high balls and balls along the ground in the wet. Confidence was everything with him. When he had it, he had glue on his hands and everything came off for him, which was the case in 2003.

Les arrived from Australia with the nickname of Horse. Whether it was because he was built like a horse or ate like a horse, I'm not sure, but the guy proved a great big, wonderful enigma who came into our environment at Bradford as a wide-eyed innocent and left a world-beater and the coolest bloke imaginable. The club brought him over to watch the 2001 final and put him up for a week at the Cedar Court in Bradford. Once the boys got wind of this after the final it was party time every night at the hotel, all on Les's tab. Les himself was none the wiser. Besides, he was too busy enjoying himself, until it came time for him to check out. He was presented with a bill for £8,000 in extras and phoned Abi Ekoku, our chief executive, in a state of panic. The hotel staff refused to let him go without paying. I think even Abi saw the funny side of it. The club stumped up and Les was free to leave.

When he came back it was as a Bradford player for the 2002 season but with unfinished business from 2001, namely Bradford's first World Club Challenge appearance and the annual showdown fixture between the Super League and NRL Grand Final winners. Everyone was writing about life after Henry for the Bulls. Could we be as good without him? It made for good headlines, but the sense in the dressing room was having moved on from Henry, a feeling that I shared. Our three seasons at Bradford had been wonderful, but this was a new phase for me and the club. It began with the acquisition of the title of World Club champions at the expense of Newcastle Knights. No mean feat against

Australian opponents starring Andrew Johns, the holder of the Golden Boot as world player of the year.

If the Grand Final was the perfect match, a 41-26 win over Newcastle was not too far behind, in keeping with the sense that this match was an extension of our 2001 season. We were breaking new ground but a filthy night in Huddersfield played into our hands. I was captain but Jimmy Lowes was our on-field leader and he was on fire that night. He did not yell or talk even, just led by example. A suggestion on Sky Sports by a fellow member of the hookers' union, Mike "Stevo" Stephenson, that Jimmy might be over the hill had got his goat. "Not bad for an old fat fella, eh Stevo?" he barked at a television interviewer when collecting his man of the match award. I lasted 38 minutes of the match but scored two tries in sliding on to a kick by Paul Deacon and working a move with Mick Withers off a scrum, in which we changed roles and Mick came in to stand off.

It all clicked into place, until the moment I took a knock on the head and felt a stinger shoot through my neck. I had experienced this pain before, as far back as 1997 when pinching a nerve but the pain would come and go. I was certainly susceptible in that area because I suffered a similar injury reaching to pick up a phone on one occasion, while years of wrestling in training did me no good at all. As I found, the older you get the less bendy and more breaky you become. Nor did it take long for the high of being crowned World Club champions to end.

Stronger, leaner, faster

As a younger player I used to think, ok I'm 23 now, I'll retire when I'm 33, so that means there are only 10 more pre-seasons to put up with. Make no mistake, pre-season training hurts. They are designed to shock your muscles and harden your minds. By the time you are 10 weeks into your pre-season programme you are just crying for a game, because that's when you know that the pain will not be around for much longer. It's tough but necessary, as Greg Brown, Huddersfield Giants' Head of Strength and Conditioning, explains here.

Pre-season philosophy

As mentioned in the previous HP section, the off season home programme is directly related to the pre-season training programme. It will have suggested exercises that help create a base fitness for the players but at a very low level. A lot of the work will cover "issue" areas like hips, back, knees and shoulders, where there is a lot of wear and tear due to the amount of grinding during running and the unpredictable collision nature of the sport. So it's a matter of getting those movement patterns back into the players prior to them coming into the pre-season. As players leave for their end of season break, they will be supplied with a "to do" list in their home programmes. This gives conditioners a three week window to set some basic foundation work in place ready for pre-season.

Age and experience needs to be taken into account regarding pre-season and needs to be adapted to the athlete's specific circumstances. If you are aged between 22 and 28, then you pretty much know your body. Most programmes will be based around this age group as they are the core of most teams. Older athletes have to be treated a little more gently and their programmes are tailored as they do not recover as fast. A close eye is kept on those 21 and younger, as they need to show competence in the gym, otherwise they could hurt themselves or somebody else. This is also the time when youngsters learn the culture of the sport and the mental toughness behind it.

The pre-season's main focus is to prepare for the continuous grind and collisions you will receive over the duration of the season. The start of the pre-season is a conditioner's dream, as the athletes are asked to perform intense weights sessions, wrestle sessions, track sessions, etc. without having the need to worry about the work/rest balance during competition time.

Pre-season lasts 8-12 weeks and different players will have different needs. Some may need to lose fat and size, some may need to gain muscle mass. Ultimately, a simple focus is to make all players stronger, leaner and faster. These are the goals I set as a conditioner.

In the gym the players will go through three major phases during pre-season, starting with quite intense strength work. Again a lot of the foundation work would have been implemented during the off season home programme. Also players should be continually undergoing the prehabilitation exercises given to them by the club physiotherapist. This should allow them to hit the ground running for the pre-season.

An appropriate pre-season weights programme is vital to help with strength, speed and power demands that are required in this game. Outlined below is a very basic pre-season programme designed as an example of how to prepare for the start of a season.

WARNING: Never lift weights without learning form and technique. There is a real danger for those who don't do this. I will advise every athlete considering undertaking such activities to first contact a qualified personal trainer to make sure their lift technique is correct. Weights not performed correctly will not achieve desired results and can cause serious harm to yourself or others in the gym.

Phase 1: Strength endurance (approximately 4 weeks)
During this period the players will lift slightly lighter weights but with higher repetitions. For some exercises the focus will be on lifting eccentrically (not the dynamic lifts). Eccentric training is the lowering phase of an exercise – for example, in a biceps curl the action of lowering the dumbbell back down from the lift is the eccentric phase of the exercise. Eccentric training with light weights helps build muscle size and strength. Below are a few sample sessions using a very basic approach to help describe the three different phases.

Strength endurance

Lower body
(DB=Dumbbell)

Exercise	Sets	Repetitions	Time/distance
Squat	4	8	-
Shrug pull	3	8	-
High pull	3	8	-
DB push press	3	8	-
DB static alternate lunges	3	6	-
Walk plate lunges	2	-	20 metres
Plate windmills	2	6	-
Dumbbell crucifix hold	2	-	Max length time

Upper body

Exercise	Sets	Repetitions	Time/distance
Wide grip chins	4	8	-
Flat bench press	3	8	-
DB single arm row	3	6	-
Incline DB bench press	3	6	-
Supine pulls	3	8	-
Press ups	2	-	Max
DB bent over reverse flys	2	8	-
DB bicep curl super set with tricep dips	2	8	-

Phase 2: Strength (approximately 4 weeks)

Quickly we move from strength endurance to an out and out strength phase in getting the players to lift big weights and deliver a lot more force (this is also replicated on the track and in the wrestle gym with shorter wrestling sessions). The philosophy for the strength phase is that we are trying to get them to produce some really big strong lifts at that point and big strong movements.

The importance of doing the strength endurance stage right cannot be underestimated as it sets the foundations for success during this strength

Young and fresh faced for the inaugural summer Super League season in 1996.
(Yorkshire Post Newspapers)

Happy chappie - celebrating winning the 1996 Challenge Cup semi-final in qualifying for Wembley.
(Yorkshire Post Newspapers)

Nervous tension in the Wembley tunnel before the 1996 Challenge Cup final with Bulls chairman Chris Caisley and Bradford legend Brian Noble ready to lead us out.

I escape the clutches of St Helens hooker Keiron Cunningham in the 1996 Challenge Cup final.
(Yorkshire Post Newspapers)

Rock star moment - my celebration after scoring an historic Wembley hat-trick of tries in the 1996 Challenge Cup final.
(Yorkshire Post Newspapers)

How to stop Billy Whizz? Jason Robinson carried the greatest attacking threat for Great Britain, but New Zealand still managed to win the 1998 Test series 2-0, with the last match drawn. (PA)

Bad breaks are part and parcel of rugby, but watching from the sidelines was never easy. (Yorkshire Post Newspapers)

On the run for the Bulls against Sheffield Eagles in 1998. (Yorkshire Post Newspapers)

He did it! Henry, Lance Todd Trophy winner as man of the match in the 2000 Challenge Cup, points at me. (Yorkshire Post Newspapers)

Brothers in dreamland - Henry looks on as I lift the Challenge Cup in 2000 after Bradford defeated Leeds in the final at Murrayfield. (Yorkshire Post Newspapers)

In the clear - UnstoppaBULL Bradford against Wigan in 2001.
(Yorkshire Post Newspapers)

Happy brothers
through to another
final - celebrating
with Henry after
Bradford
beat Warrington in
the 2001 Challenge
Cup semi-finals.

Lifting the Super League trophy with Henry in 2001.
(Picture reproduced with kind permission of the Telegraph & Argus, Bradford.
www.telegraphandargus.co.uk)

Below left: Strike the pose - a Paul-esque study in concentration for Bradford in 2002.
(Yorkshire Post Newspapers)

Below right: Ball on the line - battling Newcastle Knights and beating the NRL champions to the World Club Challenge with Bradford in 2002.
(Yorkshire Post Newspapers)

Celebrating Bradford's 2003 Challenge Cup triumph
on the pitch at Cardiff with our kids.

Kissing the cup that cheers - the Challenge Cup was the competition in which I
made my name and the thrill of winning it never leaves me. (Yorkshire Post Newspapers)

Up with the cup! Lifting the Challenge Cup in 2003 after winning the trophy at the Millennium Stadium, Cardiff.
(Yorkshire Post Newspapers)

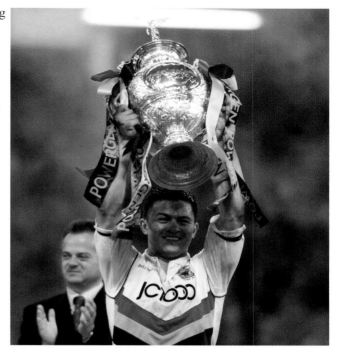

After the Grand Final at Old Trafford in the same season.
(Picture reproduced with kind permission of the Telegraph & Argus, Bradford.
www.telegraphandargus.co.uk)

Grand Final
heartache - the
agony of losing to
Leeds at Old
Trafford in 2004.
(Yorkshire Post
Newspapers)

Posing at Old Trafford
before the 2004 Grand
Final with Leeds
captain Kevin Sinfield,
who I hold in the
utmost respect as a role
model professional.
(Yorkshire Post Newspapers)

Eye on the ball - posing with Bulls team-mates in 2004. (Yorkshire Post Newspapers)

Bradford's incredible 2005 Grand Final triumph was built on team spirit. Here we are during that season on a superheroes, priests and army outing. I'm the commando fourth from left on the back row.

You cannot be serious! Giving vent to my feelings mid-match.
(Yorkshire Post Newspapers)

A trio of Lance Todd Trophy winners with the Challenge Cup. Ellery Hanley (Wigan, 1989), Alex Murphy (Leigh, 1971) and Yours Truly (Bradford, 1996).
(Yorkshire Post Newspapers)

A Lilliputian maybe but happy to be a Giant. (Yorkshire Post Newspapers)

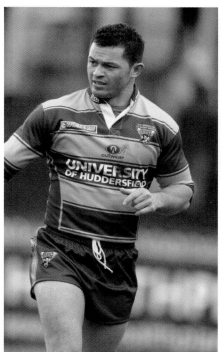

Sporting the Claret and Gold - a little bloke in the land of the Huddersfield Giants. (Yorkshire Post Newspapers)

Happy hooker, well sometimes - distributing the ball for Huddersfield from dummy half. (Yorkshire Post Newspapers)

On Super League duty with Salford City Reds in 2009. (PA)

My hands on another trophy... helping launch the 2012 Northern Rail Cup in my capacity as a Northern Rail ambassador. (Yorkshire Post Newspapers)

Smiles all round with Leigh Centurions after narrowly beating Halifax in the 2011 Northern Rail Cup final. (Simon Williams)

Celebrating with Mia, Iesha and Natalie after picking up my last piece of silverware, the 2011 Northern Rail Cup trophy. (Simon Williams)

Looking the business in 2012. (Matt Johnson)

phase. If not done correctly, it will not return the correct results and may even cause injury.

Lower body

Exercise	Sets	Repetitions	Time/distance
Deadlift	4	6	-
Hang clean	3	6	-
Barbell push press	3	6	-
DB single arm high pull	3	6	-
DB curls and press	2	6	-
DB step ups	2	6	-
DB side raises	2	6	-
Farmers walk	2	-	20 metres

Upper body

Exercise	Sets	Repetitions	Time/distance
Weighted mid pronated grip chins	4	6	-
DB flat bench press	3	6	-
Barbell bent over row	3	6	-
Mid grip incline bench press (superset) close grip medicine ball press ups	3	6	-
Weighted supine pulls	3	6	-
DB single arm bench press	2	4	-
Weighted alternate grip chins	2	4	-
Barbell reverse grip curls (superset) barbell supine grip curls	2	6	

Phase 3: Power (approximately 4 weeks)

The final phase is a power phase. At this point we may decrease the weight a little bit and the volume of the training, but you will be trying to move the weights as fast as physically possible whilst never compromising your technique and form. At this point you will enjoy training a lot more because you will have a good base level of endurance and base level of conditioning. Also at this phase you will be doing less time and repetitions, but your intensity is far greater in this phase because what you are doing is focussed on being dynamic and explosive. This whole phase is about acceleration, getting from point A to point B and back again as quickly as possible, with good rest in between sets.

Lower body

Exercise	Sets	Repetitions	Time/distance
Squats superset with body weight jumps	4	4	-
Shrug pull from the floor	3	4	-
Powerclean press from hang	3	4	-
DB alternate lunges Superset bench counter movement jumps	2	4	-
DB single arm snatch	2	4	-
Plate woodchops	2	4	-
Dumbbell swings	2	6	-

Upper body

Exercise	Sets	Repetitions	Time/distance
DB bent over row	4	4	-
Flat bench press superset clap press ups	3	4	-
Weighted grip chins superset medicine ball slams	3	4	-

Supine floored DB single arm bench press superset supine medicine ball chest throws	3	4	-
Weighted supine grip chins superset band reverse grip flys	2	4	-
Resistant band press ups	2	6	-
DB Zottman curls superset medicine ball alternate press ups	2	4	
		and superset med ball alt press up 6 times	-

At this time also we are nearly at the start of the season – indeed, we may have already played a pre-season match – so a lot of what is being delivered is about tapering training down and there is also a focus on recovery to balance energy levels for competing in games.

RH-P: At this point you will probably be ripping your hair out desperate to get on to the field and use the machine you have been developing over the past 8-12 weeks. As you will be at the peak of your physical prowess, this is the ideal time to record your strength on all of your lifts in the gym, your sprint speed over a number of distances, your body mass index (BMI) and your fitness. You can then use these measurements as a bench mark for yourself to see where you are at during the season.

For further information on off season training or to contact Greg follow him on Twitter at either his personal account @GregBrowny or at his business account @ExtremeCon

Chapter 12

UnbeataBull Year

The beauty of sport is its sheer unpredictable nature. It can lift you up and dump you straight back down. Nothing is set in stone and the human element is as capricious and unforgiving as it can be beguiling at times. The joyous scene of our dressing room at Old Trafford after the 2001 Super League Grand Final could not have been more different 12 months later. It would have been easy to kick stones and feel sorry for ourselves after the 2002 final – the "grand larceny" as some people saw it – but sport being the wonderfully fickle old beast it is, the fates mercifully smiled on Bradford throughout the following 2003 season.

Win or lose, though, Old Trafford was part and parcel of Bradford's year for five consecutive seasons under Brian Noble, whose swagger about the place was infectious. Losing at Valley Parade to Leeds in the fourth round of the Challenge Cup, eight days after we had beaten Newcastle Knights in the World Club Challenge fixture, was not the most auspicious of starts to the 2002 campaign, but in his second full year in command Nobby generally had his finger on the Bulls' pulse, with a singular exception.

Lesley Vainikolo was a challenge to Nobby. "Coach, don't you like me coach?" was Les's plaintive response to Nobby's frustration on occasions. Nobby, on the other hand, just wanted Les to pull his finger out, except that Les had never been spoken to in such an abrasive way. He has a heart of gold and is a big softie, but Les loved to be loved at that formative stage of his career. Without that love as he saw it, his confidence plummeted. As the season progressed, his faith in himself dropped down through his boots. The more mistakes he made, the more the crowd got on his back, the more Les would beat himself up. It was Nobby who picked him up. Down Under, he would just have been dropped, but Brian persisted with Les, worked on his character and confidence and eventually saw him flourish. He would call him into his office and give him a piece of his mind and Les would emerge shaking his head. However, Nobby knew what he was doing. He did a lot of one-to-one stuff with him. It was life coaching more than anything. He knew the talent he had at his disposal and he was determined to bring it out in Les. But that was Nobby, a supreme man manager, who thrived on his dealings with the players and the cut-and-thrust of competition, none more so than when it came to St Helens.

The rivalry was one that we all thrived on. Who can forget our encounter in the 2000 play-offs when we led 11-10 at Knowsley Road, the siren having gone, when Saints somehow kept the ball alive for a winning try by Chris Joynt that went down in the annals of Super League history? Fortunately, we didn't repeat that mistake on their old ground two years later in the qualifying semi-final. Both clubs had finished on the same number of points at the end of the 28-match regular season, seven points ahead of Wigan. We were two highly sharpened teams in a competition in which Leeds were off the mark at that stage and Wigan were still struggling to find themselves after the pre-Super League glory days. Bradford and St Helens had the best core of players who respected one another. My outlook on life is always rosy but I never detected any antipathy between Bradford and Saints. I admire quality and their key trio of Paul Sculthorpe, Sean Long and Keiron Cunningham were all at the height of their considerable powers. We squeezed past them 28-26 in qualifying for the final in lumbering them with the scenic route to Old Trafford via the final eliminator. They threatened a comeback from 24-4 down, and had Sculthorpe converted Anthony Stewart's try three minutes from the end, the tie would probably have been the first Super League play-off match to go to extra time. "Miss it, I kept thinking," Nobby told reporters. "This is a tough Bradford team. We're not going to relinquish our title easily."

Nor did we in the most controversial of title showdown matches at Old Trafford. Nothing in my career was more disappointing than losing the 1996 Challenge Cup final. Everything pales by comparison with that desolate feeling, but the devastation in the dressing room after the 2002 Grand Final loss to St Helens was acute. Everyone felt let down, none more so than Paul Deacon, my half back partner, who suffered my experience at Wembley of collecting the Harry Sunderland Trophy as man of the match in a beaten side. This after he had scored a try that would have put us 12-0 clear but which was ruled out by Gerry Kershaw, the video referee, for an apparent knock-on in a previous set of tackles by Jamie Peacock. Our grievance over that decision proved justified less than 24 hours later when Stuart Cummings, the RFL match officials director, said he could find no knock-on and that the try should have stood. It was among a catalogue of rulings that went against us on a fateful evening. Bradford chairman Chris Caisley, who felt that we were similarly "robbed" by the video official in the 1999 final, told reporters: "To paraphrase Oscar Wilde, to lose once is unfortunate, twice is careless, except that the carelessness belongs entirely to the match officials. Anyone with half a brain would have seen that it was a try by Deacon. Do the RFL send their officials to Disneyland before a game? What happened was sheer make-believe."

The only fantasy that night belonged in the St Helens dressing room. Nobby had warned in the press that a bounce of the ball or an official's call could swing the game, but even he was flabbergasted by an extraordinary turn of events in the last minute. We were locked at 18-18 when Sean Long, who had sunk us with his touchline goal three years before, dropped a goal 49 seconds from time. Saints' captain Chris Joynt looked to be winding the clock down when he flopped at the feet of Deacs and Lee Gilmour. The scream went up for a voluntary tackle. Russell Smith, the referee, had none of it. Had he given the penalty, Deacs would have had a 35-metre attempt to win the title. Instead, St Helens had got the better of us in a fifth league and cup final in seven years. "We are sat here again, having been dudded in the last minute," a disbelieving Nobby said at the media conference. "Great play by them for the dropped goal, but I thought we were the better team."

Jimmy Lowes was apoplectic and had to be restrained by one or two of the lads from getting to Russell Smith, the referee, while the St Helens players danced around and hugged one another. Jimmy was supposed to be retiring and all he could see was that this was how his career would end. It turned out to be a factor in him continuing the following season, with Nobby talking him out of hanging up his boots. The rage I felt myself initially was not especially helped by the RFL's admission that the video official got the Deacs try decision wrong, but I never allowed the drama of 2002 to affect me personally. You cannot change results or what happened although, six days later, I did achieve some sort of small moral payback in beating St Helens at Knowsley Road with a New Zealand XIII in the first match of the Kiwis' tour that year.

Curiously, the one trophy I lifted in 2002 came at Twickenham in rugby union's prestigious Middlesex Sevens, for which the Bulls had been entered six years after Wigan had taken the tournament by storm. Even more bizarrely the tournament kicked off just 14 hours after five of us had lost a league match for the first time in our two-season spell at Valley Parade to guess who? Saints walloped us 50-22, with a point made that they still might harbour some sort of grudge for a £25,000 fine imposed on them for sending a skeleton team to Bradford the week before the Challenge Cup final in April, which we had easily won 54-22. It was the first time that St Helens had beaten us at home in the seven years of Super League, a bitter pill to swallow as we made our bleary-eyed way to London in the early hours after the match. This after the first bus broke down and we crawled into our hotel at 5am. I woke up a couple of hours later wondering how on earth I was going to get through the day. But we needed some success after what Saints had done to us and just set to work.

"Despite the fraught build-up, the Bulls proceeded to give a sevens master-class in front of 26,000 sun-drenched supporters," one report said. "Their approach to defence, in particular, proved their trump card. Confident in their ability to make one-on-one tackles, Bradford merely fanned out across the field, rugby league-style, whenever the opposition had the ball. They then waited for opponents to run up blind alleys once too often, usually spilling the ball in the process, and promptly took full advantage. In Robbie Paul, Leon Pryce, Michael Withers, Nathan McAvoy, Brandon Costin and Tevita Vaikona, the Bulls had players with the skill and awareness to transform defence into attack with deadly efficiency."

Our defence was pretty shocking in the first match against Leeds Tykes but once we began approaching it like a rugby league game and scrambled hard for each other, we encountered little difficulty in beating Henry's Gloucester and the British Army in reaching the final. Wasps, our opponents, had plenty of England international talent with the likes of Josh Lewsey, Phil Greening and Paul Sampson, but we cruised home 42-14. "The Bulls will not automatically be invited back next year, but I'd imagine after that quite a lot of people would like to see them again," Charles Hogbin, the chairman of the tournament organising committee, said.

We never did return but there were bigger fish to fry in 2003. Having completed the three-match Test series against Great Britain in the autumn, the club said that I need not report back until the new year. Most of the lads, though, had been in since November. I did not know what to do with myself and so turned up for training, to the surprise of everyone. I had no break whatever from the rugby and, as I was to discover later, it was detrimental to me physically. When you are feeling fit, healthy and raring to go, nothing is going to stop you. In the December I signed a contract extension until the end of the 2006 season, on the premise that I wanted to see out my career at Bradford. There was a fresh air of excitement at the club, partly because, after two years away at Valley Parade, we were back at a refurbished Odsal.

More than that, we also had a group of guys genuinely starting to hit their peak. If there was one year in which all our stars were going to align, 2003 was it. Leon Pryce was desperate to be in the middle of the park alongside Deacs. An opportunity opened up with Michael Withers out injured at full back, where Nobby, as part of the Great Britain coaching staff, had seen me play for New Zealand in the 2002 Test series. I liked the position with the Kiwis and loved the thought of playing in a back three with Tevita Vaikona on one wing and Lesley Vainikolo on the other. The "Volcano" was ready to erupt, too. He had lost some weight, was more mature as a person and just had a great hunger to prove himself. In starting like a house on fire that season, the crowd were enraptured. The love Les craved he got in spades and it just further inspired him. With two spectacular wingers and me as the window wiper at the back, the three of us would put on some special plays. I was basically a half back operating in back field with two guys who could run like the wind and were built like front rowers. All you had to do was feed Les, who would get a quick play-the-ball, have opponents on the back foot and burn them off. Sometimes Tevita would hit me with the ball for easy yards, or he would simply dummy and go. In a match against Wigan, I got possession and ran towards Tevita who turned upfield in drawing his opposite winger, then kicked back out before I linked with him again in creating a two on one. Tevita's work-rate was phenomenal and working with those two guys kyboshed my public speaking line about wings being just muscly linesmen.

It was an irresistible combination. Les and Tevita, both being Tongan, shared a common bond. They were both men of religion, trusting, welcoming, hilarious, honest guys with massive hearts, and were a pair of monsters for us on either flank. Les and Joe Vagana were so naturally powerful that they didn't do weights with the rest of us. While we worked on being as powerful as they were naturally, they worked on their fitness. In working with such a role model as Tevita, Les learned his responsibility to the team. I would put Les in the same sentence as Jason Robinson as a wing who could turn a game on its head. Single-handedly, he was the most influential player in terms of winning a game that Bradford ever had.

2003 was a season of two halves for me. I loved the first half, when everything was going perfectly, right up until the point that I broke my arm in the June. A second half of the campaign of pain and frustration ended in triumph ultimately, but before that all roads in April led to Cardiff and the first Challenge Cup final to be played under the roof at the Millennium Stadium. We beat Wigan in the semi-finals in setting up a derby final against Leeds, with whom we were running neck and neck at the top of the league. Mick Withers was due to be at full back but had woken in the night screaming with a hernia problem. It was over breakfast on cup final morning that Nobby informed me that I would be at full back, with Leon and Deacs in the halves and Scott Naylor drafted in to partner Shontayne Hape, who was playing in his first final at centre. When we emerged into the cauldron, it was like no atmosphere I had experienced before. It was like wading through treacle with the roof closed, such was the intensity of it, while the noise was such that it was hard to even think.

We had been without Jamie Peacock in our cup run since the fifth round defeat of Hunslet, after which Jamie ended up slicing the tendons of two fingers and breaking his knuckles when shoving his hand through a plate-glass door, after he'd had a few too many beers. The change in JP after that incident was noticeable and not just in the final. He knew he had let the team down and grew up into the great leader he subsequently became for England and Great Britain. The start of that process was evident in Cardiff. He was hugely grateful to play that day and delivered a great performance, one that fell a single vote short of depriving Gary Connolly, the Leeds full back, of the Lance Todd Trophy. As far as we were concerned, JP was man of the match by a country mile in an unbelievable game.

Tevita put me over for the first try and Leeds hit back through Connolly in setting the tit-for-tat tone of a bruising encounter. Les and JP got quickfire tries in putting us 20-14 ahead after we had trailed 14-

8. Leeds got back on level terms when Kevin Sinfield converted a David Furner try in setting up a pulsating last quarter. To be honest, we were out on our feet and Sinfield saw that when a chance fell to him in the 73rd minute to put over an equalising penalty. Rather than kick for goal, he backed himself and his Leeds team to run the ball and grab the winning try. Somehow we rode out four sets of tackles on our line. Someone in the crowd blew a klaxon that we presumed was the hooter. Indeed, people were running on to the field to erect the dais for the presentation. Some of us were jumping up and down celebrating, not realising that the game was not quite over. When it eventually ended, the relief was palpable.

John Ledger wrote in the *Yorkshire Post*: "If great finals were judged purely on the collective resilience, defiance and determination of the two teams involved, together with outstanding acts of individual bravery, then the 2003 Challenge Cup final would be up there with the best. Rarely can two teams have combined to feature in a final so full of nervous tension, drama and calamity than the one which unfolded beneath the closed roof of Cardiff's Millennium Stadium. The true Yorkshire grit displayed in defence by both Bradford Bulls and Leeds Rhinos throughout an epic derby tore at the emotions of every onlooker, all 71,212 of whom left south Wales in the knowledge that they had witnessed team sport at its very best."

Sinfield, unfairly, took a lot of flak for his decision not to go for goal. As a young captain in his shoes, I would have done exactly the same. As an older and, hopefully, more mature leader, I would have gone for the two points. There are no certainties in sport and life, and you have to take the scoring opportunities when they are presented like that, but I could not help but admire Kevin's attitude at the time. My dad was in the crowd and gave me stick afterwards for not putting Lee Gilmour away when I had the chance in the closing moments. "We were winning and I didn't want to make any mistakes," I said, to which he replied: "That's not the attitude of the son I brought up." I knew what he meant, but clutching that wonderful silver trophy for a second time was all that mattered to me there and then.

The mentality instilled in Henry and I by dad was always to have a go. Be fearless. With a minute to go in a cup final and the priority keeping the ball away from Leeds, I like to think that a moment of conservatism was where the maturity aspect came in. The difference between playing in a final and sitting watching one is immense. You do get caught up in the pre-match hype but out on the field it is a different world. It is a world of systems, adrenalin and trying to strike the balance between thinking strategically and emotionally at the same time. Instinct can take over from logic and vice versa. Maturity is the watchword, though, and in Daniel Gartner and JP that day we had two forwards who were immense for us, while the memory etched on that final is of Les streaking down the flank, then suddenly airborne and slamming the ball down. The Volcano had landed.

The Challenge Cup final remains the sport's great carnival and day out. I ran to the sidelines to grab my two girls and Henry's son Theo to take them on to the pitch. Iesha and Mia had been to Les's hair stylist to get their hair braided with the Bradford colours like him. The Rugby Football League did not want us to take our kids on the pitch, but who honestly was going to prevent us? I knew that it was Jimmy's last season and that he was joining the coaching staff for 2004. "We're not guaranteed to reach the Super League final, so will you lead us up and pick up the trophy?" I asked him. He didn't actually reply but the emotion in his face said it all. One of the strengths I had as a player was being a team man, I liked to think, and that was the right thing to do. Jimmy was playing a year more than he was supposed to do, due to the simple fact that there was no-one else out there to touch him as hooker of rare quality. He was playing out of his skin, week in, week out.

Jimmy approached every game that season as if it was his last. We both scored hat-tricks in a home game against Halifax and Jimmy set up half-a-dozen tries, including the sweetest of chip kicks for me to ground. He was not fast or especially agile, but Jimmy was powerfully built in all the right places and he was intelligent. He recognised when players were tired, when to use the guys around him and to deploy a great short passing game to engage the markers. The ball would float from his hands in the tackle and put support runners through gaps. Nor did anyone mess with him. His ethos was that if anyone squared up to him, then they would get the Jimmy treatment: he would grab the head of his opponent, pull him in tight so they could not hit him, then snap, snap. Jimmy never asked questions, he would just administer two quick punches to the chin. You would see the victim's head rock back twice and know that they had been Jimmied.

The emphasis on Jimmy continuing to do the business for the Bulls became even greater that season. I loved playing at full back and my season could not have gone any better until fate intervened in a home game in June against St Helens. We must have put every pass down, whereas everything they attempted came off in blowing us away 35-0. It was as I was trying to mop up a grubber kick by Sean Long into our in-goal area that it happened. My philosophy in the back field was that it was up to me to get out of there and give the forwards a bit of rest. I could see Les in a better position than me and gave him the ball. As I passed, however, Paul Sculthorpe came in to tackle me by pinning both arms to my sides. We came back down to earth on the greasy surface, with Scully on my back and the rather incongruous sight of my arm shooting off at a very odd angle where it is supposed to bend. My initial instinct was that I had dislocated my wrist, but when Anna Fitzpatrick, our physiotherapist, got to me, she just uttered one word. "Shit". I was led to the sidelines where Roger Brown, the club doctor, diagnosed that the inside bone of the arm – the radius – had been shattered. The impact was such that it had mulched the bone around it.

There was a friendly face at Bradford Royal Infirmary in Brian Noble's sister, who was on duty. "What do you think, six to eight weeks out?" I said. "I don't know," came her reply. "To be honest Robbie, in my career I have only seen one broken arm worse than this, and that was in a car crash." Someone had mentioned to Nobby that my career could be over, but in a state of shock, or whatever, I was certainly not thinking that way. Anthony Watters, the consultant, looked gravely at me and said that I could be struggling to play again and that I should wait and see. Wait and see, what exactly did he mean? My state of mind was not helped by the fact that surgery had to be delayed by a serious road accident the following day. A painful night followed before plates were eventually inserted into the arm, with me at no point giving in to the fears of others that I might have to call it a day. The only date on my mind was that the play-offs were 12 weeks away.

My recovery began in a hyperbaric chamber on the Isle of Man. I will play again, no worries, was my way of looking at the injury. This particular decompression chamber was popular with TT riders suffering injuries and I spent a week in Douglas undergoing two sessions a day. The device allows more blood-rich oxygen to circulate throughout the body in helping promote quicker rehabilitation time, for anything from muscle pulls to broken bones. When I arrived and hired a car at the airport, I was driving one-handed. By the end of the week I could grip the steering wheel with both hands. Your ears pop and eyes feel like they are going to explode in hyperbaric chambers, but their popularity with athletes is that they can shave weeks off recovery time. I was on a tight timetable. When I was not sleeping off the effects of the treatment I was hammering the bike in the hotel gym.

Injuries test your resolve as a player. I'd had a bit of practice over the years. You can feel pretty worthless, so my solution was always to throw myself into promotional and marketing work for the club. If not on the pitch, I needed to do something to try and benefit the organisation. That at least helped justify my wage, because watching from the sidelines is never easy. The boys winning the League Leaders' Shield unfortunately passed me by, though not the hilarious sight of Les doing a lap of Odsal on a bicycle, his big hair flopping everywhere and the crowd going crazy for him. It just fuelled my desire to be back. An X-ray indicated that the plates were taking all the strength and that the new bone was not forming quite quickly enough. The two weeks before us beating Leeds in the qualifying semi-final and the Grand Final was a small window of opportunity for me to get on the field. The consultant advised against it, but in my mind I just saw the green light go on from him. Nobby sat me down. "Do you think you can do it? This is what I want you to do. I want to bring you off the bench to give Jimmy a rest." Anna Fitzpatrick made a plaster cast of my arm and created a malleable plastic protector that fully encased the arm. I trained wearing it and did not feel any weakness. "It is a massive call, the biggest I've ever had to make, but Robbie is a world-class player with huge big-match experience," Nobby told reporters. I was good to go for Old Trafford.

Wigan were more obdurate opponents than they had been two years previously in the Grand Final, but the relentless power game of Stu Fielden, Joe Vagana and Paul Anderson up front ground the Warriors down. Stuart Reardon, a local lad who had seized his opportunity at full back with my injury, had a dream final in capping his man of the match display with a game-breaking try in a 25-12 win. Stuart represented a new generation in a match that brought a fitting end to the time at the Bulls of Jimmy, who had burrowed over for his 99th try for the club, along with two other great servants in Mike Forshaw and

Daniel Gartner. It left me as the only survivor of our original Super League line-up in 1996. I filled in for Jimmy for 25 minutes of the match, felt no discomfort and got to raise the trophy with him, the last of the great old-fashioned hookers. I do not look back at the achievement quite as fondly as I do 2001, simply because I missed such a large chunk of the season, but the class of 2003 was the best team I played in. No side had won all three domestic trophies in the Super League era. The reasons Bradford cleaned up that year were teamwork, belief and a master coach.

JP was named Man of Steel, Nobby won the coach of the year award and Les, ever the showman, took the awards night by storm in a powder blue suit and with his hair bigger and bouncier than ever. It was a stronger team without Henry, which is no disrespect to him, simply because there was a different dynamic across the board. 2003 was also a season when so many players were at their best, whether near the start of their careers such as Stuart Reardon or the end like Mike Forshaw, who was also known as Wrestling Royce, a trailblazer for that particular training routine.

Throughout my career I never encountered a more gifted player than Leon Pryce, for whom 2003 was a testing year off the field. We named him the Prince of Bel-Air after the American sitcom *The Fresh Prince of Bel-Air*. I presented him with an award when he was 13. He was head and shoulders above his peers. I gave him a lift a year later. He failed to tell me that he lived in the completely opposite direction. He had to walk home half-an-hour but as he told his mates, "I got a lift with Robbie Paul". When he came into the Bradford set-up at 16, I immediately knew that he was someone special. I did my best to get him across for a try on his home debut but he got held up. I got into trouble from the coaching staff because I could have scored myself, but the two of us had a close friendship from the start at Bradford, Leon's home town club. He was charged with unlawful wounding following an incident at a bar early in the season, which badly affected him and hung over him until he was sentenced at the end of the year to 120 hours' community service after he had pleaded guilty.

Leon's problem was that he was talented in too many positions. He saw himself as an outright stand off, but the trouble was that he was equally good playing on the wing, at centre or full back. If we didn't have Mick Withers, I think that Leon would have been made the

Bradford full back, but the straw that broke the camel's back for Leon was the signing of Iestyn Harris, whose arrival from rugby union mid-way through the 2004 season had an unsettling impact. After the year in which everything had gone right, things at Bradford began to go wrong.

Maintaining the HP peak

As mentioned in the last HP section, it is important that as the season develops athletes must have a way of understanding where they are at physically. Keeping aware of how the athlete is travelling will help them stay injury free. As a majority of professional sports organisations' financial resources are invested in the performance department in a club, having injured players on the sideline is viewed as a waste of money. To stay fit you need to stay strong. Greg Brown, Huddersfield Giants' Head of Strength and Conditioning, offers his thoughts here.

Philosophy

Different conditioners have different philosophies in terms of maintenance, but something most agree on is the importance and need of a measurement and monitoring system in pre-season to use as a benchmark for maintenance. As each athlete is different, we will be looking at strength levels, looking at a player's weight, speed, testing their skin fold to know how much body fat they are carrying, etc. Coming to the end of pre-season you should be at your strongest, leanest and fastest. These are the perfect measurements to benchmark yourself against during the coming season. We know that the athletes will not be able to stay exactly at these premiums, but staying near these benchmarks should be the goal.

Maintenance is about going through mini-cycles of training similar to pre-season training. It's about readdressing **strength endurance**, readdressing **strength** and readdressing **power**. But as you are training and playing it is really important to get your recovery/work balance right. Again the prehabilitation programme needs to be continuous throughout the whole season.

We know that all players are different and to get them to be their strongest, leanest and fastest is an individual process. It is important that to maintain your peak performance you continually focus on the areas that got you to your peak in the first place. This area is about the strength and discipline of the individual. For the most part, professionals will understand what it is they need to do individually, in addition to what is supplied by the conditioners' programmes. If not, the physical demands of the sport will leave them behind.

RH-P: Training programmes are developed with the team in mind and can be quite generic to cover as much of the team's needs as possible. The approach to maintaining your HP peak is to understand your body and what it needs. Understanding your metabolism can be a starting point.

Can you afford to eat fatty foods? Will your body burn it off? Throughout my playing career, I always had a fast metabolism and would burn through everything I consumed quickly. I ended up having to force-feed myself and spend extra time and effort in the gym to make sure I kept my size up, whereas big guys at Bradford Bulls such as Joe Vagana concentrated on just staying lean as he was naturally a big specimen.

If my focus slackened, it would have physically affected my performances. The philosophy here is to stay focussed and stay as near to your physical peak as possible and continue to test and measure where you are at. You need to be disciplined enough to sacrifice physical pleasures like fatty foods, socialising, or whatever it has taken personally for you to reach your HP peak, in order to stay competition-ready and avoid injury. No-one said it was going to be easy!

For further information or to contact Greg Brown follow him on Twitter at either his personal account @GregBrowny or at his business account @ExtremeCon

Chapter 13

Worst of Times, Best of Times

Leaving the jokes out, what makes a good hooker? That was the question in my mind once Jimmy Lowes retired and I resumed playing after a bone graft to make the arm I broke in June 2003 stronger. The 2004 season had got off to the perfect start for the Bulls with a second World Club Challenge triumph, this time at the expense of Penrith Panthers, but I did not resume playing until the March. The lads described me as the most expensive water-carrier in rugby league history. As well as bringing on the water bottles, plus the school visits, mentor schemes and doing a radio show to keep me busy, I turned to Jimmy and Steve McNamara for help. I had never properly played hooker before, so what makes a good one tick?

I spent a good portion of that season learning to pass the ball off the ground. Boom and away, boom and away. My problem was that I had never played the position properly. I had filled in now and again, but after starting the season with Aaron Smith in the role, Brian Noble's expectation was that I become the new Jimmy Lowes. They were enormous boots to fill. Nobby had found no-one suitable in scouring the world for a replacement and settled on my pace being a key factor for us in getting out of acting half back. As an old hooker himself, albeit one from the sport's dark ages, who was I to argue?

The trouble was that I saw myself as an offensive player. But when you have Joe Vagana, Stu Fielden, Paul Anderson and Lee Radford around you in the middle of the park, and you are the smallest bloke among them, who are the opposition going to target? They would run at me all day. When I had the ball it was all go, go, go. Basically I blew up and ran out of juice. I just thought that it was a matter of fitness. I would do more and more cardiovascular work but without any improvement. It was a long time before I learned the lesson from Brad Drew at Huddersfield that the position is one that is as much about energy conservation. "Go tell the forwards to do the work, they will do it," Brad said. "But if you put your hand up every time, they are going to stand back and take a rest." I was playing the position like a crazy madman, not appreciating at that stage that you needed to bulk up physically in order to burn less energy.

It was the most frustrating year of my life. The more I ran in games, the more exhausted I became. The more miles I clocked up on the treadmill, the leaner and more vulnerable I was, as I only later learned. Hooker was now my position but nothing came naturally to me, as it did in the halves. I was not alone in being frustrated that season. Leon Pryce had the stand off position he had always craved, but in the July the rumours and speculation about Iestyn Harris returning to rugby league from rugby union in Wales were proved right when he joined us on a four-and-a-half year contract that was reportedly worth £1 million. Nobby had always wanted someone like Henry back in the No 6 position and Iestyn was the solution. Nobby was none the wiser, but Leon felt his nose had been put out of joint by Iestyn's signing as a specialist stand off. There was no other position that Iestyn could play effectively, as was underlined when Nobby unsuccessfully ran him a few times at hooker. Leon's versatility, which Nobby saw as a big plus, had again counted against him. Iestyn moving in at stand off was unsettling for everyone.

Having spent three years learning to play union, Iestyn discovered that the world of league had moved on in his absence. The game had become much more direct. In union he could kick over the top and find space, but league defences were scooping that space up. He did a lot of long looping passes but when he made one of those Sydney Harbour Bridge passes, defences would just slide off it. It was too easily defended. Basically, Iestyn had to learn all over again to play league and we had to get used to playing alongside him. Nobby fought hard to get him to Bradford and so had to give him every chance. Iestyn certainly did not hit the ground running and it was not until the following season that he had properly worked everything out.

Iestyn was a good bloke, who did everything right to fit in and get himself up to speed. However, the extra baggage the deal for him cost began to weigh the club down. It was a portent of things to come with finances at Bradford. Well before his signing, Leeds made it clear that in the deal struck with the Welsh Rugby Union for Iestyn to move to Cardiff in 2001, it was stipulated that should he ever return to league, he would do so with the Rhinos. A High Court judge ruled in 2005 that Iestyn had failed to honour a clause in his contract which gave Leeds first call on his services as a league player. Nonetheless, it was not until three years later that the two clubs settled the legal dispute and Bradford apologised and agreed to pay compensation. Amid the plethora of embittered headlines throughout an unsettled second half of the 2004 season, it was remarkable that we marched on Old Trafford for a fourth successive year. But as Iestyn found his feet and we climbed the table, it boiled down to us beating Leeds twice.

Once again we got the direct route through to the Grand Final by winning at Headingley in the qualifying semi-final. Two weeks later, though, it was a different story against a Rhinos outfit who had long moved on from their own Iestyn Harris era with home-grown talent in the likes of Danny McGuire, Chev Walker, Richard Mathers and Ryan Bailey. In a season to forget, it was a final to forget for me. I played an hour in the middle of the park at hooker and was shattered. At one stage I moved back into the halves, but I was so tired that when running with the ball it slipped from my grasp. We had been right in the middle of the arm wrestle and Leeds went on from my mistake to complete a 16-8 win from a McGuire try. I had been a hero before and enjoyed my share of heady moments. This was the flipside, I was the scapegoat and, yes, it hurt, no matter how much you reconcile yourself to rolling with the punches. I said in the immediate aftermath: "I consider myself a big-game player, so when you drop the ball six minutes from time, two points behind, and you concede a try, it hurts."

No-one who saw Kevin Sinfield raise the trophy that night could possibly have envisaged that he would do so time and again in the years that followed. To get my hands on it for a fourth time, I knew one thing for certain, that I no longer wanted to play at hooker. In the 2005 pre-season I told Nobby as much. He said not to worry because the hooking position was all sorted. Ryan Hudson had been on Nobby's radar for a long time. He had been playing phenomenally for Castleford and offered the perfect solution. With Mick Withers injured, the intention was for me to start the season at full back. We had a great warm weather training camp in Portugal. Everything looked good and I was driving to London for a promotional event when I got a call from Nobby. "Mate, it's not been announced yet, but Ryan's tested positive for a performance-enhancing drug." It was like an anvil had struck me in the stomach.

A few weeks later, Ryan's three-year contract with the club was terminated after a urine sample was found to contain the banned steroid stanozolol. He was a lovely guy who made a terrible decision. Having done the crime, he had to do the time of a two-year suspension. I was reinstalled as our number one hooker, on the basis that there was no-one else suitable, while Leon was shifted to cover at full back. I wasn't happy, but for a solid month I did a crazy amount of fitness work to prepare. Part of me was driven by Brian McDermott having told me once that Jimmy Lowes was a secret trainer. He went off and did road running. Whether true or not, I hit the treadmill in pounding out the miles, not appreciating the fact that I was doing myself more harm than good. There was a definite lack of science at that stage and no-one to blame, simply because we did not know any better. The fact is that playing hooker is more an anaerobic activity with fitness mixed in. You explode, wrestle, then rest. It is not about how many miles you can run.

However, Nobby had seen me doing all the extra work and how fit I was and said in pre-season: "I think we are going to have a big season out of Robbie." What I was doing was for the greater good, or so I imagined. But I kept blowing up in games, we struggled to get in the top six early in the season and when Nobby experimented with Iestyn at hooker, the situation went from bad to worse. Iestyn was just a headless chicken there. Paul Deacon was also put in at No 9 and got hammered. It was not until the arrival of Ian Henderson, a specialist in the hooking position, that matters began to improve. He had the worse pass in the world from a technical perspective. Importantly, though, Ian got us on the front foot. The pressure was released for me and I settled into another role off the bench covering for both Ian and in the halves, although far bigger problems were starting to erupt.

At the start of the season, Nobby had appointed Jamie Peacock as team captain and retained me as club captain, which smacked me as a little odd. I knew that JP was interested in joining Leeds and he was far from alone in wanting to leave. I had held the captaincy from 1995, but in this newly-defined role I would do all the publicity stuff as a captain but with none of the on-field responsibility. I was also out again, this time with a broken hand. Spells on the sidelines were always low points for me emotionally and this one amplified personal problems. I went on a night out and kipped at one of the lads' houses. I had been drinking until late and managed to turn up for training at 9am wearing the gear I had gone out in, the worse for wear. Had I arrived in my training kit, perhaps I wouldn't have stuck out like a sore thumb. But we were just going to have a fun day playing cricket and, I thought, what the heck.

Nobby came in, took one look ay my glazed eyes, and said: "You, you can go home." "No, I'm not," I said, which began a verbal pantomime in front of everyone. Sod it, I thought. I went down to the field to watch the cricket. "I told you to go home," Nobby shouted. "You turn up in the state you're in, you shouldn't be here." All the boys stopped to watch us. I told him that I would wait in the office for him. I was injured, hungover and pissed off. When he came in I reminded him that when another player had turned up worse for wear for a video session there had been none of this fuss in front of everyone. I told him that I was angry that he had taken the captaincy off me. In a tired and emotional state, I dissolved into tears of anger and frustration. "On top of that, I'm playing for you in a position I don't want to play in," I shouted. We quickly made our peace, but Nobby knew that something else was eating away at me. It was only after he phoned Debbie Charlton at the club to ask what was wrong that he discovered the extent of the problems in my home life. In the hyper masculine environment of the dressing room, you did not go round telling your woes to all and sundry.

The proverbial hit the fan at the club in the aftermath of a televised fifth round Challenge Cup defeat at Hull, after which the Bradford Bulls would never be quite the same. There were nine or ten players whose contracts were up at the end of that season. Nobby was involved in those negotiations as part of an extended role as head coach. He was very much piggy in the middle of all the various talks and the target of a great deal of bitching among some players at a barbecue after the Hull cup tie. Having forked out big money for Iestyn, the club simply did not have the resources to support the cost of a world class team. The kids who had grown in the Bradford system were no longer kids but fully fledged first teamers, many of them internationals, who were not on £35,000 contracts any more.

There have never been big financial backers of the Bulls. As a club it has depended on backsides on seats and simple mathematics. I knew that problems existed. However, I was taken aback by the extent of the moaning and backbiting. Once you start telling one player that you are going to be paid so much and another that you cannot afford X amount, the news spreads around the camp like wildfire. Nobby found himself in a peculiar situation of conducting contract negotiations while coaching, with him cast as the villain of the piece by some of the lads. I could see that night that the team was in danger of falling apart. Players weren't unhappy with each other but with the organisation itself.

A good smart business owner knows that if you have a happy workplace people will be more productive. The brand values needed to be driven from the top, the hierarchy of the club, but they weren't. It created an us-and-them mentality, with the players no longer believing in the identity and values of the club's administration. There were individuals who no longer felt valued. That is why I am so supportive of more players becoming administrators in the sport, simply because they understand about delivering the core product on the field. Players began approaching me for advice. As club captain and someone who believed fervently in the Bradford Bulls, it was incumbent on me to say something, bearing in mind that, as well as being the coach, Nobby was my mate. It was as I was about to go in and speak to him that he pulled me into his office the Monday morning after the Hull game. "We're head and shoulders above them. Why did we lose to them?" he asked, at which point I held up my hand.

I was brutally honest with him, simply because I had to be. I was conscious not to hurt his feelings, but he had to know the truth that he was losing the dressing room. "Mate, you need to do something about it and you need to do it quickly," I said. "You're stuck in the middle of this mess and shooting yourself in the foot." When I returned to the gym, JP said that he admired my honesty. He didn't know whether he would have had the balls to have been quite so blunt. Two things were uppermost in my thoughts, one that this was my club and the other that Nobby was my friend. Bradford and the legacy of success there, under Brian Smith, Matty Elliott and, above all, Nobby, was one of the main reasons why I had stayed in rugby league. I felt bound to the Bulls, as part of their story, and bound too to a coach for whom I had endless respect but who needed to change his approach.

Being into Anglo-Saxon history, Nobby had two swords made. If he had one of the swords out, you knew you were in trouble. Sometimes he would walk into a team meeting wielding it. Sometimes we would be training on the pitch at Odsal and he would plant the sword into the grass at the top of the hill as a visual metaphor for us. The trouble was that many of us had seen him with the sword for five years and it had lost its impact. When he was walking around with it, he became something of a cartoon character. The hard truths I delivered were because I loved and admired the bloke. It was hard for me, too. He was my mentor and you don't teach mentors. But something needed to be said, I was the one to do it and the effect it had was instantaneous.

Nobby called in JP, who confirmed my assumptions, whereupon he gathered the players together and delivered one of the best speeches I had ever heard. It was impassioned, forthright, inspiring and cleared the air in a matter of minutes. He withdrew from all contract negotiations, which would be handled by Chris Caisley, the chairman. "My hat's out of that ring," he declared. "I didn't know this was going on and I didn't know you guys felt this way." I knew that several of the players in the room had either signed for or were talking to other clubs, but what counted for us all at that time was the here and now of winning another title. The greatest of Nobby's triumphs began to be fashioned in that one moment, notwithstanding our meagre standing in the league table. He put away his sword for one more tilt at glory.

Having stepped away from the administrative duties at the height of the crisis to focus on the coaching, he became the inspirational Nobby of old. There was a steady stream of confirmations to say that Leon Pryce was off to Saints, Jamie Peacock to Leeds, Lee Radford to Hull and Stuart Reardon and Rob Parker to Warrington. Nobby himself got a two-year extension on his contract in continuing to combine his part-time role as Great Britain coach. The death of club legend Trevor Foster, after his 67-year involvement as a player of rare distinction, coach, director and, latterly, timekeeper at Odsal, only further galvanised us in terms of our prime motive. We were a tight-knit team on a one season mission which, until we met Leigh in mid July, looked to be mission impossible.

After 20 rounds of the regular season we had won ten matches, lost nine and drawn one. We stood fifth in the table, 13 points behind Leeds at the top. That left us with eight matches to the play-offs, starting at home against Leigh. Having won only one of our previous five matches, we managed to beat Leigh easily enough. Salford came close to derailing us at the Willows before we swept aside Frank Endacott's Widnes with 13 tries and repeated our earlier win at home against Salford. Whether Leeds had their mind on their Challenge Cup final appearance the following week or not, our resurgence was duly noted after a 42-10 victory at Headingley. "A clear case of Cardiff-itis for Leeds has to be tempered by the undeniable evidence that Bradford are on an irresistible roll," *The Times* reported. "We've been building steadily," Nobby said. "Once we had our team back on deck, I knew we could shake it up."

That victory took us to third in the table, a position from which no side had won a Grand Final, but at least gave us a shot at it. The momentum continued with further wins over Hull, who Les blasted apart with a six-try haul, Huddersfield and St Helens going into the end-of-season jamboree. During this period there was also the surreal arrival from Australia of Adrian Morley, the Great Britain prop, on a short-term contract from Sydney Roosters. That did not exactly impress Lee Radford and Rob Parker, although who does not want a player like Moz on their side? Bradford was not the only club to exploit a loophole in snapping up leading players on short-term deals, whose clubs had failed to qualify for the NRL play-offs. Andrew Johns joined Warrington, and New Zealand international Sione Faumuina signed for Hull. In addition, Nobby, wearing his Great Britain hat, had Morley with him early and match fit for the forthcoming Tri-Nations series, playing alongside JP and Stu Fielden, his fellow Britain pack members.

It was weird because Moz was surplus to requirements coming into an unbelievably together squad. Much was made by the media of the fact that Adrian could become the first Englishman to emulate the treble of former Australia forward David Furner in winning Australian and British Grand Finals and the Challenge Cup, which Moz had won with Leeds in 1999. He was an outsider coming in, but being the humble guy he is, he dealt with it well. He was fiery and loose as a young fella, but he had learned to deliver consistently in letting his athleticism do his talking for him. He came into our system and made an impact off the bench with big runs and even bigger defence.

As we piled up the wins, my own future at the club came under discussion. I was contracted through to 2006 and had not looked beyond that date. But when Huddersfield quietly emerged on the radar, David McKnight, my manager, trotted out his usual line that you should always be willing to have a conversation with people. It transpired that Jon Sharp, the Giants coach, saw me playing for him in the halves at Huddersfield. That possibility certainly excited me. Although I lived in

Mirfield, a short distance away, it is fair to say initially that it was not a club that I saw myself at. They made me a two-year offer. Jon also spoke about the potential of me joining the coaching staff there. That did not really interest me but, potential scope to get involved on the administration side at some point did. I was apprehensive at the thought of leaving, but my position was clarified by Nobby, who had been discussing my future with Jon, who was then his Great Britain assistant. Nobby was honest: "If you stay at Bradford, you're going to have to continue to play at hooker. We can't get rid of Iestyn. He's been too big an investment. Paul Deacon has solidified his position. The only position for you in 2006 is chopping and changing with Ian Henderson at No 9."

As with several others, I now knew that my future lay elsewhere and, like them, it only fuelled the fire to end on a high. The odds favoured a St Helens-Leeds final, as the top two finishers, and were stacked against us. It was a circuitous route to Old Trafford, but we easily beat London Broncos and then Hull 71-0 at home, after which John Kear, their coach, said: "I've a couple of quid in my pocket and I'm going to put it on Bradford." A trip to Knowsley Road followed to face a St Helens team who had won the League Leaders' Shield but finished second best to us on the night. A late drop goal by Deacs and a Shontayne Hape try from a floated pass by Iestyn proved just enough for us to make Old Trafford for the fifth year running.

The news about me going to Huddersfield was out by then. The Grand Final was to be my 305th and last game for the Bulls at the age of 29. Nobby said at the traditional Monday final press conference at Old Trafford: "Because he's a Kiwi international, what people forget about Robbie is that he's a product of our system. He's a superstar bred in Britain. He's given this club a big profile and won us a hell of a lot of big games. When Robbie runs at defenders he can still burn them. The last couple of years he's had a lot to contend with, but he's ready to perform. Sometimes in life it's right to move on."

There was nothing for Bradford at the Man of Steel awards ceremony. Faith in ourselves was all that mattered. We felt indestructible and unbeatable going into the showdown with Leeds. We walked into that game with a swagger. There was not a player among us who felt we would lose that day. The confidence that drove Leeds the previous year was not evident this time. We were a white-hot team who wanted to end an era in the right way, especially for the nine of us leaving. We had created our own destiny, as JP observed afterwards. None more so than Leon, who collected the Harry Sunderland Trophy. It was scruffy and tense but a 15-6 victory felt as sweet as if we had won by 100 points. I was devastated and very emotional afterwards, knowing that it was over but appreciative of the fact that it was mission accomplished. From the worst of times, to the best of times, all in one season.

"If they get fed up of Bulls at Odsal, Bradford Believers would serve as an apt replacement," *The Times* wrote. "Belief, confidence and momentum irresistibly swept the Bulls and Brian Noble, their record-breaking coach, to a third and easily most significant Grand Final triumph in five years. Chelsea's pursuers in the Premier League could take a leaf from Bradford's book in rising off their knees and achieving what was regarded in rugby league as impossible. The play-offs help dreamers to dream, of course. But conventional wisdom that only the top two finishers after the regular season can possibly win the championship went out of the window with Bradford's brilliantly gritty triumph. How do a team languishing in fifth place in early August, whose task amounted to a climber attempting Mount Everest without crampons, come to lift the trophy? The secret to Bradford's success in reaching every final since 2001 is timing. When blackberries start to ripen, the season of mists and mellow fruitfulness fills the Bulls' nostrils."

The next morning, we opened up the bar in Cleckheaton at 9am and put on a keg of beer and bacon sandwiches for the lads. Some of our fans joined us, many of whom we had grown up with. They were part of a great big Bradford family, who I would shortly be leaving. It was a special dynamic, the sort you do not get often in sport. We travelled to the stadium, which was packed. A stage had been set up in the middle of the pitch and I just sat to one side in trying to keep a check on my emotions. Had I grabbed the mic in time-honoured fashion, I would only have started blubbing. Leon got up and addressed the crowd: "This team has been awesome and we have been through a lot, but the success of the Bradford Bulls down the years comes down to one man, that little fella sitting down there, who has been here from the start. If it wasn't for him, this club would not be the club it is." Those sentiments meant so much to me coming from a guy who I admired so much, notwithstanding Leon's attempt with Ian Henderson to drag me up to try and say something. It is not often in life that I am lost for words.

My lasting image of that day is of Les getting out of the limos we were driven in round the perimeter of the pitch and surfing his car. We thought, though, that the big man had overstepped the line when we met up beforehand in the media room at Odsal, where the club had laid on more beers. The guy did not know his own strength at times. At a particularly tense training session once, Nobby told us how we were going to try and beat Leeds. "This is how we beat Leeds," Les cried in leading with his shoulder straight into Nobby, who got launched in the air. Everyone was still rolling around when Nobby dusted himself down, fury still burning in his eyes. He admitted later that it broke the tension and probably did us some good, but Nobby was built to take a shot. Not the journalist who wandered into the media room while we were downing a few bottles. "You can't come in here unless you scull a beer," someone shouted. "Ok," the guy said. He had just necked the beer when Les hit him in the solar plexus. As he came down, the room suddenly went silent. We honestly thought that Les had done some real damage this time. The guy, somewhat dazed, rolled over and muttered, "Bugger me, that wasn't nice". The room dissolved into laughter.

That family of ours still has reunions. Bradford went on at the start of the following season to win the World Club Challenge for a third time, but one by one people left: Chris Caisley stood down as chairman, Stu Fielden and later Mick Withers and Deacs joined Wigan, and Les and Shontayne Hape eventually crossed to rugby union, while the great Joe Vagana hung up his sizeable boots. The club entered a spiral of decline that culminated in a financial crisis that resulted in the club entering administration in the summer of 2012, despite £500,000 raised by supporters, all of which was difficult for me watching from the sidelines after a 12-year association.

Nobby left his beloved Bradford in April 2006 to take up the coaching job at Wigan, six months after my departure. We later returned to the bookshop where we used to meet as the Bulls book club for a coffee and chat about the good times and life generally. He remains my mentor, my mate and fellow television pundit. Had I stayed on at the club playing at hooker, I would probably have ended up blaming him for it. He did me a good service as a fellow professional and friend in telling me to move on, a decision that I never regretted for a minute. I got to pull on a Bradford shirt one more time for my testimonial match the following January, while one of the greatest honours bestowed on me was my inclusion at stand off in Bradford's team of the century, as voted for by the fans. I was privileged to play alongside seven others who were nominated in that great mythical Bradford team: Shontayne Hape, Lesley Vainikolo, Paul Deacon, Stuart Fielden, Jimmy Lowes, Joe Vagana and Karl Fairbank. A team coached by Brian Noble, who else?

The word is acceleration

To survive in professional rugby you are going to need to be quick. Quick in mind and quick in body. Mum and dad had blessed me with a quick pair of feet, but as I was training on my own in the early days at Bradford, I didn't really know what weights and exercises could increase your speed.

When Brian Smith and Matthew Elliott joined Bradford Bulls they brought with them cutting edge training programmes developed from the Australian Institute of Sport in Canberra. Once I was exposed to these systems, my professional game changed almost instantly. I not only became faster, I became more powerful and explosive.

It stopped just being about flying over the grass once you hit top speed, but became about getting to top speed faster, more dynamically, then being able to sustain it once you got there. Again I have enlisted Greg Brown, Huddersfield Giants' Head of Strength and Conditioning, to give an insight into these processes.

Philosophy

The foundation work for speed has come as part of the overall pre-season process starting in the gym. The weight training and endurance work is tailored to help you become more explosive to help produce force and movement.

Hip movement

As a sprinter in rugby, you want to go through certain movement patterns that allow you to have good hip mobility and good hip range. This will allow you to produce greater force and accelerate at pace. This ultimately will be your first goal.

Running

From there you will start your running programme by running longer distances at slower speeds. For example, you may run 50 metres at 50 per cent. Then shorten it to 30 but run at 75 per cent, then you will start to look at running more game-specific distances. For the most part in rugby you will sprint 10-20 metres at a time (if you are on the edge or at full back it may be longer but most positions it should be about 10-20 metres). So by using this as a framework to move forward you will need to shorten your training sprints down to 10-20 metres but sprinting at your top speed, 100 per cent.

The word is acceleration

Speed is not the word any more. The word is **acceleration**. It's about getting off that line and out of the "blocks" as fast as physically possible. It is about how fast can you get to the break down; as soon as the ball rolls clear, how fast can you get to it; when the ball's kicked down field, how fast can you get down there; and how quickly can you get out of acting half and into top gear. It's not just about running. Acceleration is about the explosiveness of your shoulder burying itself into the midsection of your opponent as you crunch them in a tackle. All of this energy is produced from the floor up through your legs.

The recipe for this is multifaceted. To produce top acceleration you must work on your technique and power in the gym, on the track and on the field. All of these aspects come together to create acceleration and this is what you'll need if you want to make it as a 21st century rugby player.

Programme

Below is an example of simplified sprint sessions that professionals may use as part of their training programme.

WARNING: Preparation prior to running fast is vital to protecting yourself from injury. Spending that little extra time preparing the muscles, raising your heart rate and core temperature will only aid performance.

Purpose	Time	Activity
Stride development / warm up	-	Walking lunges, A skips, B skips, high knees, fast feet, shuttle runs (string out at below 50%) Dynamic movement for backs, hamstrings, calves, and groins
Over the weeks you are aiming to progressively increase your speed and acceleration.	-	-
Session	Week 1	Over 40 metres at 75% x 8 efforts with walking recoveries
Session	Week 2	Over 30 – 40 metres at 75 – 90% x 8 efforts with walking recoveries
Session	Week 3	Over 20 – 30 metres at 90% x 6 – 8 efforts with 45 – 60 secs recovery
Session	Week 4	Over 20 metres at 90 – 100% x 6 efforts with 60 secs recovery

For further information or to contact Greg Brown follow him on Twitter at either his personal account @GregBrowny or at his business account @ExtremeCon

Chapter 14

Food for the Soul

One small step, perhaps, but one Giants leap. For someone who would toss themselves into new ventures quite fearlessly, I was more than a little nervous leaving Bradford for Huddersfield. Twelve miles separate the two clubs but it might as well have been 12,000 miles. As a professional rugby player, all I had really known was Bradford. From my arrival there in 1994, the only people left were Chris Caisley, the chairman, and Freddie Robinson, the legendary kit man. Huddersfield didn't have a Freddie Robinson to wash and dry your training gear and polish your boots. You cleaned your own kit.

Mind you, I had seen the culture difference at Bradford in respect of how Freddie was treated by a new generation of players. When you came in from training, you put dirty kit into different baskets for Freddie to sort. It rightly hacked him off that some of the younger players would scatter their kit everywhere and leave it for him to pick up. People like Freddie are the lifeblood of a club and their passion, commitment and endeavour cannot be under-estimated. He walked into the dressing room at Odsal as Brian Smith was launching into us one time before a training session. Everyone turned to look at Freddie, who deliberately stared up at the light and blew it out. The room went pitch black. Even Smithy had to laugh. Freddie broke the tension that day and we had an awesome session.

At Bradford we never did anything before 10am, but at Huddersfield we began team run throughs at 8am. For the lads coming across the Pennines, it was a crack of dawn start. I was used to an environment inhabited by world class players, but when I met Jon Sharp, the head coach, I was impressed more with his and the club's approach than the actual team itself. Huddersfield had an up and coming side and Jon had specific plans for me. "This is how I see you, in the halves controlling us with Brad Drew and Chris Thorman," Jon said, in a language that I had not heard for a long time. "There are areas of your game Robbie where I believe that you can improve. You never change the tempo or style of your running. Teams know the footwork you're going to do on them. What I want to develop are your ball-playing skills."

What made the transition to Huddersfield easier for me was the sense of me being reinvented as a player. I worked a lot with Kieron Purtill, Jon's assistant, who was a half back himself. Playing at hooker, I had grown used to going at a million miles an hour and jumping out of the line while half my team-mates were still winding up. Brian Noble's instruction to me was to run or pass, don't do both. Jon and Kieron's philosophy was, "We want you to run, pass and add elements to your game." An old dog being taught some new tricks made joining Huddersfield a no-brainer. For all the trepidation I felt leaving Bradford, it was one of the best moves I made. The silverware was not really there any more but it was more about what was right for me at the time – my beloved food for my soul.

My reputation at Bradford as a bit of a party boy didn't sit well with me, while in 2006 my relationship with Antonia finally ended for good. It wasn't a painful break-up. We had just come to the realisation that we were not right for one another. We had given it every chance. It was ingrained in me that we should be there together for the girls, but when we spoke about what was best for one another we came to the conclusion that it would be best for everyone to end it. I knew that there was no going back, just as there was no going back in moving to a new rugby life at Huddersfield where none of the guys really knew me. It offered a fresh start on a variety of fronts, despite a new environment at the Giants feeling alien at first.

I had come from a hugely competitive team that pushed and challenged from within, in order to scale fresh heights. My first thought was that these players were good at fitness and skill work, but where was the internal competition and drive? In the gym, it simply did not exist. There were also some off-hand remarks about the Bulls "being on the gear" to which my response was, "Don't get pissy because you think Bradford are on drugs, which we weren't, sort your gym methods out." The players simply lifted weights at Huddersfield. They did not push one another to the extreme, as Bradford did, with a singular exception. I quickly identified that Chris Thorman was someone I could compete with in the gym. A Geordie lad who had discovered rugby league as a kid and spent a season in the National Rugby League at Parramatta Eels, Chris was cut out to compete in Ironman. He just possessed a huge ticker, lung capacity and an infinite ability to run and run. I worked out with Chris and teased the forwards. "Is that all you're lifting." They knew they had to be bigger and stronger, because at the hour mark in games we would run out of steam. If it was a running race, we would run further than any team, but the balance between aerobic and anaerobic training had to alter. When the club released the trainer mid-way through the season and appointed his assistant, Ben Cooper, improvements began.

A lot was expected of me, similar to when Bradford rose to prominence. I loved that feeling again. A lot of people say that I won four Super League titles, the Challenge Cup twice and the World Club Challenge with Bradford and sod all at Hudderfield, but that was not the way I felt at all. Suddenly I was the go-to man again. It was like being 18 all over again. I had not felt this way since before I broke my arm three years previously, just in terms of purely enjoying playing. I loved being back in the halves. Even when I got put in at hooker after Paul March tore a cruciate ligament, it wasn't so bad, because Brad Drew started teaching me the position properly. Rather than me doing the work all the time, I learned to delegate, mix up the play and work on my strength.

We were riding in fifth place in Super League when the time came to go back to Odsal. Playing against Bradford was unusual, to say the least, but the crowd reaction was something else. They began to chant my name, to the point during the game when I wondered whether I had the wrong shirt on. It was a dislocating experience mentally and a wake-up call physically. I'd spent five years at the Bulls watching hapless tacklers try to stop a rampaging Lesley Vainikolo. Now it was my turn. I was at marker and tried to grab the big man. He launched me in the air and I stared up as he trampled all over me and I thought, wow, he is explosive. A 52-18 loss put a spanner in our works in terms of the league, but we were still motoring nicely in the Challenge Cup.

Familiar surroundings at Odsal for the semi-final certainly helped, but we were heavy underdogs against a fearsome Leeds side. It was an exciting experience for the club to reach the last four stage and there was no real expectation of us making the final. Crucially, we were unencumbered by pressure, unlike Leeds who were cut to bits by Brad Drew from dummy half. Stuart Jones and Stephen Wild just kept belting every Leeds player who had the ball and Steve Snitch put on the special footmark that always marked him out as the niftiest of forwards. Chris

Nero and Stuart Donlan ran some great lines, picked up two tries apiece and before I could even catch my breath after a 30-12 victory, I was rushed from the field to the temporary BBC studio. I was still dripping sweat and in my kit and boots alongside Clare Balding, Jonathan Davies and Nobby, which must have looked surreal. Having got to five finals in the competition before, a sixth was not quite the huge deal it was for the club, although it was not long before I got caught up in the momentum of Huddersfield's first Challenge Cup final appearance for 44 years.

After the semi-final, Jon Sharp asked us to go home and write one thing down about every team member, which proved a smart piece of thinking. However, the time until the final was the longest month, occupied by far too many meetings, which all seemed to start with the words, "We don't want you to worry and over think the final ..." Everyone was on tenterhooks, walking on broken glass. The more meetings we had, the more it stoked the tension. I knew what to expect but to watch the guys around me so on edge was worrying. By the time we reached Twickenham, most of the lads had played the game in their heads on a continuous loop. The place held some bad personal memories from the last Challenge Cup final, when Bradford were beaten by our old nemesis St Helens, who were on another irresistible roll under Daniel Anderson five years later. The Twickenham surface, bad enough last time, was worse. Batley's Mount Pleasant at its muddiest would have been better to play on. The final had been due to be staged at the new Wembley but because of building delays was switched. With most people having already booked hotels in London, Twickenham was the only available alternative and the pitch had only just been relaid. Any field, any time, anywhere, I know, but ideally not Twickenham.

The one liners that we had written about each other a few weeks before were laid out with our kit. It was a great touch that gelled us together in the crucial moments beforehand in the dressing room. "He delivers what we expected him to," someone had written about me. Inspired, perhaps, we emerged all guns blazing. "Some bookies were offering the Giants at 6-1; they might have felt differently after the first five minutes, during which St Helens were hit by 13 claret and gold piledrivers," the *Sunday Times* reported. "It wasn't so much Leon Pryce's mistake, handing the Giants possession from the kick-off, which set the tone. Twice given the chance to clear their lines, Saints, perhaps the most creative and inventive team currently playing the game, couldn't do it and Brad Drew made them pay, creating the space for Martin Aspinwall to cross in the corner."

We only trailed by six points at the break before a familiar failing. We ran out of juice as Saints cranked up the pressure in rattling off five second half tries, two of them by Jon Wilkin, despite having his nose rearranged and looking like the Phantom of the Opera with his face bandaged. At one point I flew in to collar Sean Long, who picked up the Lance Todd Trophy for a record third time, only to find that he had put on his trademark big left foot step and gone. My try after 70 minutes meant nothing more than guaranteeing my name in the papers the next morning. It provided meagre consolation after losing to Saints for a sixth time in a major final, but as I told reporters afterwards: "It was a real cauldron for some of the younger players and St Helens showed that they are a world-class team. Ninety per cent of our squad had never had the experience of playing in an occasion like this before. But there are real characters in this side and, hopefully, we'll come back stronger than ever." It was my dad who pinpointed our real weakness that day. "You're a bunch of racehorses," he declared. "You can run all day, but where's your power?"

The remainder of the season felt like a case of after the Lord Mayor's parade – indeed, we ended up ninth in Super League – although that first year at Huddersfield brought the best out of me. It had given me the chance to reinvent myself. I stopped going out as much and went teetotal for the first half of the season. The few occasions I did go out I went at ramming speed in terms of the drink, but that year, significantly, I met my wife Natalie. I had been single for a while and was out in Huddersfield at a bar with a couple of team-mates. I glimpsed a beautiful girl walk past with a friend and remarked to one of the lads how stunning she was. A short while later, the two of them turned up in the bar. Her mate knew who I was but Natalie is no rugby fan. Curiously, she had come across me before when working at a Wacky Warehouse where I used to take the girls. We chatted, exchanged numbers and went out for a cup of tea the following weekend.

A few coffee dates later, we had grown close but with me wary at first that she was 10 years younger than me, though I should add, 10 years more mature. Natalie was 19. As a father of girls of 12 and 10, that made me uncomfortable initially. We went for dinner before she returned to her second year of English and psychology studies in Dundee. I had been expecting her to say that it was a long distance away, she had her own life at university and what really was the point. I asked her whether it was worth giving it a go and, to my surprise, she said yes. At 19 you are supposed to be enjoying yourself at university, I pointed out. "You're not going to stop me enjoying myself at university. I'm just aligning myself with you," she replied. I probably knew even then that I had met my soulmate.

Before she returned to Scotland, I invited some friends over to help with Iesha and Mia's introduction to Natalie. Iesha was cool with it but Mia was on to me like a shot. "Daddy, is this friend your girlfriend?" to which I hesitated. "She's my friend and I want you and Iesha to meet her." When Natalie arrived, Mia must have picked up on the energy between us straight away. "You said it wasn't your girlfriend and it is," she said, in floods of tears. It wasn't long, though, before Natalie and the girls were playing on the trampoline together. "I didn't want to like her," Mia told me years later, "but I really did like her." That endorsement was important for me. My relationship with Natalie went from strength to strength, despite the physical distance between us.

We kept in touch via the wonders of Skype and in December went for a one-week cruise down the Nile. It solidified our relationship and underlined our common interests in art and art history. Players would organise end-of-season trips to Amsterdam where I would be more interested in visiting the likes of the Rijksmuseum and Van Gogh Museum. When Natalie and I visited the Sistine Chapel in Rome to see Michelangelo's painting of the chapel ceiling, especially The Last Judgment fresco, the wonder of it brought tears to my eyes. Surely this could only have been created by God? Until you appreciate that it is the work of man.

Proportionality in my life was also changing. If you measured my socialising to that with the boys, it was well under control. Measured against drinking socially with Natalie, I was still learning. Whereas she would be ready to go home at midnight, I wanted to carry on. It took time for me to get the balance right. When I joined Salford I deliberately drove there so that I wouldn't be tempted. The players gave me respect that I was no longer a party animal. I effectively retired the other me, who I had labelled "Fun Bobby". Looking back, I feel that I would have enjoyed my professional career more had I drunk less. Outside the Bradford circle, in which we did have a lot to celebrate, the drinking at Huddersfield was not as regular or pronounced. The culture now is still not right, though, when it comes to alcohol. Rugby players need to treat themselves like boxers do in the months preparing themselves for a fight. That means respecting their bodies through the season and cutting out the drink. There were a few occasions when Natalie saw me drinking with team-mates and that was frightening for her. "You can't behave like that, you're a professional sportsman," she would say. She was dead right.

Making the 2006 Challenge Cup final had been a stepping stone for Huddersfield Giants as an organisation and I was raring to go for the following season. We effectively had only a couple of weeks off because we were given a growth training home programme by fitness coach Ben Cooper. It was based on what my old Bradford mate Carl Jennings was doing with Penrith Panthers in Australia and designed to turn Huddersfield's racehorses into bigger, stronger animals. Known as Hypertrophy Specific-Training, the tension loading of muscles through progressive loading basically tore the fibres in two directions. It was power-based, intense weight training to put some timber on us, and it worked. That work was combined with a new defensive pattern that Jon Sharp brought back with him from a fact-finding mission Down Under.

It was an incredible system that took us two months to learn. When the ball began moving wide, we would close in like a clothes line. As we wedged in, it was a strangulation defence that forced opponents to try and come over the top of us. It was hard to perfect, to the extent that we did little else that pre-season. We spent almost no time on our offensive work and for the opening seven games of the season we didn't win. The frustration was that we lost all those games by small margins, with the reality that we were sat at the bottom of the table. Sharpy had no hair on his head to tear out but knew that the wins would come. The week before we played York City Knights in the fourth round of the Challenge Cup, he just had us playing games and working on our attack. All the frustrations poured out of us in a 74-point demolition of York. It was the first of eight successive wins, including the club's first league defeat of Bradford for 35 years.

However, it was not all a bed of roses. There was a fall-out between

Jon and Brad Drew. They were intelligent people who happened to have some fundamental disagreements but the upshot was that there was no communication between our off-field and on-field leaders. It left me as piggy in the middle between two blokes I admired and it did have an effect on the team as we bounced up and down the table. To an extent, what they were both saying was right but the impetus was for Brad to look for another club, which was a huge pity because he was so engaged with the club and the fans loved him. He just didn't see eye to eye with Jon, but the fact is that it must always be the coach's way. He is the one with his head on the block. You either go with him or get going. That is why Brad thought it best to move on at the end of the season.

It was during a 9-9 draw at Hull that I first hurt my neck. I went in to make a tackle and everything went numb on my right side. A burning pain shot up my upper back. I had no strength in my right arm, came off the pitch and was ordered to rest for a week. When I tried to do weights I could not push my arm beyond a certain point. In attempting to push it I managed to drop a 35kg weight on my head. Maybe it was the impact, because I immediately tried it again with the same result. Basically, I had hammered one of the discs in my neck that had swollen and squeezed a nerve. It wasn't until six months later that the disc broke apart, leaving me in a world of pain. A bit like dropping the weight on my head a second time, I knew then that I could have called it quits, although an actual opportunity to retire came as a bolt from the blue.

I went in to see Jon to have a talk about the next couple of years. My contract was up at the end of the 2007 season and I wanted to know what my future held. I appreciated that I was no spring chicken at 31 and I could see the club moving forward with the signings that they were making. The former Wigan scrum half Luke Robinson was recruited for 2008 from Salford and Kevin Brown's ball skills had seen him converted from centre to stand off. The club also had back up in Ryan Hudson at hooker, a position that I had learned to love in being bigger, stronger and smarter. I had a good game in a win at Harlequins when Jon told me that I did not figure in his plans for the following year. You could have knocked me down with a feather. For the first time in my career there was no prospect of ongoing rugby. I almost didn't catch the other words that Jon spoke. Something about the club having another proposition.

The reassurance I sought came from David McKnight, who told me he knew of another club interested in signing me. That club turned out to be Salford City Reds, but what Huddersfield had to say got me thinking further. The role the Giants had in mind was a marketing one. However, that would mean retiring. Was I really ready to hang up my boots? It was a surreal spell playing with a team who climbed the table again at the back end of the season, finishing fifth and qualifying for the play-offs for the first time, while contemplating the end of my career. The Giants gave me a couple of weeks to make my decision, during which I had lunch with Ken Davy, Huddersfield's chairman, who shared his fascinating rags to riches story from leaving school at 15 without academic qualifications, working as a photographer on P&O cruise ships, setting up a commercial photography business and diverting into the financial advice sector.

The Giants would not be where they are without Ken, who has been instrumental in the club's revival during the Super League era. I have always been inspired by him and thought that here was a man I could work for. The package was a good one, I spoke with mum and Natalie and, in my head, I was already retired when the day eventually came to put pen to paper. That day I also received two phone calls, the first from David to say that Salford had a contract offer and the other from Henry. "Dave's told me everything," he said. "You know what bro, I'll support any decision you make. But you need to ask yourself one question. Don't answer it straight away but think about it. Are you ready to retire?" And it hit me amidships. This was the guy I had been with all my life, not telling me not to retire but just asking me to ask myself the question. Once you retire, you retire for the rest of your life. You'll stop playing for the rest of your life. That prospect is a hard one to contemplate.

Half-an-hour before I was due to put pen to paper I rang Ken. "I want to thank you for the opportunity," I said, "but I've asked the question whether I'm ready to retire – and I'm not. I love this game too much and still think I've something to offer. Sorry but I'm not ready." Ken understood my dilemma as did Richard Thewlis, the chief executive, while I also made a call to Bob Cryan, Vice Chancellor of the University of Huddersfield, the club's shirt title sponsors, to apologise that I could not at that stage take up the ambassadorial role that would have been combined with the marketing job at the Giants. I told Bob at the same time, though, that I very much wanted to begin studying at Huddersfield during the 2007-08 academic year.

Not that many first year undergraduates forego the pleasures of freshers week to train. My degree in public relations and sports marketing at the University of Huddersfield and pathway in higher education opened up a whole new world for me, but not before a fond farewell to the Giants – alas marked by elimination at the hands of Hull in the play-offs – and the start of a new life in the lower division at relegated Salford, plus a whole new pain in the neck.

They won't stop us laughing

Throughout my career I have always enjoyed fitness. Not so much the gut-wrenching pain that one goes through in the middle of an especially gruelling session, when the lungs burn and the world spins. It was rather the post work-out feeling when my body would reward me with an endorphin release and, more importantly, the sense of smug satisfaction that I had survived what they had thrown at me, chewed it up, spat it out, then went looking for more.

I remember once with Bradford Bulls training with Graeme Bradley and Bernard Dwyer on the sand dunes at Cronulla beach – famous in Sydney and feared by those flogged up and down them. We were in the middle of a true flogging session, forced to sprint up and down the dunes, with the sand giving way underfoot.

Everyone was in a world of pain, with tears in their eyes. We thought we were nearly finished, only to have Matty Elliott, the coach, scream at us: "All right, you want to cut corners (someone had obviously tried to cheat), let's start it all again."

We couldn't believe what we were hearing, but as a good leader does, Bradley shouted in his commanding Aussie accent: "Let's go boys, don't let them beat you. They'll never stop us laughing."

Then everyone started shouting, "They'll never stop us laughing". This became a mantra for the Bradford team for more than a year. It meant they couldn't break us. This is the approach to fitness I've always had: be unbreakable and enjoy the rewards. BRING IT ON!

Interval training is really important to fitness work for rugby players. The nature of rugby is that the game is naturally a stop-start affair: short intense explosive efforts followed by an undetermined rest period. The following sessions are some I have used during pre-season and during season training. These are all sessions that can be participated in individually, or as a group and are all based on the interval training approach. As winter can sometimes be a drab affair, I will start with sessions that are performed in a gym.

In the gym

Session 1

Elliptical (cross) trainer intervals:
1 min low level – 1 min high level.
1 min low level – 2 min high level.
1 min low level – 3 min high level.
1 min low level – 5 min high level.

Bike:
1 min low level – 1 min high level.
1 min low level – 2 min high level.
1 min low level – 3 min high level.
1 min low level – 5 min high level.

Treadmill:
5 km run with a gradient level 1 (under 15-20minutes. Aim to run 5k in 20 minutes, then try to beat your time).

Session 2

Static rower:
10 x 200-300 metres row under 1 minute with a minute rest (Start at 200m, then push the distance up as you become fitter).

Treadmill:
5k run with a gradient level 1 (under 15-20 minutes. Aim to run 5k in 20 minutes, then try to beat your time).

Outdoors on field

Session 3

Find a 20m section of playing field and mark it out with cones, placing a cone at 0m, 10m and 20m. Starting on your stomach in the middle at the 10m mark, sprint forward to the 20m mark and hit the ground on your stomach again. As soon as you hit the ground, jump straight back up again turn and sprint back to the 10m. Again hit the ground on your stomach and get back up again, running towards the 0m marker. Again hit the ground and straight back up again and turn and sprint back to your start position. That is one rep. You then receive a 30 seconds rest, then start another rep. Repeat this activity, so the least you will do is six reps. You get a 30 seconds rest after each rep.

Session 4

Warm up
10 min athletics warm up.
10 min lower body stretch.

Done on a pitch try line to try line
10 X 400m (each one in under 90 seconds with 90 seconds recovery).
10 min lower body stretch.

Track work

Session 5

Warm up
10 min warm up jog.
10 min lower body stretch.

6 X 100m on the minute (aim for under 20 seconds per run then remainder of minute is rest time).
4 X 100m on the minute (all sub 16 sec).
10 X 40m on the minute (all sub 8 sec).
20 X 20m sprints on the 20 seconds (sub 4 sec).
1000m jog warm down (15 min stretch down).

Session 6

5 min dynamic stretch.

On the start line
Working off a whistle
8 X 400m Sprint
(Must complete the 400 metres run, then walk to the next 100m point in 3 minutes. Expand the recovery time, or shorten the run if needed).
8 X 200m Sprint (must complete the 200 metres run, then walk to the next 100m point in 2 minutes. Expand the recovery time, or shorten the run if needed).
1 Lazy lap and thorough stretch.

Ultimately, fitness is an attitude activity. The more you put in, the more you'll receive from it. The aim of this HP section is to offer you a couple of sessions from different environments that you may want to undertake. I ask you to work out at your desired level and mix and match the different sections together. There are many other ways to improve your rugby fitness, like wrestling, boxing, swimming etc., but what I have provided you with are a couple of my favourites that use a mixed approach.

Like every other skill or physical-based HP section, technique is everything. Unless you perform these activities using the correct form or the equipment properly, then you will take longer to achieve, or potentially not even reach your desired goals. You also run the risk of injury to yourself or someone else. I can't reinforce enough the need to learn correct technique before undertaking the challenges.

Chapter 15

Pain, Pills and Silver Pots

I noticed the wastage on my right side in the mirror one morning. All the extra work I was doing in training with Salford was making no difference to me physically. I simply could not generate power on my right side. I stepped up the training but it made no difference. Little did I know but the impact work and wrestling we were doing was increasing the pressure on the bulging disc in my neck and breaking it apart. I had spurned the opportunity to retire and walk straight into a job with Huddersfield Giants. Time and again I just felt electricity firing through me as the disc finally gave way, although at the time medical staff were unsure what exactly was happening to me. Was this my body telling me that I had made a bad decision? You know something is wrong when you go on holiday with a transcutaneous electrical nerve stimulation or TENS machine for pain relief.

The pain was so intense at times that I took massive doses of painkillers to get me through the day. As well as popping paracetamols, ibuprofen and codeine, I used anti-inflammatories to help. I also took a lot of diazepam and baclofen as muscle relaxants and tramadol as a painkiller too, all of which can be addictive drugs. They were pills that I perhaps turned to too readily at times but it was a case of anything to alleviate the pain. I would use the diazepam to help me sleep but it was habit-forming. It was a case of going cold turkey for a couple of days to get off the pills. Once I did, it induced feelings of depression for no fathomable reason, in which case I would take myself straight off to the gym for an endorphin release. I have always found the effects of exercise, not medication, to be far more beneficial.

I have always been a big fan of American comedians and Henry got me tickets for a Chris Rock concert. The neck was so bad, however, that every time I laughed electricity shot through my spine and across my upper body. I sat through two hours of pain, after which I was exhausted and wet-through with sweat. It was a blur trying to live with it, then we were off to the United States for pre-season training in Jacksonville, Florida. I did not do any weights, just some ball work, while most of my time was spent swimming to help maintain fitness. I had convinced myself that it was nothing more than a muscle issue that I would get over in the course of time.

On our one night off in Florida I had far too many drinks with Malcolm Alker, our stalwart captain and one club man who might have ended up at Bradford – Brian Noble was always a big fan of Malc's – but had his heartstrings pulled by Salford. It ended with the two of us wrestling on the hotel room balcony and head coach Shaun McRae catching us out. Goodness knows what Bomber thought of me. I was barely training, swimming on my own and complaining about the pain I was suffering, yet here I was drunken grappling. I was embarrassed and vowed the next day to return to full contact training. I hit the tackle pads as hard as I could. If I got the adrenalin pumping, maybe the pain would go away. Needless to say, it just made it worse. It was not until we returned home and I saw a specialist at the Alexandra Hospital in Cheadle that the magnitude of the problem became clear. I had a prolapsed disc, two vertebrae needed to be fused together and a section of my disc was resting on my spinal cord, which was triggering the electric shock waves. I was looking at between 10 and 12 weeks out. So much pain and discomfort entered my world at that time that I just existed until the surgery. Taking into account that even if I coughed or shouted the piece of disc resting on my spinal cord would move and spark electric shocks over my upper body, I survived on adrenalin.

From the moment surgery was completed I felt a new man. It was as if a ten storey block had been lifted from my shoulders. I no longer feared a cough, sneeze or chuckle. I was still on all the painkillers and in la la land much of the time, which wasn't much good for my university degree work at Huddersfield. My fellow students probably thought they were studying with Frankenstein's monster. I tried to keep a scarf around my neck to hide the great wound across the jugular that was held together by 17 staples. Managing recovery, training and playing on a full-time contract while studying proved problematic.

My neck, although eventually good to go, has never been right since. Having the two vertebrae fused meant those joints and discs around the fusion had to take even more pressure and work harder, which led to a further operation in 2011. I sat out the first two months of Salford's season in the 2008 Co-operative National League One and made my return in the Northern Rail Cup at home to Bramley. I bagged a couple of tries in getting off to a reasonable start back in what was, in effect, a Super League team operating at Championship level, containing the likes of Malcolm Alker, Craig Stapleton, Phil Leuluai, John Wilshere, Paul White and Karl Fitzpatrick, plus a couple of blossoming English half backs in Richie Myler and Stefan Ratchford, both later to make their names at Warrington.

I had joined at the Willows on a two-year contract with the deliberate intention of being back in Super League for 2009, based on the new licensing system for clubs and an expanded competition to 14 teams. The midsummer announcement that Salford and Celtic Crusaders would be part of the new Super League structure from 2009 was a vindication of all the club's efforts. With the bolts out of my neck, so to speak, I also had a ball, first winning the Northern Rail Cup in a 60-0 demolition of Ellery Hanley's Doncaster at Blackpool and reaching the National League One Grand Final at Warrington. We lost heavily to the Crusaders at home in the play-offs, which meant we had to beat Whitehaven to meet the Welsh side again in the final. It turned out to be one of the best finals I played in.

"Salford stared down the barrel before they came up trumps in a remarkable final over 100 minutes," *The Times* reported. "Celtic Crusaders, the Bridgend club who, along with Salford, have already been accepted into the Super League next season under the new licensing system, were 20 seconds from victory until they conceded a crucial penalty that led to extra-time. The Crusaders had twice come from behind and were grimly hanging on to an 18-16 lead when Darren Mapp held down Richard Myler, the Salford scrum half, in a tackle. The forward's interference enabled the prolific John Wilshere to step up from 38 metres. His last kick of the 80 minutes sailed between the uprights and left a shaken Crusaders side to face an additional 20 minutes. A reprieved Salford went on to secure the league title with quickfire tries by Ian Sibbit, who latched on to Robbie Paul's teasing kick, and Paul White's second touchdown on the left wing. Myler's late try gave a misleading impression in terms of the score [36-18], but as Shaun McRae, the Salford coach, said: 'We've gone through every emotion, from an easy win to a tight one and being beaten. They just never went away.'"

Having started the match at stand off, I rotated with Malcolm at hooker and, after 100 minutes, barely had enough breath to celebrate.

Being in a winning environment had certainly fired my enthusiasm and the prospect of a last fling in the Super League was an exciting prospect for the 2009 season. What began so promisingly, though, ended in tears on another pre-season trip to Florida, this time lasting two weeks and involving a game against Leeds in Jacksonville. We trained solidly for the first 11 days. If you can imagine 30 blokes living in each other's pockets and thinking of home, it is not surprising if they let off steam when given the chance. Everyone was tired and on edge. Add alcohol to the mix and you have something pretty combustible. It was a boys and beer thing that kicked off, and one that I didn't even witness having gone off to do my own thing. But when reports of players fighting got home, the club decided to take Malc's captaincy away from him.

From a public relations perspective they felt that they needed to show a wider public that they were in full control, but in stripping him of the captaincy it just felt like an over-reaction. As I was the most senior player, they turned to me to take over as captain. Not only did I not want the role, I did not feel it was my place to accept it, especially under the circumstances. A situation had got a bit daft and out of hand, so what? Was it really worth taking the captaincy off the club's most loyal servant? From a selfish point of view, too, I did not want the extra responsibility. I was anxious simply to enjoy my last season in the top flight. I said as much to Bomber in America, but agreed with him, as a one-off as the vice-captain, to lead the side in a pre-season game with Widnes. After that, it was up to the club to name a new captain.

Rob Parker got the job and led the side to an opening weekend win over Celtic Crusaders. In trying circumstances, Rob did an excellent job. Six weeks later, Malcolm was restored as captain and Rob was simply told that his service in the role was no longer required. It wasn't handled well – the least they could have said to Rob was that they were making Malcolm the on-field leader again but giving him the club captaincy – but there was no discussion. There is a right and wrong way of doing things and Rob, having stepped into the breach, was simply instructed to stand down. Captaincy is an emotive role and cannot be treated with casual disregard. As a supermodel, Rob makes a good rugby player; he ran around with a fractured skull for a while before they found what was wrong with him. But he had great energy and a great heart that sucked you in. He deserved better.

Malcolm's return coincided with a run of three victories, but mostly we bumped along the bottom of the Super League table. I knew that I wasn't cut out for another season at top level after this one. Even training took its toll on me, while as late as the Friday, I still felt physically tired from the previous weekend's game. Generally, senior players at clubs are treated a little differently and are given more time to recover, but that wasn't Bomber's philosophy. From the view of an outsider it is perfectly right that all players should put in the same amount of training in terms of their contractual responsibilities. But the fact is that a 30-plus player cannot do what a 19-year-old, with testosterone coursing through his body, can. Certainly not this creaking 33-year-old. At Huddersfield, Jon Sharp had the confidence in me not to complain if I ducked out of some of the training. It is about being smart in terms of looking after your body in order that you can deliver your best performance on the field and not still be in recovery mode.

When I sat down with Bomber in his office and explained that I was knackered and struggling, his reaction was that it would send out the wrong message to younger players if I didn't train like them. I could understand the methodology behind what he was saying – Bomber recognised that as a squad we were not as naturally gifted as a lot of other teams, but that by dint of hard work we'd compensate by being one of the fittest sides in Super League – but I had hit a wall. I wasn't able to balance recovery with the amount of fitness work expected, although I did accept what he said. He was the guy under a heap of pressure in a results-based business and did not want to compromise the need to work our backsides off.

Some players had pre-warned me about Bomber's video sessions. The big fella is a great orator and pundit. He would talk eloquently, for up to two hours at a time. The guy can talk as much as me. Saying that, I had nothing but respect for Shaun. We crossed swords only once and then I felt we were simply caught up in a case where a couple of journalists were trying to create some headlines. I was asked on the BBC's Super League Show what was up at Salford and mentioned that there was a bit of dressing room upset. That related to relationships between some players and the club, not Bomber. A journalist rang Shaun for his reaction. He had not seen the programme but responded. In turn, another reporter called me to respond to what Shaun had said about me. It all got out of hand, as I told Bomber when I rang him to say that it was something and nothing.

One problem at Salford was an us-and-them mentality between the team and the club itself, which was something I had not experienced before. I came from Bradford where we were one big family – players, club staff and supporters – and Huddersfield, where a sense of togetherness similar to the Bulls was developing. I felt that the Salford club operated separately to the players during my spell there. The only time we spent at the Willows was match days and for promotional events. I was used to making myself a nuisance with the administration staff in offering my assistance, but at Salford there was a clear division of responsibilities. The real separation actually came from the players, as there was a feeling of mistrust that I had never seen before. It was a pity because it did not promote brand value in terms of the City Reds. A small thing, perhaps, but it did not help that our pre-season training gear failed to arrive until January. Some players would train in other clubs' kit. It was hardly the professional ethos I had come from at Huddersfield where on day one back you would be presented with all your gear and told that it was your responsibility to care and look after it.

During my first year at Salford we trained on school playing fields next to Sedgley Park rugby union club, where our gym was separately based. We moved the following season to Salford University where there was also a swimming pool on campus. However, the chopping and changing did not help with unity between the players and club. On occasions I found myself acting as the conduit between the two, but the fact was that my own attitude was changing thanks to education. My studies at university, which Salford were always very understanding about, could involve me staying up working until 2am. I would meet up at 6am with Paul White and Jordan Turner, the two other Yorkshire-based lads, for the car pool over the Pennines. Striking the balance was not easy but university had opened my mind to the fact that the bubble we were operating in wasn't the real world.

The world beyond rugby operated a different set of values. Studying in my 30s meant that I was one of the more mature of even the mature students at the University of Huddersfield. Talking to a fellow undergraduate one day, he mentioned how much he disliked another guy because he was arrogant and had deliberately walked into him. "Why don't you chin him?" was my snap response. He looked at me strangely. In the rugby world, that's how you dealt with someone who was out of order. But the look on the bloke's face baffled me. "What do you mean, he looked at you weird," Natalie said. "That's normal. You just can't go round hitting anyone." I knew it was illegal to strike someone in any culture, but in the closed rugby world that sort of thing was part of the norm. It got me thinking about all sorts of different things and a sense of disengagement from the world outside, such as the ritual of Mad Monday, when players at the end of each season turn into gibbering teenagers.

By educating players better, they have a greater understanding of who they are, their responsibilities in the world and the responsibility to themselves as brands in their own right. My role as a former athlete is to promote the players and the sport, because they are the best tools we have. Rugby is like making love – even when it's bad it's good – but the sport needs nurturing and the players are best positioned to help make it grow. If athletes know more and understand better, they will deliver. Some players still do themselves more harm than good through their use of social media. Be thoughtful and insightful on Twitter, for instance. As I tell players, post as if you are posting to your mum. Think of those supporters who are following you, kids and families, and identify with their values.

Amid these changes in my life, I was enjoying playing but struggling physically with the training demands. Wins were few and far between, but Salford's first victory at Leeds for 40 years was a notable one. Unfortunately it was one of only seven in the Super League all year. Compared with what I had been used to at Bradford and Huddersfield, the players were not always au fait with what our system was supposed to be. We didn't train that element enough because we were so busy working on being as fit as we could possibly be. I was also trying to work out how to speed up my university education while continuing to play and still pay the bills. My joints were intact, even if recovery from matches took an awful lot longer. The obvious compromise was a return to the Championship.

During my final year at Salford, I talked to Leigh Centurions and Halifax, who were more interested in developing a young pup than having an old dog at half back. I had earlier run into my old Bradford team-mate Simon Knox, who was flying out with Leigh for a game at Toulouse the same day we were travelling to Perpignan to play Catalan Dragons. He said that the Leigh coach Paul Rowley was interested in my experience taking them forward. The flexibility of joining Leigh part-time was attractive in that I could also pursue my university studies, media commitments and after dinner speaking work. The club also recruited an old hand there in Ian Millward for the 2010 season, a coach who I had heard some great and some not so great things about. As with all such things, I would make my own judgement.

Ian had hacked a lot of people off in his time at St Helens and won admirers in equal measure. His Saints side had tormented Bradford enough times, so I was fascinated to see the bloke at work. He was utterly ruthless. Basil's not the world's biggest bloke, he's a ginger-haired little dude, and the way he spoke to some of the boys, I just thought, Basil, you're tip-toeing a thin line. He ranted, he swore, he turned bright red, but everything he said made perfect sense. He saw the team going in a certain direction and me as the most senior player being the captain. This time I accepted the role. Just as when Brian Smith first arrived at Bradford, I saw in Ian an innovatory coach with an ability to improve a team and, yes, even at my age, improve me as a player. He had a goal and wanted me to lead on the field. Off it, it was his way or no way. Everyone was quickly brought up to speed and everyone improved. Invigorated for his second spell in the British game by a wealth of knowledge and new thinking in the National Rugby League from his time as assistant coach of North Queensland Cowboys, Ian poured his enthusiasm and expertise at us.

It was a total pleasure playing under him. He had me operating in the halves alongside Martyn Ridyard, who was going from strength to strength, but made me a more direct player. He was always in our faces but we learned and grew as a team, basically the same team that had finished ninth the season before and thought that they had been relegated. It would certainly have been a come down playing in the third professional tier in Championship One, but Leigh were spared demotion once Gateshead Thunder asked to remain in the lower division after suffering financial difficulties. Ian had us playing out of our skins from the start. We lost just one of our first 14 games. I was learning and loving my time at Leigh, until a painful episode at Bradford. It was not so much a 58-16 loss in the Challenge Cup to my old club that hurt but a knee in the balls. You get that occasionally but my testicles were tested, so to speak, by a run of three such incidents.

Natalie would like me to have retired from Huddersfield in 2007.

She had seen me in agony with great pins in my neck, having undergone a shoulder clean out and a young surgeon reckoning that I was only fit for the knackers yard, and now my bollocks were black and blue. After the last incident, I woke up to discover my nether regions grossly swollen and purple and a dull ache in my stomach. Despite that, I managed to squeeze in another game at Whitehaven before going to hospital for a scan. I had split a testicle. I rang Natalie, who got me booked into Pinderfields Hospital in Wakefield, where the doctor told me: "There are three possibilities when I go in to look. One, the testicle is split, I can shave some off it and sew it up; two, I go in, it's black and blue and dead, in which case I remove it for a fake ball; three, I go in, they're both black and blue, I bring both out and put two fakes in and you're on hormone tablets for the rest of your life." My prayers for it to be option one were fortunately answered. I'm not the man I was though; I'm down a third of a ball.

Ian took the team that year from the bottom to near the top, although we ultimately ran out of juice. I would car pool with Ricky Bibey, who had a great season and agreed that Ian was better than nine out of ten coaches in the Super League at that time. In the likes of Stuart Donlan, John Duffy and Mick Nanyn, he had established heads, he brought on the young guys and was judicious in the way he drafted in Jacob Emmitt, Matty Blythe, Lee Mitchell and Tyrone McCarthy on dual registration. Chris Hill and Tony Tonks were the best props in the Championship for us. He made a great signing in Jamie Ellis for 2011, while I let Basil know early that it would be my last season. Importantly, it was about finishing my career in a good competition with a progressive club and also on my terms.

I say on my terms because I didn't want the game to end me. It nearly did on February 20, 2011, in the third Northern Rail Cup group game of my 18th and final rugby league season. Jamie Ellis was Ian's big project and I had reverted to hooker in rotating there with John Duffy. I got a try in the opening win at Batley and was rested for the next tie at home to Swinton for a big game the following week against Sheffield Eagles. "I need you as fresh as possible because I want you to play a big part this whole season," Basil said. We were playing well, I came off the bench after 20 minutes, helped lay on two tries, then suffered a rush of blood to the head. Menzie Yere, the Papua New Guinea centre, who glories in the nickname of The Jukebox – because he has so many hits – carried the ball from acting half back and I flew out of the line to put a shot on him. I went for the shoulder but as he sidestepped me, his forehead hit my temple. I hyper extended my neck and came down on my face out cold.

There were a few occasions when I had been briefly knocked unconscious but not for this length of time. I came round in the dressing room some minutes later. I noticed that I had a neck brace on and felt as if my arms and hands were on fire. I was back in the world of pain that I had dreaded. With two of the vertebrae in my neck having already been fused, those around it had taken the shock of the impact with The Jukebox's head. The outcome was another disc bulge and damaged nerves. I had a steroid injection in hospital to calm everything down. The morphine just made me throw up. When Natalie came to pick me up, it felt as if someone was applying a blow torch to my skin. My arms throbbed and hands shook. The cold air on my skin as I walked outside just intensified the feeling. I loaded up with painkillers – all the old favourites – and when I saw the surgeon a few days later, he stressed the need for a second neck operation.

Naturally, I asked him for an alternative. "You can have a cortisone jab into the disc bulge and see how that goes in four to six weeks, but I'm telling you that you need the op," he said. I had the injection the next day and was on a diet of diazepam and tramadol. The burning sensation in my arms receded a little but when I saw the surgeon a month later, he was unequivocal. "You need the op and you need to retire." They were words I had heard before and ignored. I did the calculations quickly, 16 weeks out would mean I would get to play the back 10 weeks of the season, including the Northern Rail Cup final. "Okay," he said. "I'll let you finish then but you must promise that will be it. Your body's giving out on you." Sobering words but a promise is a promise and my focus turned to being ready for the business end of the season.

So began a familiar process. It turned out to be a partial prolapsed disc that had broken apart in one area. Again I had the big staples in the neck, a week of killer painkillers and another few days of cold turkey to get off them. My determination to finish at a time of my own choosing drove me. Big muscle spasms on my right side for several years were among the signs telling me to give up, but the prospect of one more final drove me for a final fling. The 2011 Northern Rail Cup was the last piece of silverware I was guaranteed a shot at. Being an ambassador for Northern Rail, with posters of me proudly holding the cup aloft in 2009 displayed at dozens of railway stations, the big focus for me was the final at Bloomfield Road, Blackpool.

I scored a try on my return in a league game at Toulouse, set up another against Batley and went into Blackpool on a high. This was Leigh's "Wembley" and my last "Wembley" too. I would tease the boys that it meant nothing to me when, in fact, it meant the world. I had targeted the final and been flogged on the sidelines by Paul Rowley. Fitness-wise, I was raring to go. It was typical Lancashire weather in Blackpool. It threw it down and Natalie, Iesha and Mia went off to the Pleasure Beach. They were like drowned rats when I caught up with them but sported the biggest smiles. I felt a different energy altogether. There was no police escort for the bus travelling to the ground but the old thrill was there. I had done some training with schoolchildren who were playing in a curtain raiser and went to say hello to those guys and wish them luck for their final. That allowed me to take my mind off what was to come, because when I went into the dressing room my fellow forwards were ready to rip the walls off.

The great cameo to the final was Ian Millward up against Brian Noble again after all the old Saints-Bradford dogfights. Nobby had joined Halifax on a consultancy basis a few weeks before and had transformed their defence. The drama that surrounded Leigh centred on Arthur Thomas having stepped down as chairman after his private business went into administration. Arthur was a hugely popular figure at the club and had been instrumental in the creation of Leigh Sports Village as the club's new home. His departure caused widespread anxiety, yet curiously bonded the team and community even tighter. Our bonus money for the final went back into the club while there was another big incentive that day, ticking the box for Leigh to make a Super League licence application in 2014.

Halifax went 10-0 up but it could have been double that score. We were on the back foot for 40 minutes and Ian Millward delivered one of the best half-time speeches I had ever heard. There was no ranting or raving this time. He was superbly clinical in making his point with the use of a screen and projector. "We're not doing the things we're used to doing. We all know we're not delivering, so let's have a look at what I'm talking about." He picked on just a couple of points – losing our feet in the tackle and gaining an extra half second in the tackle – but with ringing clarity and precision. Sat listening to him in the dark, we got it. It was the perfect team talk. We had been playing on raw emotion, and once we fixed up the small aspects, things began to happen.

If Basil had bawled us out, lips would have dropped lower and our knuckles started to scrape along the floor. "All you need to do is go and do what you do well," he said, which is precisely what we did. The second half was ours. I was on for the first 15 minutes, John Duffy took over, I went back on at loose forward and ended the game back at hooker after John's calf went. Jamie Ellis and Chris Hill, who had been outstanding all season, scored tries within 10 minutes of the resumption. Jamie grabbed another in reply to a further Halifax try by Rob Worrincy, which locked the score at 16-16. Both teams were basically working towards overtime when Dylan Nash nearly took Stu Donlan's head off with a lazy reach and grab. We got a vital penalty but too far for the place kick.

Everyone held their breath. There were 40 seconds remaining. Two sets earlier, we had gone for a ridiculous drop goal attempt. We tried to get as near to their posts as possible for another one-point attempt when, on play three, I connected with Martyn Ridyard, who dummied a drop goal effort in drawing the Halifax defenders off their line. Instead he sidestepped and found Stu Littler, who popped the ball up as Jim Gannon grabbed him, for Tom Armstrong to go over at the corner. The winning try, cue delirium, in what almost felt like the world going into slow motion. Nobby, Halifax head coach Matt Calland and Ian had left their seats in preparation for extra-time – poor Matt, with whom I shared my first Wembley experience, was just open-mouthed – while I could see all the Leigh people were losing their minds. Yes, it felt like Wembley again, except this time we had won. The same adrenalin rush, the same feeling. Rock god, if a somewhat wrinklier one.

Light in the dark

In the State of Mind HP section I mentioned that being injured can be some of the darkest and loneliest times for professional sportsmen and women. Inevitably, it is one of the realities of sport that at some stage you will get injured. How you deal with it psychologically will be a journey that will be different for everybody. So what do you do when you are "busted"?

Personally, I used to feel less than human when injured and I truly believed that I wasn't worth the money I was getting paid, because I wasn't doing what I was getting paid to do on the field. I used to throw myself head first into as much promotional and publicity work as the club had to offer, as this became my way of earning my keep.

Sadly, this did not help the loneliness of sitting on the sidelines as you watched the lads go to work week in, week out, day in and day out. The only thing that helped emotionally was, as I improved, getting back into the gym and working out again. There is a positive knock-on effect. As you exercise more, you become healthier, and healthier people recover quicker as well. Matthew Green explains how to deal with rehabilitation and why it will benefit you personally.

Biography

My name is Matthew Green and I am the rehabilitation conditioner at Huddersfield Giants. After graduating from university in 2007 with a degree in Sports Therapy, I was employed by Halifax Town Football Club as a rehabilitation and fitness coach. I have also had involvement with Huddersfield Town and Bradford City football clubs. Along with Greg Brown, I am also a founding partner of a one-to-one personal training studio in Huddersfield, Extreme Conditioning.

Introduction

If you are involved with playing sport on a regular basis, regardless of the level that you play, it is inevitable that at some point in your career you will sustain an injury. Speaking from personal experience this is an extremely frustrating time, as you are unable to take part in the activity you love. Although it is very easy to lose focus whilst away from the field of play, it is of great importance that you have the same professional approach towards your rehabilitation as you would with training and competing. What you do whilst injured will influence the risk of injury/re-injury and, most importantly, your level of performance when you return.

Be strict with early management

How the injury is treated during the early stage will play a big part in how successfully the particular injury heals and therefore how quickly and safely you return. Although it can seem a little tedious at the time, it is important that you adhere to the early management strategies given to you by the physiotherapist, such as icing the area on a regular basis during these initial stages. Common treatments, depending on the specific injury, that are advised are icing the area on a regular basis, keeping the limb elevated and resting.

Follow exactly what the physiotherapist tells you

As well as the early management strategies, a physiotherapist will be able to advise you on specific rehabilitation exercises which you will need to carry out on a daily basis. This will range from simple movement patterns and strength exercises in the early stage to more functional, sports-specific exercises during the late stage. During the time of injury, these specific exercises become as important as the strength and fitness training you carry out whilst fit and therefore demands the same level of effort and commitment.

Focus on what you CAN do, not what you can't

Just because you may not be able to play sport, run or do certain exercises in the gym does not mean that you can't still train hard. This is the time to start thinking about what exactly you can do and focusing on that. For example, if you have a shoulder injury, you are still able to use an exercise bike and do certain lower limb resistance exercises. Once you have found the exercises that are safe for you to do, the next factor that you then need to consider is intensity. To maintain as much strength and fitness as possible whilst injured, the training intensity needs to replicate as close as possible the regime when you are fit. An easy way to do this is to think about how hard a typical fitness or weights session is during training and aim for this. As with any form of training, please seek advice from your fitness coach or a personal trainer and the involved physiotherapist before doing any form of exercise to ensure it is conducted safely.

Be progressive

To ensure the injury heals successfully and that you are physically ready to return to competition, your rehabilitation, strength and fitness training needs to be progressive. It is important to find that balance between pushing yourself and not over doing it. As a general rule, if an exercise has become too easy it is no longer producing a training effect and will need progressing either by doing more repetitions, increasing resistance or increasing the complexity of the exercise. To ensure your progression is safe you will need some guidance from your fitness coach or a personal trainer.

Ensure you are physically fit before returning to the field of play

This may sound like an obvious point, but it is quite common to see athletes return only to injure themselves again, not because the injury has not healed but they have de-conditioned and therefore are at a higher risk of injury. When you have become unfit, you will also not be able to perform at the level you are capable of and it will take a while for this to improve again. Although you and your coach will be desperate to see you return as early as possible, it is far more important that when you do return you are in peak physical condition. This will help prevent injury and ensure you perform to your potential.

To find out more about rehabilitation or to contact Matthew you can follow him on his personal Twitter account @Matthewgreen14 or business account @ExtremeCon

Chapter 16

A Rugby Life Less Ordinary

I played in 20 finals and missed out on my 21st when Leigh were beaten by Sheffield Eagles in the 2011 Championship final eliminator. My lungs burned, I was exhausted and lots of me ached but there was no sadness in that loss for me. After 31 years playing rugby, 18 of them as a professional, I had reached the end of the line of that part of my life, one rich in memories and steeped in the sort of success even a New Zealand forest boy with the most vivid of imaginations would have struggled to dream up. When I awoke the morning after that last match I felt genuinely happy. I walked a path of many highs and many lows, not yet knowing where the next phase of the journey would take me. I had walked away from playing rugby on my terms, but I was more than a little nervous about the future in Civvy Street.

The death in 2010 of Terry Newton, the Great Britain hooker, was the catalyst for the State of Mind round of matches in Super League a year later. The tragedy of Terry taking his life highlighted the demons that can lie beneath the toughest of players. In Terry's case, he was trying to come to terms with life after rugby. Several former team-mates have suffered from depression in making that difficult transition and it has been a well documented issue for many professional sportsmen. In understanding the pressures that high level sport can exert and the crazy bubble and culture that you live in, it makes me angry that education and post-career options are sadly neglected by so many. One organisation that has delivered a lot for players is the GMB union, driven by Leeds scrum half Rob Burrow's dad Geoff. The GMB has worked to create vocational pathways for players to study at a number of different colleges in the north of England. Frustratingly, too many players are still living for the moment and neglecting their futures. It is the culture that has to change. I had passionately driven myself towards working in the world of sports administration once I retired. Coaching was never something that appealed to me. When you are a coach you are often controlled by people who simply aren't qualified to understand the intricacies of coaching strategies and ultimately decide your future.

I did not know Terry all that well but the news of his death, which I heard about while I was watching Chris Thorman's York team play Oldham in the Championship One final at Warrington, hit me like a sledgehammer. It also stirred all the emotions of losing one of my closest childhood friends who I played rugby with as a kid, Sharn Inu. Sharn was 22 when he took his life, an immensely talented player, a father and a young bloke who we all lost far too early.

The rate of suicides among young men is not just alarming but a scandal. It was one of the reasons I took up an offer by a friend, Andy Upton, director of Leeds-based production company Firestorm, who was working on a series of music-based short films to bring awareness of the issues surrounding young people and mental health. Having a natural aptitude for showing off and a short history of dramatics at school, I accepted. My character was seen jumping to his death from a tower block in a film called Destroyed, which was shown in schools, colleges and youth groups nationally. It was a music video in which I rapped the narrative. I spent an afternoon in London in front of a green screen pretending to fall to my death. It was a story of abuse behind a youth lifestyle that led me to pay the ultimate price. It was a powerful film with a powerful message and earned Firestorm a Royal Television Society award.

As for other thespian ventures, I have the distinction of being the only player from the Huddersfield Giants to have been given a speaking part in the local pantomime. It's the only production of *Jack and the Beanstalk* to have a Haka thrown in. I also appeared for one night in John Godber's play *Up and Under*, in Derby. I'm not sure whether the good theatre folk of Derby knew who I was but it was just another of the experiences I have always grabbed at in taking me out of my comfort zone. That included a game of strip poker once for the BBC for an especially colourful Challenge Cup tie preview. I began in a black suit and tie and ended in my birthday suit.

I am under no illusion that all my television work sprang from the 1996 Wembley final with Bradford. The hat-trick helped and, of course, there was my motor mouth. I have rarely been lost for a word or three in my whole life. A week after that first Challenge Cup final, Sky invited me on to their expert panel for a game at Wigan in which Henry was playing. It was at the old Central Park where the Wigan fans – possibly mistaking me for my brother, who knows? – gave me a standing ovation. Sky saw in me someone who was engaged with the media and open to do anything. With hindsight, I would have leveraged the opportunity better and perhaps been a little more guarded and structured in what I delivered, but I also appreciate that a raw, naive young kid so full of beans helped make good television. Mum and dad's core values made me a marketable commodity. I don't think that Eddie Hemmings and Mike "Stevo" Stephenson, Sky's rugby league double act, had encountered a player before who they simply couldn't shut up. But I loved the television work and Eddie and Stevo, along with Neville Smith, Sky's rugby league executive producer, could not have been more helpful or encouraging in those early years.

I was not the typical rugby league player, I suppose. If I hadn't been capable of putting the ball over the try line, the media wouldn't have been interested, I know that. But who on earth else in the sport would be a qualified nail technician? Like Brian Moore, the former England rugby union hooker and self-style "pitbull", who trained as a manicurist when his wife opened a nail bar, I took a similar course when Antonia opened a shop in Horsforth outside Leeds. We had invested in the business and the only way I could get engaged was by helping her out. That meant learning the science and intricacies behind nail care on a course which I somehow passed. I have the certificate to prove it, although I cannot say I exactly fell in love with the nail business. Sky came along to film me doing a manicure but I can't remember doing too many more, although my approach has always been to give new things a go. What's the worst that can happen?

When Sky asked me to be a regular panelist, Huddersfield were great in accommodating that side of my career. From an awareness-building perspective for the club, it was a good move. I was encouraged by those at Sky to continue to work for the BBC during the Challenge Cup rounds, as it would allow me to grow as a presenter. This led to the offer of being a regular pundit on the Super League Show with Harry Gration, Mr BBC Look North. By accepting the position I perhaps naively did not appreciate that I was effectively batting for both sides with the BBC being a competitor to Sky. I sensed something was wrong when Sky didn't invite me back the year I began working on the Super League Show, although I will always be grateful for Neville and his entire Sky crew in giving me my first big break and taste of an important facet of my career.

There was no particular targeted strategy with the television work. I simply loved talking rugby. The media fascinated me, as well as raising my profile. It can be a double-edged sword. It is always good to meet and talk with people who know your face, although it can be difficult when it occasionally intrudes on your privacy. One luxury, I suppose, for rugby league players, yet a downfall of the game itself, is that the sport flies under the media radar a lot of the time and players can largely ply their trade without the bizarre scrutiny that accompanies many Premier League footballers. However, a player's profile is hard to build when blinkered London-based national newspapers, for instance, have reduced their coverage of the sport, with all the difficulties that entails in trying to sell rugby league and its stars to a wider audience. Higher profile league players switching to union are put under the magnifying glass, as Henry was, but working as I do now in a business and marketing capacity at Huddersfield Giants you can't help but feel that a big part of a Londoncentric media is missing a trick with what it unfairly pigeonholes as a northern sport. It is also why it is important that London Broncos breaks the "big smoke". Should they ever do so, it would bring the sport a new audience, one that would command significant resources.

Rugby league needs to make itself newsworthy and not shy away from controversy or the sort of innovative thinking that has characterised much of the game's history. There is a problem also of the sport thinking that it is more important than it actually is. In the great scheme of things, it is not. It must realise that to move forward and develop, it must open up more. That means an end to the closed shop mentality, by operating an access all areas policy to make the sport as media-friendly as possible. It would only take a short while for players to get used to throwing open the dressing rooms to the cameras after games. Not only would it allow journalists to paint a better picture, it would create a new and dynamic insight exclusive to the sport. It was a drum I banged in an interview not long after Bradford had lost the 2002 Grand Final in the most dramatic and controversial of circumstances to St Helens. "We were livid and people were bouncing off the walls," I said. "But in the game's fight for exposure, can you imagine the agony we were going through in close-up? We've got the north but you've got to have the southern-media's backing. We can help by offering something different and opening up the changing rooms to capture the real emotion."

Cameras in dressing rooms in New Zealand and Australia are hardly a new phenomenon and that open policy, especially at Wembley until the authorities clamped down after 1994, certainly helped create greater column inches in the newspapers. In my own small way I have helped reintroduce the post-match changing room player interview as part of the BBC's Challenge Cup coverage. These days I get to ask the questions and I love it. It is cosy sitting under the nice warm studio lights giving your expert analysis, but a whole lot more testing with a microphone that is on the blink and a camera fogging up as you try and put a match winner on the spot. Hopefully, the viewers get a little of the raw emotion I was talking about all those years ago, but also an insight into the players themselves and their personalities. A lot of the BBC audience does not follow league on a regular basis. However, they can appreciate interesting sports people when they see and hear them.

Wembley and working there now still gives me a shot of adrenalin. It was a weird but wonderful sensation one year having to put down the mic and join a parade of Lance Todd Trophy winners in receiving a standing ovation. Nothing will ever compare to the shock as I emerged from the tunnel in wide-eyed wonder in 1996 behind Brian Noble, who was asked by Brian Smith to lead us out as a Bradford legend. Now I work with Nobby on television and there is no better person to sit alongside and spout a few words as a fellow graduate of that Odsal school. His approach to the game is the same as mine in that we love to articulate our unbridled love for the sport and those who play it. We had three great years together on the Super League Show sofa with the inimitable Harry Gration, another great friend and mentor when it came to learning the intricacies of television, for which I am also indebted to BBC's rugby league editor Carl Hicks and producer Sally Richardson for their patience and persistent encouragement.

I hounded the BBC to send me on a course in London with a host of potential presenters from all different fields, to learn just what it takes to make television, from manning the cameras to application of make-up. Whatever I do, I like to amass as much knowledge from every conceivable source to help make me more proficient at it. I am very self-critical of my work, a lot of it pre-game analysis for the Challenge Cup. This involves me running across the pitch as the players go through their warm-up, talking to camera, trying not to fall over, bump into or distract the players, or send the cameraman flying, while hopefully offering some pithy key messages rather than just gobbledygook. I am always mindful, too, of what my mum always says: never swear on television.

Part of my adaption to no longer playing was seeing a hypnotist shortly before I retired. I came from a predominantly male household, worked in a hyper masculine environment, but inhabited an all female house. When Iesha and Mia grew spines, suddenly dad and rugby weren't cool any more. In the blink of an eye, they went from laughing at everything I said to looking at me as if I was the strangest thing on the planet. Life happens, children become teenagers and there was a lot of changing to do myself. I would get angry and explode. Those were worthy attributes as a defensive mechanism on the rugby field, not for handling the three women in my life. Natalie was the biggest motivation to seek some guidance. She pointed out how I overreacted to even small things. Whether the hypnotherapy sessions really worked or not, I find that I am a much more passive person, although I do still have my moments.

It is a constant drive for self improvement. Don't think you have always got the answer and have no fear of seeking answers elsewhere by whatever means, counselling, hypnotherapy. If I feel any anger bubbling, I try to just chill out and compose. There's no strategic thinking in my new workplace in exploding all the time. A lot of the so-called caveman tools are not needed in the modern world and an equal society. My degree course pointed the way for me, as well as introducing me to a new type of competition – competing with myself. My first piece of university work got a mark of 51 per cent, which I was pretty happy with until Malcolm Alker pointed out that 51 per cent wasn't that good. He was right and it drove me to work harder and improve. Doing sports marketing and public relations also allowed me to put theories into practice at Leigh in looking at the whole fan experience.

A couple of months elapsed from retiring to landing a job tailor-made for me at Huddersfield as business development manager. The Giants had offered me a job when I wasn't ready in 2007 and were good enough to come up with a role when I eventually was. I have always loved the Galpharm Stadium, which sits proudly like a tank in the basin of the town, along with Huddersfield's friendly and financially astute ethos, as espoused by Ken Davy, the chairman. The club's enormous potential was the other attraction. Being part of Bradford Bulls' era of explosive growth, it is no surprise that the club is similarly being positioned at the hub of the community. Whether it is a zumba class with 40 ladies or the haka with hundreds of schoolchildren, I love being in the thick of it. Interactivity with fans, growing the Giants' brand, improving the experience for spectators so they'll be attracted back are all part of my remit. We want to be industry leaders. Nor is it all shirt and tie. The fitter and healthier you are, the more productive you are, which is why I introduced the urban atheltes programme for the administration team, who run every step of the stadium with me most days.

As well as the early morning gym sessions, without which I would be grumpy all day, art remains a huge passion for me. I move seamlessly from the sports pages in newspapers to the arts and lifestyle sections. My interest is perhaps explained best by the masterpiece I always return to, the futuristic Italian artist Umberto Boccioni's 1910 work La citta che sale, or The City Rises, which is exhibited in the Museum of Modern Art in New York. It is a dynamic combination of men and horses coming together to build a city and a symbolic sign of the old and new ways. What gets me still is Boccioni's vibrant colour scheme. Aggressive reds and yellows contrast with his use of aqua blue. It is a work that just has so much life to it. It is both life affirming and life enhancing.

Maori culture and symbolism have become a big part of my artwork. I have invariably got two or three pieces on the go at one time. One of my favourites is part of a playing contract I had blown up, complete with the Rugby Football League's official stamp, using stencils and spray paint. There are few things more pleasurable and satisfying than losing myself with a pallet, oils and brushes. It was hard at times trying to fit art work in with playing, but life drawing classes at college in Bradford proved invaluable to me. They were a reminder of my first life drawing encounter at art college in Auckland. The lass dropped her robes and I tried not to snigger. As soon as the tutor started to talk about shapes, space and tone, the human form lost its sexuality. My creative side would appear, on the surface, to be at odds with the aggressive nature of rugby, but when I think historically of rugby league emerging from a powerful landscape of mills and mines, I am instantly transported back to Boccioni's great work.

Much of my inspiration also hails from regular trips back to New

Zealand and seeing the explosive growth of the cultural aspects of the country and resurgence of Maori and Polynesian identity. That was simply not there when I grew up in the country. The pride I feel now when I go back is immense. I declare my Maori heritage loud and proud. It has infiltrated my art work and, specifically, my body, which is covered in ta moko – the Maori art of tattooing – which means the clearing of the way. The tradition was to cut the skin and apply black pigment but that is a little too painful. The cultural moko I have arose from the traditional art books I began to collect on my trips to New Zealand. The moko's return to popularity began with the likes of the singer Robbie Williams having Maori-style tattoos but I wanted something more meaningful to me.

Through tireless research I managed to find the facial moko in a book of one of my ancestors, a chieftain by the name of Kawhiti. I used it as the basis for a moko design. It is bad karma to do an exact replica because that is his life story. Mine is an interpretation, which I designed myself, and was done for me by Otis Frizell, one of New Zealand's leading tattoo artists, who put his own stamp on the design. A few years later I had more moko done by a family friend, a woodcarver by trade, on the top of my back. It took six hours and is symbolic of my parents, my children, my brother and his children and my journey to England. The specific shapes and swirls describe my life journey thus far and, as a piece of living art, is added to over time as the story continues.The first addition was done when my grandmother died in 2006. I had the top of my left arm tattooed, with the centrepiece being a design known to be typical of my Iwi (tribe) and two interlocking koru (swirls) flowing away from one another and representing both of my late grandparents on my father's side. Smaller koru fan out from these two swirls, each representing my father's vast number of siblings.

The passing of Big Nan – Mary Paul of Ngati Hine – affected me deeply. I kept a journal from learning of her death to her burial...

Day one: After a rushed journey back from England, we touch down in Auckland and three generations of Pauls – my dad, Henry and I and Henry's daughter Milan – prepared to mourn the matriarch of our lineage. I am met again by the huge Maori carving that greets everyone to New Zealand. Straight away the impact of Maoridom is slapped across my face and the sobering reminder that we are not only here for a funeral but a Maori funeral. We are met by the living matriarch of my mother's line, Mary Allen. She is a very wise lady who has the ability to make all around her feel special. My grandmother tells us that Big Nan is at Tau Henere marae in Pipiwai where our whanau (family) laid their roots many moons ago.

After a three hour drive we finally arrive and reality hits. We stand on the threshold of the marae (meeting house) doorway. I catch glimpses of faces that seem so familiar. Henry and I follow behind my father as protocol demands. I catch a quick glimpse of Nan's coffin which is housed in the main room of the marae. My father's uncle, who was in the middle of a speech when we walked in, continues to speak. It's a surreal feeling. Another face, another cousin, another aunty. Some smile, some look at us and their defences fall and start to cry. We stop before the coffin and I look down upon Nan's face. She is sleeping. I push the tears back but it's okay. Nan knows who I am, unconditional aroha (love). I kiss her forehead, say a few words silently to her and then turn to see our whanau. As jet lag starts to take effect I grab Milan and we find a small gap between cousins and squeeze in next to them and we are asleep before our heads hit the pillow in the great hall along with our family and Big Nan.

Day two: *Today people have been arriving from all over the country. Nana Paul obviously had a huge amount of mana (respect). It is a beautiful day and we have been sitting around telling yarns of yesteryear and mischief we got up to when we were young. I think to myself, I know Nan would have a big smile on her face knowing we are all smiling as well.*

Day three: *After a long day of receiving more family, my cousins put on a special church service for the young children. As everyone readies for the final night with Nan in the marae before she makes her final journey it comes to the time for the passing of the tokotoko (a carved walking stick). When you are handed the stick you are expected to say who Nan was to you and what she meant ... when it came to me I said: "Kia ora Nan. When I think of you, I think of fried bread. Ha! No, seriously, fried bread. My memories are of you in the kitchen. We all know that she who controls the kitchen controls the house. I can picture you standing surrounded by us, your mokopuna (grandchildren) dolling* *out the orders and the fried bread. Nan, even though I live on the other side of the world, I am happy knowing what a beautiful whanau and culture we have. My mission for the rest of my life is to make you proud of me and my girls. I thank you for this last gift you have bestowed, to bring all of our family and whanau to this one place in time. Kia ora Nan, aroha mai aroha atu." I finish by singing 'Toru nga mea'- a song of love and happiness and am joined straight away by the hundred or so family members I am surrounded by.*

We buried Big Nan at Perana cemetery, her ancestral home. My last memories are of my father saying these final words to her in Maori: 'You have left us and you've gone to a better place for you; go back to your beginning, the spirit world and your whanau. There they will look after you, love you and they are waiting for you, so go, go, go...

In fact I experienced that wonderful sense of coming together in New Zealand again four years later but under very different circumstances. It was always our intention to marry in New Zealand in 2010. Natalie and I checked out various venues the year before and found the perfect spot in wine country in west Auckland. We took a 30-strong barmy army from England with us for the trip of a lifetime. Natalie had put her heart and soul into arranging everything from 12,000 miles away and we soared together on a cloud of happiness on our big day, helped by our extended *whanau* in New Zealand and the English branch of the family who were blown away by the intensity of the love of everyone there. There was a Cook Island dance performed by my nieces and nephews, speeches in Maori and English, stories and so much singing anyone would think they had stepped into the strangest West End musical.

Henry was best man, naturally, and it was wonderful to have there many of the people so key to me during my playing career – Frank Endacott, Peter Brown, Stacey Jones, Tahi Reihana, Joe Vagana and Phil Leuluai, my big mate at Salford. Henry once filled in for me at an after dinner speech engagement and died. He should have just used his best man's speech; it was brilliant. We honeymooned in Fiji where it took a couple of days for me to relax and come down to earth. It was between my penultimate and last season at Leigh, which partly explained the 6am gym sessions and daily beach sprints. Sleep is something I've never been all that good at. Not with a brain that is constantly whirring. I sleep with a portable DVD next to the bed. I will turn it on three or four times a night, watch for two minutes, then drift off again.

Natalie has put up with all that and a lot more. "I don't want a husband in a wheelchair," were her words to me when I was knocked unconscious early in my last season and sustained the nerve damage which affects me now. The records for that last 2011 season were no longer for Robbie Paul but my newly-married name of Robbie Hunter-Paul in sharing Natalie's surname. My mum is pretty liberal, my dad never stands in the way of new ideas and I'm not a stereotypical rugby league player. I do what I believe is best and it was a decision we made together in five seconds. It is inclusive, a sign of our love for one another and not a bad name all round I reckon, even though I had started off with the idea of Robbie Paul-Hunter. I was quickly outvoted by Natalie, my daughters and her three sisters on that one, which is something I've had to become used to. Quite right, too. I always joke that had her name been Pumpernickle we might have had a different conversation but I'll never know.

That determination for the sport not to beat me, knowing how many friends had been retired by rugby early, sustained me through to my final game with Leigh. The feeling when the siren went for the very last time was one of just how fortunate I had been. Eighteen years is a long time for any professional sports person, from unprecedented success with Bradford to my brief stint in rugby union at Harlequins, being part of the first Challenge Cup final appearance by Huddersfield Giants for many years, trophies at Salford and another last prized piece of silverware at Leigh.

In the dressing room, I got up and thanked the Leigh players and Ian Millward. No disappointments, no regrets but with a huge lump in my throat knowing that this was the last time. As I spoke, it was to a much wider room and a far bigger audience, one with Bernard Dwyer sitting there, Stacey Jones alongside him, Joe Vagana, Malcolm Alker, Brian Noble, Matty Elliott, Brian Smith, Daniel Anderson, Shaun McRae, all the assistants, trainers, backroom and administration staff there for me down the years and, behind them, New Zealand supporters, plus the fantastic fans of every club I played for. Eighteen joyous years. It was my honour and absolute privilege. Kia Ora! And please remember: enjoy life, love your families and live your rugby.

Feed the machine

Nutrition and professional sport walk hand in hand. Getting it right is never an easy thing and it seems every day we are introduced to a new piece of science that suggests we eat this and don't eat that. As an athlete you are hopping from foot to foot trying desperately to find out what is the next new thing that will help you reach your ultimate goal and peak performance.

Leading up to games was always a nervous time for me as I wanted to make sure I had the right amount of energy in me to get me through 80 minutes of mayhem. I wanted to feel light and energised, not as if I had a stomach full of food, and walking around dragging my knuckles on the ground (this happened on many occasions).

Getting this balance right was not only a physiological strength but psychologically beneficial. It meant I went into matches switched on. Getting the energy levels correct gives you a confidence needed to deliver your best, as sports nutrition expert Graeme Close explains here.

Biography

Dr Graeme L Close BSc (Hons), ASCC, PhD is a senior lecturer in sports nutrition and exercise metabolism at Liverpool John Moores University, where he leads the sports nutrition programmes at undergraduate and masters level. Graeme has published over 30 papers, reviews and book chapters on various aspects of sports nutrition and is regularly invited to speak at international meetings on the subject.

Alongside his academic teaching and research, Graeme is also the Head of Sports Nutrition at Munster Rugby in Ireland and works with a variety of athletes, including world class runners and professional jockeys, as well as providing nutrition consultancy to several Super League and Championship rugby league clubs.

Graeme is a former professional rugby league player himself, having played in the 1990s for Warrington, Workington and Leigh. Graeme has actually played against me on several occasions, including a 92-0 defeat for

Workington in the Challenge Cup in 1999 (not one of his finest playing career highlights). Indeed, it was during this game that Graeme told me he had his eureka moment and decided that a career change was required so he embarked upon a PhD in sports science.

Nutritional preparation for rugby matches: most leave it too late

Perhaps one of the most frequent questions I am asked as a sports nutrition consultant is what should I eat for my pre-game meal? Many players, including elite Super League players, have the misguided belief that this is the meal that will prepare them for the 80 minutes ahead. It is often a surprise to players when my answer is *whatever you really feel comfortable with*, providing you have prepared properly for about 24 hours prior to the game. Indeed, it is this 24 hours that many players get completely wrong.

An 80-minute rugby game places considerable demand on a player's store of carbohydrates. Carbohydrates are the main fuel for high-intensity exercise and these stores can be completely depleted after 60 minutes of high-intensity exercise. Considering that a rugby game is often 90 minutes (including stoppage time and warm-up) this is more than enough time to completely wipe out carbohydrate stores in making high-intensity efforts impossible.

It is therefore essential that rugby players eat a high carbohydrate diet for **approximately 24 hours prior to the game**. *For those of you interested in numbers, I usually advise about 8g of carbohydrate per kg of body weight in this 24 hour period, so if you weigh 80kg you should eat approximately 640g of carbohydrate (you can find the carb content of all foods on the back of the packet).* As well as "carbing up" it is also essential that players ensure they are fully hydrated ready for the game and are not deficient in any micronutrients as both of these factors could impair their performance. Table 1 below describes a typical 24-hour period prior to a game with regards to a player's nutritional intake.

Table 1:

Time	Food	Drink
8.30 am	Large bowl of Muesli or Porridge with banana and mixed berries. 3 poached eggs, 2 slices of wholegrain toast.	Glass of fruit juice (i.e. apple juice) Glass of water Tea of Coffee (if desired)
11.00 am	Wholegrain bagel with peanut or almond butter and jam.	Glass of water
1.00 pm	Chicken and basmati rice with a tomato based sauce and garlic bread, side serving of fresh vegetables. Berries mixed with Greek Yoghurt	Lucozade Sport and glass of water
3.00 pm	2 oat based flapjacks (make your own!)	Glass of water
6.00 pm	Meat or fish with mashed potatoes (2 large), serving of steamed vegetables. Banana muffin with custard	Bottle of chocolate milk
9.00 pm	Cottage cheese on 2 slices wholegrain toast	Glass of water with electrolytes (such as Dioralyte)

On **MATCH DAY** I usually ask my players to count back 3 ½ hours from kick-off to time their pre-game meal, i.e. if it is a 3pm kick-off I would like my players to start eating about 11.30 am and be finished eating by noon. The reason for this is to give the food sufficient time to digest. Eating food later could lead to gastrointestinal discomfort and impair performance. This meal must contain a good amount of carbohydrates but you SHOULD NOT stuff yourself at this meal. If you believe this is the time to carb load, you have left it too late. *For those interested in numbers, you should be eating 1-2g per kg body weight of carbohydrate at this meal (i.e. about 160g for an 80kg player).* It is crucial that this meal consists of easily digested foods and, therefore, I ask players to avoid red meat, lots of vegetables and fruits with edible skins. I also ensure that players are well hydrated at this meal, by encouraging them to drink 1-2 glasses of water that has had some electrolytes added (often as simple as a Dioralyte sachet from the local chemist). An example of a typical game day meal plan for a 3pm kick-off can be seen in Table 2.

Table 2:

Time	Food	Drink
8.00 am	Fresh peeled fruit with Natural Greek Yoghurt Bowl of Muesli with milk 2 egg omelette with ham and tomatoes.	Glass of fruit juice (i.e. apple juice) Glass of water
11.30 pm PRE GAME MEAL	Fish or Chicken with basmati rice. Rice pudding with jam and banana.	Glass of fruit juice Glass of water with electrolytes added (Dioralyte)
2.30 pm (pre warm up)*	Carbohydrate gel or	Bottle of isotonic sports drink (i.e. Powerade, Lucozade Sport, Gatorade etc).
3.00 pm	Kick Off	
Half-time	Carbohydrate gel or	Bottle of isotonic sports drink (i.e. Powerade, Lucozade Sport, Gatorade etc).

*Occasionally players do not tolerate any carbohydrates well before a game and these players should simply drink water at this stage.

RH-P: Take it from someone who has used the above approach, I followed this to the letter and it became a huge part of my recipe for success. I am confident that "feeding the machine" properly is as important to your success as an athlete as working out in the gym. To be the best you must try to find the best balance of ingredients for what makes you compete at your peak. It will take some trial and error, but the pay-offs will be worth it.

To find out more or contact Graeme Close, follow him on Twitter at @close_nutrition

Afterword

by Henry Paul

There are stories only brothers can tell. I caught Rob once clearing his dish of mum's rice and pineapple risotto out of the pantry window. It was something we did as kids if we didn't like what she'd cooked – sorry mum! – but this night I decided to tell her. Rob begged me not to. Being the clever one, I seized the opportunity. I made little brother my slave. He spent the next two days making the breakfast, doing the fire and any menial jobs I could find for him. It was as he was doing the washing up that he exploded.

The tale of him picking up the machete, which was used for chopping up kindling, is touched on by Rob in these pages, but not what prompted him to throw it at me. A dish wasn't washed quite properly and I put it back in the sink. By that time he was broken. He didn't care whether I told mum about the risotto. I just kept calling out for mum louder and louder. When he picked up the machete, I ran outside calling him names. I ran to the other side of the swimming pool, still winding him up. It was at that point his face turned from red to white and he launched the machete at me. It flew in an arc towards my head. I barely had time to duck as it clanged into the fence behind me. Mum hit the roof. We were dragged to see dad by our ears. Rob's minor punishment was to do his homework, mine was to spend four hours with dad passing him his tools as he fixed up the car. I learned a valuable lesson that night never to wind up my brother when there's a machete to hand and dad is working on his car, because it can be a long night.

When Rob came on the scene, it was great having a brother who you could create lots of games with – floor hockey, corridor cricket, sofa tackle. But with him being two years younger, it was me who always copped the blame for anything. "Henry made me play it/do it/use it/throw it/catch it/hit it/hide under it," he'd tell mum. It made it hard not to want to bully him. Rob was too honest. He could have just made stuff up like me, but he had no cunning as a kid. He was easily talked into things, like the time we watched a rugby league match and noticed that the players had grease smeared around their eyes and over their ears. I looked in the medicine cabinet and found some stuff that looked like what the players had on their faces. I made sure the corners of Rob's eyes were really thick with it. How was I to know it was tiger balm? I rushed half blind into mum's room and Rob was crying his eyes out. Asked what happened, Rob came out with his standard response: "Henry made me do it."

Here's a list of a few things I got busted for over the years that Rob never took any heat for: climbing on to the roof of the house and bombing into the pool; catching eels in the estuary and releasing them into the pool; taking our uncle's motorbike to the beach and riding the mud flats (well, mostly me but Rob helped push start the bike); building an awesome tree hut in the park but leaving some of dad's tools there; painting a bombed out car that dad was using for spare parts into the "General Lee" from the Dukes of Hazzard (again, probably me, but Rob did remark that it was a good paint job).

We were into kung fu and karate. I was obsessed with being Bruce Lee and also took up taekwondo, for which Rob didn't have the patience. He hated me for it because I would use him to practice kicks, punches and "death grip" combinations. Oh, and I made him call me "master". If he didn't, I'd kick him round the house and tell him that it's all about learning discipline. That's if I could catch him. I always put his evasion skills down to me. When it came to rugby, I was good at winning trophies and prizes. It came as a small shock to see Rob winning those same prizes and trophies two years later. I used to count my trophies on prize day and it was always a good day if I got more than Rob. Not that he cared less. He was more interested in the cakes and sweets on offer.

Rob wasn't as dedicated a trainer as me. Rain or shine, I'd do extra kicking practice before Saturday morning games. Rob didn't kick goals, so didn't train that aspect of his game, although he still boasts about his 100 per cent Super League goal-kicking record – two from two. But rugby probably came more naturally to him. He was a foot quicker than me in any race. He didn't mind mixing it with bigger, older kids. We would work on our side-steps and spin moves and wind up the big guys who couldn't catch the two skinny, freckly kids. Rob's two best mates, Wendell and Ueta, who used to be at our home pretty much all the time, were good guys who looked after Rob, along with Warwick and Dean, his other friends, who I'd tease all the time. Thinking about it, I wonder why they ever became my friends too in the long run.

When I signed for Wakefield in 1993, I only imagined I'd be staying for four months, then returning home and preparing for my contract with Auckland Warriors. When we started to win games, there was a real feel good factor at Wakefield, plus Wigan were interested in me. Mum told me in a call home that Canberra Raiders were interested in Rob, but I told her not to rush anything. I asked David McKnight, my agent, to put together a plan to try and get Rob to England, which I thought would be a great move for him and for me having little bro with me.

Wakefield were keen for Rob and me to play together at Belle Vue but hesitated over small details. I admired Wigan's focus and commitment to secure me, while Dave began talking to Bradford Northern about Rob. They were in a hurry to sign a replacement forward due to injury. I think there was some poetic licence used by Dave to entice them to sign Rob. Bradford expected a 16 stone powerhouse prop forward from the New Zealand bush to rumble the hard yards. Instead they got a near 12 stone, 18-year-old half back who had never lived away from home.

Our first experience against one another in a Wigan-Bradford match was better for me than Rob, who was playing out of position at full back. We kicked bombs to him all afternoon. It only took a season for Rob to establish himself at Bradford. In that time the old Bradford had been reborn and rebranded by the vision of new Australian coach Brian Smith and his backroom staff. Rob became the youngest Super League captain and the Bulls became a force to reckon with. They were a major thorn in my backside and Robbie Paul, my bro, annoyingly, became their key man to watch. He was a threat with the ball in hand, because he had great change of pace and he was always in support of Bradford's big men. Rob would take advantage of their offloads and finish lots of tries off. To top it off, you had to contend with his strength. For a small guy, he had probably the best overall strength to size ratio in the Super League.

Thankfully, I wasn't always on the receiving end of Rob's game. I got to benefit from his runs and offloads when we started playing together with New Zealand. I was really proud for him when he made the Super League Nines team in 1997. When New Zealand won the competition in Townsville in Australia, I realised how much a world-class player Rob was becoming. Our first Test match together was in 1998 and it was a great playing experience. The trip Down Under was less glamorous on cattle class from northern England to Auckland, a trip of about 30 hours. The good thing about being brothers is that you can sleep on each other, and when you moan about how long the journey's taking, you know the other person has heard all your whining before.

That international against Australia at North Harbour Stadium is one I will cherish forever. Australia had a team full of Rugby League greats in Darren Lockyer, Andrew Johns, Terry Hill, Steve Renouf, Paul Harragon, Geoff Toovey, Steve Menzies, Brad Thorn, Brad Fittler, Glenn Lazarus, Laurie Daley and Wendell Sailor. Our squad were all top players in the National Rugby League competition in Australia and New Zealand, with just Rob and myself from Super League, which the Australians liked to look down on. We had worked well with Frank Endacott, the coach, in the past, and he asked Rob and I not to be afraid to have a go, work our guts out, then let the boys do the rest. We lost our prop John Lomax from the first hit up of the game, then went 12-2 down inside 30 minutes. Most people would have probably thought the game was over but we dug deep, battled up field and Rob set up a great try to make it 12-8 at half-time. As we jogged off, Matthew Ridge, our captain, taunted the Aussies that they were finished.

I earned the nickname "Crowbar" in that game, because I ran so much you needed a crowbar to get the ball off me. Rob was the best player on the pitch and had an amazing game. Two of his best runs set up tries. In defence he was everywhere, always adding to the tackle as third or fourth man, then rolling out and back in the line. Kevin Iro, a hero for both of us when we were growing up, rounded off the night with an amazing solo try out of nothing that Rob likes to take credit for with an assist pass. That night in Auckland after a 22-16 victory was great, the Kiwis were the toast of the country, Rob and I spent most of the night together catching up with friends and the 30 hour trip back didn't seem so long.

I like to think we're both generally humble people. We shared our sporting success and always acknowledged the help of others in fulfilling our goals. Sometimes there was an air of arrogance, usually brought out because we were extreme in our training regimes and total intensity was what we expected of ourselves and our team-mates. No one likes a slacker in rugby, as it just means you have to do more work on the field. We are both able to handle having the mickey taken out of us, most of the time. For instance, look at Rob. He has a big head and a little body. It's a fact that he has to step into his clothes in the morning his head's that big! I remind him often about the size of his swede. It's what brothers are for.

Rob is a bit more conservative when speaking up, whereas I like to be heard. Rob is more reflective and will spend more time considering options. When I think something needs to be said, I will quickly fire in with suggestions to fix things. This method doesn't always endear you to coaches and management. Maybe that is why I wasn't captaincy material. Rob communicates really well and he can relate to all types of people, young or old and from all sorts of backgrounds. He has an easy going manner but with a steely resolve. He had the temperament to last as a team captain for as long as he did. I can't think of any players who played with Rob who didn't rate him as a good captain.

He learned to give good direction and followed this up with his actions. Rob also tells the story in this book of us blowing up at each other during a game at Halifax. Let me add my perspective: I had tried to disobey Rob's command to kick the ball out of play and end the first half; Rob had wanted to regroup in the dressing sheds; I had seen it as a great chance to get down the field and possibly score before half-time. As I went to tap the ball, Rob snatched it from me and kicked it into touch. I was furious in giving him a mouthful as we trooped off. I continued in the changing room. Rob's body language remained relaxed and he again spelled out his case about regrouping. The next minute, Stu Fielden, James Lowes and Brian McDermott, who you don't argue with, were between us and giving me a mouthful. I backed off, sat down next to Rob and we smiled at one another as if to say, what's their problem, we're only having a chat about the game? The point was that Rob had ultimate respect within the team, his word was law and I had to get with it or get out, because he knew what was best for us. We ended up winning by 50 points.

Bradford was a good club when I joined in 1999, pieces of the Bulls' puzzle were already in place and plans were in train to make the club even better. One crucial element of a good team is quality banter in helping team spirit. There was no shortage of that at Bradford. I took plenty of stick for signing with Gloucester in switching to rugby union, but the only person I really confided in about the nervousness I felt leaving a club with great coaches, great players and a great playing system was Rob. On the face of it, Gloucester seemed a strange choice, but Rob was right behind my move after the 2001 Super League season. "Don't moan about playing in the winter again," he said. "I know you want a new challenge and to be among the first in switching from rugby league to rugby union, but be good at it. Show everyone at Gloucester what you can do – and don't kick the ball, run it."

Our last game together, as Rob has documented, was the 2001 Grand Final against Wigan at Old Trafford. Rob describes it as the perfect match. It was a dream game for every Bradford player. Brian Noble got the tactics and selection policy spot on. Rob led the team magnificently. You could hear the excitement in his voice when he addressed us beforehand. We were up against a class Wigan outfit, but the Bulls were very special that day. It was strange knowing with 30 minutes still to go that the game was won. We lifted the trophy in front of our fans, me on one side, Rob on the other. Not bad for a kid who couldn't stomach his pineapple risotto, but what a player!

Henry Paul won the Challenge Cup and Super League with Wigan Warriors and Bradford Bulls. He played for New Zealand in the 1995 and 2000 rugby league World Cups and switched codes in 2001, representing England on six occasions.

The Finals Countdown

My playing career was defined to a large degree by finals. I played in 20 of them and went through enough heartache to get the rewards – three Super League Grand Final rings, two Challenge Cup winners' medals, a World Club Challenge medal and another for winning the Middlesex Sevens, all with Bradford Bulls, including a clean sweep of prizes in 2003; Northern Rail Cup final successes with Salford City Reds and Leigh Centurions; and a Championship Grand Final victory with Salford. I'm acutely aware of the flipside to being beaten on the big stage – Bradford never managed in my time there to get over our bogey team in a final, St Helens – and while I enjoyed my share of wins over Australia, I was part of the New Zealand team that lost the 2000 World Cup final to them. All my finals, though, were in their own way memorable.

BRADFORD BULLS, 1994-2005
(Played 305, Tries 156, Goals 3, Points 630)

Honours: Super League champions 1997, 2001, 2003, 2005; beaten Grand Finalists 1999, 2002, 2004. Challenge Cup winners 2000, 2003; beaten finalists 1996, 1997, 2001. World Club Challenge winners 2002; 2002 Middlesex Sevens winners

1996 Challenge Cup Final
Wembley Stadium, April 27

Bradford Bulls 32 St Helens 40

Three tries by Robbie Paul – the first hat-trick performed in a Wembley Challenge Cup final – but alas no cigar. Bradford were 26-12 up but were undone by Bobbie Goulding's aerial bombardment that produced three St Helens tries in a devastating seven minutes. Robbie added his third with a scintillating effort in earning him the Lance Todd Trophy as man of the match, but St Helens secured their cup triumph in a classic final with Apollo Perelini's 75th minute touchdown.

Scorers: *Bradford Bulls:* Tries: Paul 3, Scales, Dwyer. Goals: Cook 6. *St Helens:* Tries: Prescott 2, Arnold 2, Cunningham, Booth, Pickavance, Perelini. Goals: Goulding 4.

Bradford Bulls: Nathan Graham; Paul Cook, Matt Calland, Paul Loughlin, Jon Scales; Graeme Bradley, Robbie Paul (captain); Brian McDermott, Bernard Dwyer, Jon Hamer, Jeremy Donougher, Sonny Nickle, Simon Knox. Substitutes: Karl Fairbank, Paul Medley, Jason Donohue, Carlos Hassan. Coach: Brian Smith.

St Helens: Steve Prescott; Danny Arnold, Scott Gibbs, Paul Newlove, Anthony Sullivan; Karle Hammond, Bobbie Goulding (captain); Apollo Perelini, Keiron Cunningham, Andy Leathem, Chris Joynt, Simon Booth, Andy Northey. Substitutes: Tommy Martyn, Ian Pickavance, Vila Matautia, Alan Hunte. Coach: Shaun McRae.

Referee: Stuart Cummings. Attendance: 75,994.

1997 Challenge Cup Final
Wembley Stadium, May 3

Bradford Bulls 22 St Helens 32

St Helens retained the cup at the expense of Robbie's Bradford in beating the Bulls for a second year. Robbie injured his foot and little went right for the Bulls, despite them leading early through tries by Danny Peacock and Paul Loughlin. St Helens were inspired by Tommy Martyn's two tries and his creation of two more, while Bobbie Goulding, their captain, landed six goals in passing 1,000 points for the club. Tries late on by Glen Tomlinson and James Lowes were never going to trouble the outcome.

Scorers: *Bradford Bulls:* Tries: Peacock, Loughlin, Tomlinson, Lowes. Goals: McNamara 3. *St Helens:* Tries: Martyn 2, Hammond, Joynt, Sullivan. Goals: Goulding 6.

Bradford Bulls: Stuart Spruce; Abi Ekoku, Danny Peacock, Paul Loughlin, Paul Cook; Graeme Bradley, Robbie Paul (captain); Brian McDermott, James Lowes, Tahi Reihana, Sonny Nickle, Bernard Dwyer, Steve McNamara. Substitutes: Paul Medley, Matt Calland, Glen Tomlinson, Simon Knox. Coach: Matthew Elliott.

St Helens: Steve Prescott; Danny Arnold, Andy Haigh, Paul Newlove, Anthony Sullivan; Tommy Martyn, Bobbie Goulding (captain); Apollo Perelini, Keiron Cunningham, Julian O'Neill, Chris Joynt, Derek McVey, Karle Hammond. Substitutes: Ian Pickavance, Vila Matautia, Andy Northey, Chris Morley. Coach: Shaun McRae.

Referee: Stuart Cummings. Attendance: 78,022.

1999 Super League Grand Final
Old Trafford, October 9

Bradford Bulls 6 St Helens 8

Hot favourites blew their Grand Final chance and opportunity to banish the St Helens bogey. Bradford began well, with Henry Paul – minus a boot – scoring a magnificent 60 metre solo effort. However, just as Robbie did at Wembley three years earlier, Henry collected the Harry Sunderland Trophy man of the match prize in a beaten cause. Whether Michael Withers touched the ball in flight or not in having a crucial score ruled out, Sean Long's touchline conversion of Kevin Iro's try sealed another Saints victory.

Scorers: *Bradford Bulls:* Try: H Paul. Goal: H Paul. *St Helens:* Try: Iro. Goals: Long 2.

Bradford Bulls: Stuart Spruce; Tevita Vaikona, Scott Naylor, Michael Withers, Leon Pryce; Henry Paul, Robbie Paul (captain); Paul Anderson, James Lowes, Stuart Fielden, David Boyle, Bernard Dwyer, Steve McNamara. Substitutes: Paul Deacon, Mike Forshaw, Brian McDermott, Nathan McAvoy. Coach: Matthew Elliott.

St Helens: Paul Atcheson; Chris Smith, Kevin Iro, Paul Newlove, Anthony Sullivan; Paul Sculthorpe, Tommy Martyn; Apollo Perelini, Keiron Cunningham, Julian O'Neill, Fereti Tuilagi, Sonny Nickle, Chris Joynt (captain). Substitutes: Paul Wellens, Sean Hoppe, Vila Matautia, Sean Long. Coach: Ellery Hanley.

Referee: Stuart Cummings. Attendance: 50,717.

2000 Challenge Cup Final
Murrayfield, April 29

Bradford Bulls 24 Leeds Rhinos 18

Four years in the making in rugby league's summer era but Bradford's heartache in major finals ended in Robbie and Henry lifting the Challenge Cup together. Edinburgh had been deluged in the days before the final and Henry emulated his brother by picking up the Lance Todd Trophy after his clever targeting of Leroy Rivett under the high ball caused Leeds to fall apart. A brace of tries by Michael Withers, another by Stuart Fielden and Henry's four goals allowed Bradford to finally throw the final monkey off their backs.

Scorers: *Bradford Bulls:* Tries: Withers 2, McAvoy, Fielden. Goals: H Paul 4. *Leeds Rhinos:* Tries: Hay, St Hilaire. Goals: Harris 5.

Bradford Bulls: Stuart Spruce; Nathan McAvoy, Scott Naylor, Michael Withers, Tevita Vaikona; Henry Paul, Robbie Paul (captain); Brian McDermott, James Lowes, Paul Anderson, Jamie Peacock, Mike Forshaw, Graham Mackay. Substitutes: Leon Pryce, David Boyle, Bernard Dwyer, Stuart Fielden. Coach: Matthew Elliott.

Leeds Rhinos: Iestyn Harris (captain); Leroy Rivett, Richie Blackmore, Keith Senior, Francis Cummins; Daryl Powell, Ryan Sheridan; Darren Fleary, Dean Lawford, Barrie McDermott, Adrian Morley, Anthony Farrell, Andy Hay. Substitutes: Lee Jackson, David Barnhill, Marcus St Hilaire, Jamie Mathiou. Coach: Dean Lance.

Referee: Steve Presley. Attendance: 67,247.

2001 Challenge Cup Final
Twickenham, April 28

Bradford Bulls 6 St Helens 13

The 100th Challenge Cup final at the home of English rugby union in the second year away from Wembley while the new stadium was built proved as drab as the weather. Bradford failed to summon up a try as St Helens maintained their hex over them in major finals. Sean Long was an overwhelming Lance Todd Trophy winner as first half tries by Tommy Martyn and Keiron Cunningham secured St Helens their eighth Challenge Cup success in a century. All the Bulls could muster were three penalty goals by Henry Paul.

Scorers: *Bradford Bulls:* Goals: H Paul 3. *St Helens:* Tries: Martyn, Cunningham. Goals: Long 2. Drop goal: Long.

Bradford Bulls: Michael Withers; Tevita Vaikona, Scott Naylor, Shane Rigon, Leon Pryce; Henry Paul, Robbie Paul (captain); Joe Vagana, James Lowes, Brian McDermott, Jamie Peacock, Daniel Gartner, Mike Forshaw. Substitutes: Paul Deacon, Paul Anderson, Lee Gilmour, Stuart Fielden. Coach: Brian Noble.

St Helens: Paul Wellens; Sean Hoppe, Kevin Iro, Paul Newlove, Anthony Sullivan; Tommy Martyn, Sean Long; Sonny Nickle, Keiron Cunningham, David Fairleigh, Chris Joynt (captain), Peter Shiels, Paul Sculthorpe. Substitutes: Tim Jonkers, Vila Matautia, Steve Hall, Anthony Stewart. Coach: Ian Millward.

Referee: Russell Smith. Attendance: 68,250.

2001 Super League Grand Final
Old Trafford, October 13

Bradford Bulls 37 Wigan Warriors 6

Rated the perfect match by Robbie as Henry signed off from Bradford with an exhilarating performance in harness with his brother. The Bulls' sibling half back combination was the heartbeat of a superlative Bradford display. After two Grand Final losses to St Helens, Robbie savoured the moment as he lifted the trophy. The game was over at half-time when Bradford led 26-0 after a hat-trick of tries in 31 minutes by Michael Withers after an early touchdown by James Lowes. Bradford put the game to bed after the break.

Scorers: *Bradford Bulls:* Tries: Lowes, Withers 3, Fielden, Mackay. Goals: H Paul 5, Mackay. Drop goal: H Paul. *Wigan Warriors:* Try: Lam. Goal: Furner.

Bradford Bulls: Michael Withers; Tevita Vaikona, Scott Naylor, Graham Mackay, Leon Pryce; Henry Paul, Robbie Paul (captain); Joe Vagana, James Lowes, Brian McDermott, Daniel Gartner, Jamie Peacock, Mike Forshaw. Substitutes: Stuart Fielden, Paul Anderson, Shane Rigon, Paul Deacon. Coach: Brian Noble.

Wigan Warriors: Kris Radlinski; Brett Dallas, Gary Connolly, Steve Renouf, Brian Carney; Matthew Johns, Adrian Lam; Terry O'Connor, Terry Newton, Harvey Howard, Mick Cassidy, David Furner, Andy Farrell (captain). Substitutes: Paul Johnson, Neil Cowie, Denis Betts, Chris Chester. Coach: Stuart Raper.

Referee: Stuart Cummings. Attendance: 60,164.

2002 World Club Challenge
McAlpine Stadium, Huddersfield

Bradford Bulls 41 Newcastle Knights 26

In the first match after Henry's departure, Robbie produced a wonderful two-try display in leading Bradford to being crowned World Club champions for the first time. Robbie's first half brace put the Bulls on course to glory on a filthy night when Andrew Johns, the Golden Boot winner as world player of the year, found himself upstaged by Bradford's captain. The quick thinking and vision of James Lowes continued the good work in the second half as Lesley Vainikolo crossed for a try on his debut and Michael Withers added his second.

Scorers: *Bradford Bulls:* Tries: Paul 2, Gartner, Withers 2, Vainikolo. Goals: Deacon 8. Drop goal: Deacon. *Newcastle Knights:* Tries: Smith, Johns 2, M Gidley, Buderus. Goals: Johns 3.

Bradford Bulls: Michael Withers; Tevita Vaikona, Scott Naylor, Lee Gilmour, Lesley Vainikolo; Robbie Paul (captain), Paul Deacon; Joe Vagana, James Lowes, Brian McDermott, Jamie Peacock, Daniel Gartner, Mike Forshaw. Substitutes: Stuart Fielden, Paul Anderson, Leon Pryce, Brandon Costin. Coach: Brian Noble.

Newcastle Knights: Robbie O'Davis; Josh Smith, Matt Gidley, Mark Hughes, Kurt Gidley; Sean Rudder, Andrew Johns (captain); Josh Perry, Danny Buderus, Matt Parsons, Daniel Abraham, Steve Simpson, Bill Peden. Substitutes: Matt Jobson, Clinton O'Brien, John Morris, Clint Newton. Coach: Michael Hagan.

Referee: Stuart Cummings. Attendance: 21,113.

*** Robbie was injured for Bradford's 22-4 defeat of Penrith Panthers in the 2004 World Club Challenge at Huddersfield.**

2002 Middlesex Sevens Final
Twickenham, August 17

Bradford Bulls 42 Wasps 14

Robbie's Bulls put on an exhibition in the prestigious rugby union sevens event at Twickenham in which they swept all-comers aside, including brother Henry's Gloucester in the quarter-finals. The Army was dispatched in the semis and Wasps simply could not handle Bradford in the final. Their tries by Paul Sampson and Josh Lewsey were meagre consolation after Tevita Vaikona had toyed with them for the opening try, followed by Leon Pryce going over and Michael Withers claiming two tries and Nathan McAvoy and John Feeley scoring others in a tour de force.

Scorers: *Bradford Bulls:* Tries: Vaikona, Pryce, Withers 2, McAvoy, Feeley. *Wasps:* Tries: Sampson, Lewsey.

Bradford Bulls squad: Robbie Paul (captain); Tevita Vaikona, Leon Pryce, Lesley Vainikolo, Michael Withers, Brandon Costin, Rob Parker, Nathan McAvoy, Lee Gilmour, John Feeley, Mark Sewerby, Jon Skurr.

2002 Super League Grand Final
Old Trafford

Bradford Bulls 18 St Helens 19

A highly controversial Grand Final for an ending in which St Helens captain Chris Joynt dropped to his knees on the last play and Bradford's appeals for a voluntary tackle were waved away by referee Russell Smith. Rather than a penalty to win the game, the Bulls had lost to a Sean Long drop goal with 51 seconds left on the clock. They were also denied a try by Paul Deacon, which officials later admitted they got wrong. The second of Bradford's three tries by Robbie proved a false dawn for his team.

Scorers: *Bradford Bulls:* Tries: Naylor, Paul, Withers. Goals: Deacon 3. *St Helens:* Tries: Bennett, Long, Gleeson. Goals: Long 3. Drop goal: Long.

Bradford Bulls: Michael Withers; Tevita Vaikona, Scott Naylor, Brandon Costin, Lesley Vainikolo; Robbie Paul (captain), Paul Deacon; Joe Vagana, James Lowes, Stuart Fielden, Daniel Gartner, Jamie Peacock, Mike Forshaw. Substitutes: Lee Gilmour, Paul Anderson, Brian McDermott, Leon Pryce. Coach: Brian Noble.

St Helens: Paul Wellens; Darren Albert, Martin Gleeson, Paul Newlove, Anthony Stewart; Paul Sculthorpe, Sean Long; Darren Britt, Keiron Cunningham, Barry Ward, Mike Bennett, Tim Jonkers, Chris Joynt (captain). Substitutes: Sean Hoppe, Peter Shiels, John Stankevitch, Mick Higham. Coach: Ian Millward.

Referee: Russell Smith. Attendance: 61,138.

2003 Challenge Cup Final
Millennium Stadium, Cardiff, April 26

Bradford Bulls 22 Leeds Rhinos 20

Robbie grabbed Bradford's opening try in the first indoors final. The roof of the Millennium Stadium was shut and the atmosphere electric as the two West Yorkshire giants traded blow for blow. Jamie Peacock was magnificent for the Bulls and unfortunate to miss out on the Lance Todd Trophy to Gary Connolly, one of three Leeds try scorers. Kevin Sinfield spurned a kickable penalty in the 73rd minute when two points behind and paid the price as the Bulls defended for their lives in a thrilling finale.

Scorers: *Bradford Bulls:* Tries: Paul, Vainikolo, Peacock. Goals: Deacon 5. *Leeds Rhinos:* Connolly, McKenna, Furner. Goals: Sinfield 4.
Bradford Bulls: Robbie Paul (captain); Tevita Vaikona, Scott Naylor, Shontayne Hape, Lesley Vainikolo; Leon Pryce, Paul Deacon; Joe Vagana, James Lowes, Daniel Gartner, Lee Radford, Jamie Peacock, Mike Forshaw. Substitutes: Paul Anderson, Lee Gilmour, Karl Pratt, Rob Parker. Coach: Brian Noble.

Leeds Rhinos: Gary Connolly; Mark Calderwood, Chris McKenna, Keith Senior, Francis Cummins; Kevin Sinfield (captain), Andrew Dunemann; Ryan Bailey, Matt Diskin, Barrie McDermott, Chev Walker, Matt Adamson, David Furner. Substitutes: Rob Burrow, Danny Ward, Willie Poching, Wayne McDonald. Coach: Daryl Powell.

Referee: Russell Smith. Attendance: 71,212.

2003 Super League Grand Final
Old Trafford, October 18

Bradford Bulls 25 Wigan Warriors 12

A superhuman effort by Robbie in returning from a badly broken arm, interchanging at hooker from the bench with James Lowes, with whom he raised the Super League trophy on another heady Old Trafford night for Bradford against Wigan. The Bulls, under Brian Noble's inspirational stewardship, became the first club to win the Challenge Cup and the Super League Grand Final in the same season. Lowes poached his 99th Bulls try and Stuart Reardon, an unknown at the start of the season, completed a remarkable first season in collecting the Harry Sunderland Trophy.

Scorers: *Bradford Bulls:* Tries: Reardon, Hape, Lowes. Goals: Deacon 6. Drop goal: Deacon. *Wigan Warriors:* Tries: Tickle, Radlinski. Goals: Farrell 2.

Bradford Bulls: Stuart Reardon; Tevita Vaikona, Michael Withers, Shontayne Hape, Lesley Vainikolo; Karl Pratt, Paul Deacon; Joe Vagana, James Lowes, Stuart Fielden, Daniel Gartner, Jamie Peacock, Mike Forshaw. Substitutes: Paul Anderson, Lee Radford, Leon Pryce, Robbie Paul (captain). Coach: Brian Noble.

Wigan Warriors: Kris Radlinski; Brian Carney, Martin Aspinwall, David Hodgson, Brett Dallas; Sean O'Loughlin, Luke Robinson; Quentin Pongia, Terry Newton, Craig Smith, Mick Cassidy, Danny Tickle, Andy Farrell (captain). Substitutes: Paul Johnson, Terry O'Connor, Gareth Hock, Mark Smith. Coach: Mike Gregory.

Referee: Karl Kirkpatrick. Attendance: 65,537.

2004 Super League Grand Final
Old Trafford, October 16

Bradford Bulls 8 Leeds Rhinos 16

It was not to be for Bradford in a third major final in four years against their arch derby rivals. Robbie audaciously looped a pass behind his back in helping set up an early try for Lesley Vainikolo, before Matt Diskin pulled one back. Shontayne Hape struck back for the Bulls but the pressure told on Bradford when Robbie dropped the ball late on as he shaped to pass. Leeds needed no second invitation from the scrum as Danny McGuire took Keith Senior's pass for the decisive touchdown, with Kevin Sinfield adding his fourth goal.

Scorers: *Bradford Bulls:* Tries: Vainikolo, Hape. *Leeds Rhinos:* Diskin, McGuire. Goals: Sinfield 4.

Bradford Bulls: Michael Withers; Stuart Reardon, Paul Johnson, Shontayne Hape, Lesley Vainikolo; Iestyn Harris, Paul Deacon; Joe Vagana, Robbie Paul (captain), Stuart Fielden, Jamie Peacock, Logan Swann, Lee Radford. Substitutes: Paul Anderson, Karl Pratt, Rob Parker, Jamie Langley. Coach: Brian Noble.

Leeds Rhinos: Richard Mathers; Mark Calderwood, Chev Walker, Keith Senior, Marcus Bai; Kevin Sinfield (captain), Danny McGuire; Danny Ward, Matt Diskin, Ryan Bailey, Chris McKenna, Ali Lauitiiti, David Furner. Substitutes: Willie Poching, Barrie McDermott, Rob Burrow, Jamie Jones-Buchanan. Coach: Tony Smith.

Referee: Steve Ganson. Attendance: 65,547.

2005 Super League Grand Final
Old Trafford, October 15

Bradford Bulls 15 Leeds Rhinos 6

Self belief coursed through the Bulls as they completed their unlikeliest of Grand Final triumphs from third place in Super League – a 12th successive win in an unstoppable run from July. It was the last hurrah for several of their players, including Robbie, and out of the turmoil at the club in the middle of the season came arguably the Bulls' greatest triumph. It was completed with tries by Leon Pryce and Lesley Vainikolo, while Paul Deacon landed three goals and Iestyn Harris a drop goal in marking Robbie's farewell to the club after 12 years.

Scorers: *Bradford Bulls:* Pryce, Vainikolo. Goals: Deacon 3. Drop goal: I Harris. *Leeds Rhinos:* Try: McGuire. Goal: Sinfield.

Bradford Bulls: Michael Withers; Leon Pryce, Ben Harris, Shontayne Hape, Lesley Vainikolo; Iestyn Harris, Paul Deacon; Jamie Peacock (captain), Ian Henderson, Stuart Fielden, Paul Johnson, Brad Meyers, Lee Radford. Substitutes: Adrian Morley, Jamie Langley, Joe Vagana, Robbie Paul. Coach: Brian Noble.

Leeds Rhinos: Richard Mathers; Mark Calderwood, Chev Walker, Chris McKenna, Marcus Bai; Danny McGuire, Rob Burrow; Ryan Bailey, Andrew Dunemann, Danny Ward, Gareth Ellis, Willie Poching, Kevin Sinfield (captain). Substitutes: Barrie McDermott, Ali Lauitiiti, Jamie Jones-Buchanan, Matt Diskin. Coach: Tony Smith.

Referee: Ashley Klein. Attendance: 65,537.

HUDDERSFIELD GIANTS 2006-07
(Played 60, Tries 14, Goals 0, Points 56)

Honours: Challenge Cup beaten finalists 2006.

2006 Challenge Cup Final
Twickenham, August 26

Huddersfield Giants 12 St Helens 42

Huddersfield set off like a house on fire and led early through a Martin Aspinwall try. The Giants only trailed 12-6 at the interval to tries by Willie Talau and Sean Long, who collected a record third Lance Todd Trophy award. However, the Giants ran out of steam and Saints applied their afterburners. Jon Wilkin defied a broken nose to cross twice and there were further tries by Maurie Fa'asavalu, Jamie Lyon and Jason Cayless, which all rendered Robbie's 70th minute second try for Huddersfield meagre consolation as Saints get the better of him one final time.

Scorers: *Huddersfield Giants:* Tries: Aspinwall, Paul. Goals: De Vere 2. *St Helens:* Tries: Talau, Long, Wilkin 2, Fa'asavalu, Lyon, Cayless. Goals: Lyon 7.

Huddersfield Giants: Paul Reilly; Martin Aspinwall, Chris Nero, Michael De Vere, Stuart Donlan; Chris Thorman (captain), Robbie Paul; Paul Jackson, Brad Drew, Jim Gannon, Eorl Crabtree, Andy Raleigh, Stephen Wild. Substitutes: Steve Snitch, Stuart Jones, Paul Smith, Wayne McDonald. Coach: Jon Sharp.

St Helens: Paul Wellens; Ade Gardner, Jamie Lyon, Willie Talau, Francis Meli; Leon Pryce, Sean Long; Paul Anderson, Keiron Cunningham, Jason Cayless, Jon Wilkin, Paul Sculthorpe (captain), Jason Hooper. Substitutes: Lee Gilmour, James Roby, James Graham, Maurie Fa'asavalu. Coach: Daniel Anderson.

Referee: Richard Silverwood. Attendance: 65,187.

SALFORD CITY REDS, 2008-9
(Played 51, Tries 9, Goals 0, Points 36)

Honours: Northern Rail Cup winners 2008. National League One Grand Final winners 2008.

2008 Northern Rail Cup Final
Bloomfield Road, Blackpool, July 6

Salford City Reds 60 Doncaster 0

Salford's full-timers blew away the part-timers of Doncaster, from a division below in National League Two. Robbie, in harness at half back with Richard Myler, pulled the strings as the City Reds racked up 10 tries, all of them converted by John Wilshere. The team's defensive effort was also outstanding in keeping Doncaster scoreless. Paul White completed a hat-trick of tries on the left wing. Myler chipped in with a couple more and Robbie joined in the romp with a 66th minute touchdown.

Scorers: *Salford City Reds:* Tries: Fitzpatrick, Stapleton, Myler 2, Sibbit, White 3, Sidlow, Paul. Goals: Wilshere 10.

Salford City Reds: Karl Fitzpatrick; Matt Gardner, Stuart Littler, John Wilshere, Paul White; Robbie Paul, Richard Myler; Adam Sidlow, Malcolm Alker (captain), Craig Stapleton, Steve Bannister, Luke Adamson, Jordan Turner. Substitutes: Paul Highton, Stefan Ratchford, Ian Sibbit, Phil Leuluai. Coach: Shaun McRae.

Doncaster: Shaun Leaf (captain); Dean Colton, Andreas Bauer, Zebastian Luisi, Wayne Rettie; Kyle Briggs, Luke Gale; Alex Benson, Corey Lawrie, Michael Hayley, Chris Buttery, Craig Lawton, Peter Green. Substitutes: Kyle Wood, Scott Jones, Jason Hart, Mark Castle. Coach: Ellery Hanley.

Referee: Ronnie Laughton. Attendance: 6,328.

2008 National League One Grand Final
Halliwell Jones Stadium, Warrington, September 28

Salford City Reds 36 Celtic Crusaders 18
(after extra-time; 18-18 after 80 minutes)

A final that ebbed and flowed was ultimately decided in 20 minutes of extra-time. The teams were locked at 18-18 after the regulation 80 minutes, with Salford only just pulling level seconds from time with a penalty by John Wilshere. The Crusaders had twice come from behind in a fascinating showdown between the two best sides in the division, but had no puff left when it came to the extra periods. The Reds powered home with unanswered tries by Ian Sibbit, Paul White and Richard Myler.

Scorers: *Salford City Reds:* Tries: White 2, Gardner, Fitzpatrick, Sibbit, Myler. Goals: Wilshere 6. *Celtic Crusaders:* Tries: Blackwood, Dyer, James, Tangata-Toa. Goal: Lennon.

Salford City Reds: Karl Fitzpatrick; Matt Gardner, Stuart Littler, John Wilshere, Paul White; Robbie Paul, Richard Myler; Paul Highton, Malcolm Alker (captain), Craig Stapleton, Ian Sibbit, Luke Adamson, Jordan Turner. Substitutes: Stefan Ratchford, Steve Bannister, Lee Jewitt, Phil Leuluai. Coach: Shaun McRae.

Celtic Crusaders: Tony Duggan; Luke Dyer, Josh Hannay, Mark Dalle Court, Anthony Blackwood; Damien Quinn, Jace Van Dijk; Jordan James, Neil Budworth, David Tangata-Toa, Chris Beasley, Darren Mapp, Terry Martin. Substitutes: Aaron Summers, Ian Webster, Mark Lennon, Neale Wyatt. Coach: John Dixon.

Referee: Ben Thaler. Attendance: 7,104.

LEIGH CENTURIONS, 2010-11
(Played 40, Tries 8, Goals 2, Points 36)

Honours: Northern Rail Cup final winners 2011.

2011 Northern Rail Cup Final
Bloomfield Road, Blackpool, July 17

Leigh Centurions 20 Halifax 16

Robbie's last final in which Leigh were 10-0 behind and staring down the barrel at the break after conceding tries to Miles Greenwood and Steve Bannister. The Centurions emerged with a new vigour and purpose. Jamie Ellis and Chris Hill scored within nine minutes of each other, before Rob Worrincy's try put Halifax back in control. Ellis's second try set up a grandstand finish. There were just seconds left when Leigh moved the ball wide and Tom Armstrong scored the winning try.

Scorers: *Leigh Centurions:* Tries: Ellis 2, Hill, Armstrong. Goals: Nanyn 2. *Halifax:* Tries: Greenwood, Bannister, Worrincy. Goals: Jones 2.

Leigh Centurions: Stuart Donlan (captain); Steve Maden, Stuart Littler, Mick Nanyn, Dean McGilvray; Martyn Ridyard, Jamie Ellis; Chris Hill, John Duffy, David Mills, Andy Thornley, Tommy Goulden, James Taylor. Substitutes: Robbie Hunter-Paul, Stephen Nash, Tom Armstrong, Adam Higson. Coach: Ian Millward.

Halifax: Miles Greenwood; Paul White, James Haley, Jon Goddard, Rob Worrincy; Danny Jones, Ben Black; Jim Gannon, Bob Beswick, Neil Cherryholme, Paul Smith, Steve Bannister, Jacob Fairbank. Substitutes: Dylan Nash, Makali Aizue, Sean Penkywicz (captain), Sam Barlow. Coach: Matt Calland.

Referee: Matthew Thomason. Attendance: 8,820.

NEW ZEALAND 1997-2006
(Played 33, Tries 18, Goals 2, Points 76)

Honours: 1997 World Nines winners; 1999 Test series winners against Great Britain, 2002 Test series draw against Great Britain; 1999 Tri-Nations series beaten finalists; 2000 World Cup beaten finalists.

1997 World Nines Final
Stockland Stadium, Townsville, February 2

New Zealand 16 Western Samoa 0

The draw seemed tailor-made for an Australia v Great Britain final but New Zealand turned the tables against Australia and Western Samoa upset Britain in the other semi-final. New Zealand's one defeat of the tournament came in the group stages against Britain but they encountered little trouble winning a one-sided final. Stacey Jones held the ball up for Tony Iro to claim the first try, Quentin Pongia followed him over and Ruben Wiki crushed Samoan hopes with the third New Zealand touchdown.

Scorers: *New Zealand:* Tries: Tony Iro, Quentin Pongia, Ruben Wiki. Goals: Marc Ellis 2. Attendance: 15,000.

1999 Tri-Nations Final
Ericsson Stadium, Auckland, November 5

New Zealand 20 Australia 22

The Paul brothers cut the Kangaroos to pieces early on, Robbie going over for the Kiwis' first try from Henry's break after 10 minutes but being controversially denied a second. Tries in response by Mat Rogers and Andrew Johns ensured that Australia had their noses in front at the interval. But with Henry in great kicking form and a try by Lesley Vainikolo giving New Zealand the lead, they were desperately hanging on when Wendell Sailor came up with the decisive try just over five minutes from the end.

Scorers: *New Zealand:* Tries: R Paul, Vagana. Goals: H Paul 6. *Australia:* Tries: Rogers 2, Johns, Sailor. Goals: Rogers 3.

New Zealand: Richie Barnett (captain); Nigel Vagana, Ruben Wiki, Willie Talau, Lesley Vainikolo; Henry Paul, Robbie Paul; Joe Vagana, Richard Swain, Craig Smith, Matt Rua, Stephen Kearney, Logan Swann. Substitutes: Gene Ngamu, Jason Lowrie, Nathan Cayless, David Kidwell. Coach: Frank Endacott.

Australia: Darren Locker; Mat Rogers, Darren Smith, Matt Gidley, Wendell Sailor; Matthew Johns, Brett Kimmorley; Darren Britt, Craig Gower, Jason Stevens, Bryan Fletcher, Nik Kosef, Brad Fittler (captain). Substitutes: Ryan Girdler, Shaun Timmins, Jason Smith, Michael Vella. Coach: Chris Anderson.

Referee: Russell Smith (England). Attendance: 22,500.

2000 World Cup Final
Old Trafford, November 25

New Zealand 12 Australia 40

Robbie came off the bench after 58 minutes in a World Cup final in which New Zealand had fought back to within six points of Australia through quickfire tries by Lesley Vainikolo and Tonie Carroll, both converted by Henry Paul. But once Vainikolo was denied again the Kangaroos bounced back to life in an unstoppable last 14 minutes in which they racked up 22 points. Wendell Sailor equalled the record for tries in a World Cup final with a decisive brace in four minutes and Mat Rogers set a record in landing six goals.

Scorers: *New Zealand:* Tries: Vainikolo, Carroll. Goals: H Paul 2. *Australia:* Tries: Gidley, Hindmarsh, Lockyer, Sailor 2, Fittler, Barrett. Goals: Rodgers 6.

New Zealand: Richie Barnett (captain); Nigel Vagana, Tonie Caroll, Willie Talau, Lesley Vainikolo; Henry Paul, Stacey Jones; Craig Smith, Richard Swain, Quentin Pongia, Matt Rua, Stephen Kearney, Ruben Wiki. Substitutes: Nathan Cayless, Joe Vagana, Logan Swann, Robbie Paul. Coach: Frank Endacott.

Australia: Darren Lockyer; Wendell Sailor, Matt Gidley, Adam MacDougall, Mat Rogers; Brad Fittler (captain), Brett Kimmorley; Shane Webcke, Andrew Johns, Robbie Kearns, Gorden Tallis, Bryan Fletcher, Scott Hill. Substitutes: Jason Stevens, Darren Britt, Nathan Hindmarsh, Trent Barrett. Coach: Chris Anderson.

Referee: Stuart Cummings (England). Attendance: 44,329.